The 106 Common Mistakes Homebuyers Make

(& How to Avoid Them)

SECOND EDITION

GARY W. ELDRED

John Wiley & Sons, Inc.
New York • Chichester • Weinheim • Brisbane • Singapore • Toronto

Copyright © 1998 by Gary W. Eldred, Ph.D.
Published by John Wiley & Sons, Inc.

This publication is designed to provide accurate and authoritative
information in regard to the subject matter covered. It is said with
the understanding that the publisher is not engaged in rendering legal,
accounting, or other professional services. If legal advice or other expert
assistance is required, the services of a competent professional person
should be sought.

Library of Congress Cataloging-in-Publication Data:

Eldred, Gary W.
    The 106 common mistakes homebuyers make : and how to avoid them /
Gary W. Eldred. — 2nd ed.
        p.   cm.
    Includes index.
    ISBN 0-471-19999-0 (pbk. : alk. paper)
    1. House buying. I. Title.
HD1379.E43   1998
643'.12—dc21   97-36016
                                                            CIP

Printed in the United States of America

10 9 8 7 6 5

Preface to Second Edition

The success of the first edition of *106 Mistakes* proved that this book hit the mark. The first edition received highly favorable reviews (a special thanks to Robert Bruss); it has been condensed by *Reader's Digest;* it has been cited in many leading publications such as *Business Week, Money Magazine, Your Money,* and *Bottom Line;* and reader feedback has produced much gratifying praise.

Now, in this newly revised and expanded second edition, we've kept everything that contributed to this book's original success. But we've also responded to reader suggestions. Not only have we incorporated all of the latest developments in the field of home buying, we've added examples and information that will help you:

1. Identify homes that offer great value.
2. Avoid discrimination.
3. Negotiate lower mortgage costs.
4. Ensure a smooth closing.
5. Recognize whether your real estate agent and loan representative are providing the services and advice they should.
6. Obtain the property inspections, disclosures, and warranties that will provide you peace of mind.

Plus, because "failing to buy" still ranks as the number one mistake of renters, this new edition provides you with 50 ways to become a homeowner when you're cash short. It also includes a comprehensive explanation of the terms that you will encounter in the home-buying process and sources for more information (such as the Internet addresses of some of the most popular real estate sites). And, to make sure you don't forget anything important, this new edition offers a full checklist of the financing, home, and neighborhood features that you should bring into your decision making.

All told, we believe this new edition of *106 Mistakes* will guide you through a more satisfying and more profitable home-buying adventure. And if you have further questions or comments, please give me a call at (800) 942-9304 (X-20691). Good luck. I wish you the best as you move toward the all-important goal of home ownership.

Introduction

YOU CAN PROFIT
FROM THE EXPERIENCES
OF OTHER HOMEBUYERS

Are you thinking about buying a home? Good for you. You're going to make one of the best decisions of your life—if you do it right. And that's precisely why you should take advantage of the many experiences and home-buyer mistakes discussed throughout the following pages.

By reading through these enlightening (sometimes funny, sometimes sad) stories, you will gain the knowledge accumulated through dozens of my own property transactions as well as the transactions of hundreds of other renters and homebuyers. Naturally, like most people, you want to own, but maybe you fear one or more of the following:

1. Getting turned down for a mortgage, or paying too much in interest, fees, and costs.
2. Overpaying for your house.
3. Buying a house or neighborhood that comes with "hidden" and unwelcome surprises.
4. Being taken advantage of by a real estate agent or loan officer.
5. Suffering discrimination.
6. Buying a house that doesn't appreciate much.
7. Running into problems at (or on the way to) closing.
8. Buying a house that doesn't meet your needs, wants, or budget.

Because I've heard hundreds of homebuyers voice these types of concerns, I have written this book. Through firsthand experience, I have learned not only your concerns but, more important, how you can make home buying and home ownership an enjoyable and profitable adventure. The secret to successful home ownership is just like success in other activities of life: Learn to profit from the experiences of other people.

Unlike other books on home buying, the discussions here don't dwell on step-by-step general principles, simplistic questions, or a "home-buying process." Instead, *106 Mistakes* illustrates what you need to know through dozens of examples. Through these examples, you'll see how to conquer your confusions, become more confident, and make the right home-buying decision.

The Origins of This Book

Throughout the past 20 years I've taught college courses (graduate and undergraduate) in real estate; professional education programs for Realtors®, home builders, and mortgage loan officers; and STOP RENTING NOW!™ seminars that are directed especially toward first-time homebuyers. In these courses, one of the most favored classroom topics has been "How to prevent mistakes in home buying."

Although just about everyone knows that real estate, and particularly home ownership, stands out as one of the best ways to build personal wealth, a growing number of people now recognize that successful home buying does not occur easily. It requires education. Shopping for a home, negotiating, arranging financing, and qualifying to buy have become much more complex. There are many ways to get bamboozled. Naturally, then, learning about the mistakes of others has proved to be one of the best precautions to ensure a happy and profitable home-buying experience.

At first, when I began to discuss mistakes in home buying with my classes, I relied on many of my own experiences (and mistakes). Over time, though, students were eager to broaden their knowledge and learn firsthand about the mishaps, misfortunes, and mistakes suffered by others. As a result, I incorporated "interview papers" into my class assignments. To carry out these assignments, students would interview Realtors, home builders, loan officers, and recent homebuyers.

The students would ask their interviewees to describe in concrete detail the home-buying (or real estate investing) mistakes that the interviewees had made themselves or had seen others make. Next, the students would write up their conversations and we would schedule a class session or two to discuss what they had learned.

These classroom discussions became quite popular. Accordingly, many students suggested that they would like to see the most common (and costly) mistakes that I've collected brought together in a book. Fortunately, John Wiley & Sons, Inc., and senior editor Michael Hamilton agreed. In this book we've aimed to help you benefit from the experiences of hundreds of persons who have been involved in home buying.

Second Edition

Many of the examples presented here have come from the interview papers written by my students. Others are based on mistakes that I've seen made in some of the 100 or so real estate transactions in which I've been involved as a buyer, seller, or consultant. In addition, this updated second edition includes much more information on financing and valuation. Mistakes in either of these areas can cost you tens of thousands of dollars.

In many instances, to protect the privacy of individuals, I've changed names and specific identifying facts. But all told, these experiences are real. Read through these examples and apply the lessons to your own situation. You'll enjoy a more profitable and more satisfying home-buying adventure.

Contents

4 Locate a Great Neighborhood 93

5 Is This Home for You? 124

8   Become a Satisfied Homeowner   221

CHAPTER 1

Explore Your Possibilities and Priorities

Before you set out on your expedition into home ownership, make sure you fully explore your possibilities and priorities. In my STOP RENTING NOW! seminars, I have talked with thousands of renters who have foolishly delayed their home buying for years. These individuals and families have wasted tens (sometimes hundreds) of thousands of dollars on rent because they mistakenly believed (1) "it costs us less to rent than own," (2) "we can't qualify for a loan," (3) "we don't have enough money for a down payment," (4) "we can't afford the neighborhood we want," or (5) "the future's too uncertain." In other words, these renters wanted to own *someday,* but they failed to put a plan into action. You won't make this mistake.

Once you've read through this chapter, you will see how, regardless of your present situation, the power of knowledge, motivation, and goals can move you into the home you want.

You will also see why you can profit by fully exploring various neighborhoods, price ranges, types of homes, and home features. Even if you think you can describe (and afford) the "perfect" home, the mistakes in this chapter will show you why you should still expand your knowledge of the market. Quite often, greater knowledge will cause you to rethink your priorities. With greater knowledge, you will find the home and home finance plan that are right for you at this stage of your life.

Now, let's look at the "possibilities and priorities" mistakes of others. By avoiding these mistakes, you will travel smoothly into profitable home ownership.

— 1 —

MISTAKE # **1**
—

We want to own, but we pay less to rent.

LESSON: *Over time, you will pay far more to rent than to own. Plus, homeowners gain the wealth-building power of home equity.*

Do you believe you'll pay more to own than to rent? If so, you're experiencing the same confusion that troubles many of the renters who attend my STOP RENTING NOW! seminars. They want to own, but they hesitate because "owning costs too much."

But here are the facts: After you consider income tax deductions, personal freedom, rent increases, and the accumulation of wealth through growing home equity, you will see why renters not only pay more, they also stand to lose tens (and often hundreds) of thousands of dollars of net worth.

Benefit from Tax Deductions

As a homeowner, you will be able to deduct most of your monthly mortgage payments from your taxable income. As a result, your actual out-of-pocket home costs will run—depending on your combined federal, state, and local income tax rates—25 to 40 percent less than the amount of the check you write each month to your mortgage lender.

Let's say your house payment (principal, interest, property taxes, and insurance) will run $1,000 a month. Chances are, after considering the tax benefits of owning, that $1,000 may only cost you about $700. An $1,800-a-month mortgage payment may cost you around $1,200 a month. Or looked at in terms of rent, for example, if you're paying your landlord $600 a month, you may be able to afford $750 to $800 a month for your own home. To get a general idea of your potential savings, look at Table 1.1.

Your rent-versus-own cost figures may differ somewhat from those above. But the point should be clear. Don't assume that owning costs more than renting. Talk to a Realtor or tax advisor. Run through specific

Table 1.1	**Monthly Rent-Equivalent Mortgage Payments**			
	Marginal Tax Bracket			
Monthly Rent	*.15*	*.25*	*.33*	*.40*
$ 450	$ 530	$ 600	$ 672	$ 750
600	706	800	896	1,000
750	882	1,000	1,119	1,250
900	1,058	1,200	1,343	1,500
1,200	1,412	1,600	1,791	2,000
1,500	1,765	2,000	2,239	2,500
1,800	2,118	2,400	2,687	3,000

figures for your area. Quite likely, you'll discover owning costs no more than renting—and frequently much less.

Escape from Renter's Jail

After buying her own home, Yolanda Jones told me, "I can't believe it. Not only am I saving money each month and building equity, but I feel like I've escaped from renter's jail." When I asked her what she meant by "renter's jail," Yolanda explained, "For the first time in my life I feel free. No more landlords to tell me how I can decorate, who I can have over, or whether I can get a dog. This is my home now. I'm free to do with it what I want. Even if it costs me more it'd be worth it."

Yolanda brings out a second point many renters overlook. When you own, you don't just buy a home, you gain freedom. You escape from renter's jail. If you're like Yolanda, the benefits of owning will far surpass the benefits of renting. So when figuring your rent-versus-own cost comparisons, don't leave the enhanced benefits of owning out of your equation.

Think Long Term: Rents Will Go Up

We've all heard dozens of times how America's corporate management focuses on the short term instead of the long term. Renters often make a similar mistake. In some high-cost areas of the country, even after allowing for tax benefits, the monthly costs of owning still may look higher than renting. If that's your situation, think long term. In fact, no matter where you live, the most important reason to buy a home is *not* to save money today. It's to save hundreds of thousands of dollars over the rest of your life.

Let's take an extreme case. Say you're paying $1,000 a month to rent. To buy (even after allowing for tax deductions) will cost you $1,500 a month. Sure, renting looks cheaper. But this is a trap you don't want to fall into. Think: If you've got a fixed-rate mortgage, your monthly payments won't go up—and when at some later date you refinance at lower interest rates, your monthly costs of owning will actually go down.

On the other hand, over the longer term, rents can only be expected to increase. Over time, your rents will come to match your mortgage payments. After that—even at relatively modest rates of inflation—rent levels will be heading off to the stratosphere. Table 1.2 provides several examples of how rents will increase at rates of four, six, and eight percent a year.

Some of these rent figures look impossibly large. But consider the rent levels of the 1940s and 1950s. In most parts of the country, you could rent a house for $25 to $75 a month. Average house payments were $40 to $60 a month. Today's rent and mortgage payments often run 15 to 20 times higher than the amounts of those earlier years. Similarly, you can safely bet that when remembering back 20 or 30 years, people in the future will be talking about the ridiculously *low* rents of the 1990s. In contrast, today's homebuyers will still enjoy mortgage payments at those "ridiculously" low 1990s prices well into the twenty-first century. Those who didn't buy will be paying (if they can afford them) rents three to ten times higher. And if we get more years of double-digit inflation similar to those that occurred in the past, rents could shoot much higher than even the figures in Table 1.2. Over time, owning costs far less than renting—and the benefits are far greater.

Homeowners Build Wealth

We will talk more about the investment benefits of home ownership in Chapter 2. For now, though, at least recognize the great wealth-building power of home ownership—even in periods of relatively low inflation. True, throughout our country's 200-year history, home prices have

Table 1.2 **Escalating Rents**

Future Monthly Rents with Annual Increases of 4%

| *Today's Monthly Rent* | Years | | | |
	10	20	30	40
$ 500	$ 740	$1,095	$1,620	$2,400
750	1,100	1,642	2,430	3,600
1,000	1,420	2,190	3,240	4,800

Future Monthly Rents with Annual Increases of 6%

| *Today's Monthly Rent* | Years | | | |
	10	20	30	40
$ 500	$ 895	$1,600	$2,850	$ 5,140
750	1,342	2,400	4,275	7,710
1,000	1,790	3,200	5,700	10,280

Future Monthly Rents with Annual Increases of 8%

| *Today's Monthly Rent* | Years | | | |
	10	20	30	40
$ 500	$1,075	$2,230	$ 5,000	$10,850
750	1,612	3,495	7,500	16,275
1,000	2,150	4,666	10,000	21,700

proved cyclical: sometimes fast appreciation, sometimes slow; sometimes recession, sometimes depression. Yet, over time, homeowners have always built more wealth than renters.

As you make your monthly mortgage payments, your loan balance steadily falls—slowly at first, then more rapidly. So, even if your home doesn't appreciate (a highly unlikely event), at the end of your mortgage term (15, 20, 25, or 30 years), you will own a valuable asset free and clear. But at rates of appreciation (say three, five, or seven percent), your home equity will grow to hundreds of thousands of dollars (see Figure 1.1). Now you can see that as renters become poorer through rising rents, as a homeowner, you will become richer through growing home equity. Without a doubt (and in more ways than one), continuing to rent will cost you dearly.

Figure 1.1 Building Home Equity

— 6 —

MISTAKE # **2**

We want to own, but we don't have enough for a down payment.

LESSON: You don't need much savings for a down payment. You may not even need a down payment.

Here's another major mistake made by millions of renters. Put aside forever the idea that you must have saved a large amount of cash for a down payment. Listed below are 50 ways to buy with little or no cash out of your own pocket.

Unfortunately, widespread misbeliefs about "big down payments" are too often reinforced by uncaring or unknowledgeable real estate agents. For example, I was listening to a talk-radio show recently. The subject discussed was "no-money-down" home financing. Just as I tuned in I heard an agent angrily say, "I've been selling real estate for 25 years, and I've never seen a nothing-down deal." This real estate agent went on to complain about the "hucksters" pushing nothing-down seminars, books, and tapes who had gotten rich deceiving the public. "People who attend these seminars and watch too much late-night television just waste my time," this sales agent said. "I tell 'em when they call me, 'If you don't have the money to buy, go bother someone else.'"

Work with Agents or Lenders Who Understand Possibility Analysis

Now contrast this agent's attitude to that of Realtor Joan Evans. "Anytime someone comes into our office seeking a rental," Joan says, "the first thing I do is ask them, 'Do you really want to rent? Or would you rather own?' More often than not, they say, 'Sure we would like to own, but we don't have enough for a down payment.' When I hear that, that's when I go to work," Joan says. "One of the best parts of my job is to take renters who think that they don't have enough money to own and then figure out ways to turn them into homeowners. Granted, it's not a piece of cake; sometimes it takes six months or more. But I've found many of these buyers become my most loyal clients and a great source of referrals and repeat business."

If you are cash short, look for a Realtor like Evans. Quickly drop run-of-the-mill agents who show a don't-bother-me attitude to anyone with less than a five-figure bank account.

For the past several years, dedicated Realtors, mortgage lenders, home builders, not-for-profit housing groups, and government agencies have been reaching out to cash-short renters who would like to become homeowners. You now have dozens of little- or nothing-down home finance plans to choose from:

- FHA (Federal Housing Authority) 203(b)
- FHA 203(k)
- FHA assumables
- FHA non-qualifying assumables
- HUD (Department of Housing and Urban Development) Homes
- Fannie 97
- Freddie Mac Discover the Gold
- Neighborhood Housing Services
- Central city mortgages
- Community Reinvestment Act Programs
- Rural Economic Development Programs (formerly Farmers Home Administration)
- Lease-options
- Lease-purchase
- Sweat equity
- State mortgage bond programs
- Land contracts
- Seller "trust deeds"
- Seller seconds
- VA (Veterans Administration) mortgages
- VA assumables
- VA non-qualifying assumables
- State VA programs
- Habitat homes
- New home builders
- Economic opportunity programs
- Private mortgage insurance
- Pledged collateral
- Gift letters
- Family loans
- Fannie Mae rehab loans
- Fannie Mae zero down (experimental)
- Wrap arounds
- Self-contracting
- Shared equity
- City down payment assistance
- County down payment assistance
- Co-ownership
- Create value/fixers
- Not-for-profit grants

- Employer assistance
- Government grants
- Neighborhood Advantage Mortgage
- Community Homebuyer Programs

- First-time buyer programs
- Co-borrowers
- Cosigners
- Blanket mortgages
- REOs
- Manufactured home financing

Little- or nothing-down financing is discussed in more depth in Chapter 7. Also, see Chapter 10, 50 Ways to Buy When You Are Short of Cash. And for even more home-buying possibilities, read my book *Yes! You Can Own the Home You Want* (published by John Wiley & Sons, Inc.)

To discover more ways to buy cash-short in your area, read closely the real estate sections and real estate ads of your local newspapers. Over the course of a month or two, you're likely to see many properties or finance plans that are available with little or no money down. Also, if you don't know an agent like Joan Evans, the real estate ads can help you turn up the names of Realtors and mortgage lenders (or sellers) who are willing to work with cash-poor homebuyers.

Buying when you're cash poor may not prove easy. But real estate and lending professionals who know all the home-buying possibilities will be able to help you develop the financial plan and techniques you need to become a homeowner.

MISTAKE # **3**

We can't afford to buy; the monthly payments are too high.

LESSON: *If you can afford to rent, you can afford to own.*

Before you convince yourself you can't afford to buy, make sure you compare your rent and mortgage payments on an *after-tax* basis (see Mistake #1). But if monthly payments still look too high, don't give up.

There are many ways to get over the "unaffordable" monthly payment hurdle. Here's how Doreen Bierbrier did it.

At the time she bought her first home, Doreen says, "I was earning a modest salary (by Washington, D.C., standards) as a government worker. . . . The only way I could buy a house in a good neighborhood was to find one large enough to accommodate a couple of housemates who paid rent. If everything worked out, the rental income would cover more than half my house payment and two-thirds of the utilities. Adding in tax advantages and appreciation, I figured I would actually make money. Further, when the loan on the house was paid off, I would own a valuable asset free and clear."

As time has proven, Doreen had the right idea. While many moderately paid singles and couples have mistakenly pleaded "not enough income" to buy (see also Mistake #5) others like Doreen have acted creatively and figured out ways to bridge the gap between their current earnings and affordability. In addition to taking in housemates, you might:

- Create an accessory apartment (sometimes called a mother-in-law suite) in your home by converting a garage, attic, or den.
- Reduce your monthly payments with an adjustable-rate mortgage.
- Reduce your monthly payments with a graduated-payment mortgage.
- Reduce your monthly payments by using a balloon mortgage.
- Buy a duplex, triplex, or other type of home that's already producing income that will help cover the monthly mortgage payments.
- See if you can locate a mortgage credit certificate (MCC) program in your area. Through MCCs, the federal government gives you a mortgage "subsidy" of $2,000 to $3,000 a year.
- Get a part-time job.
- Ask your employer for a raise or housing assistance.
- Buy with someone else.
- Secure an interest rate buy down.
- Assume a low interest FHA or VA loan.
- Assume a low equity adjustable rate mortgage.

Generally, these techniques either reduce your monthly payments or increase your income. But to really boost your borrowing/buying power, look for ways to reprioritize your spending (and savings!).

Match Your Spending to Your Goals

Whenever renters say that they can't afford to own, I ask them to list all of their average monthly bills. Nine times out of 10, this list reveals spending patterns that wildly deviate from these renters' professed priorities. In other words, they nearly all say that they value home ownership highly. Yet, they spend their money on "luxury" rentals, cars, boats, jet skis, travel, entertainment, furniture, vacations, electronics, eating out, and many other wasteful and lower priority items.

So, before you delay buying your own home, fill in the blanks below so you see where your money goes each month:

Rent	$_____
Electricity	$_____
Gas	$_____
Cable TV	$_____
Internet charges	$_____
On-line charges	$_____
Telephone(s)	$_____
Car payment no. 1	$_____
Car payment no. 2	$_____
Gasoline	$_____
Automobile insurance	$_____
Groceries	$_____
Child care	$_____
Clothing	$_____
Electronics	$_____
Lunches	$_____
Dining out	$_____
Entertainment	$_____
Tobacco	$_____

Alcohol	$_____
Other vices	$_____
Health club	$_____
Magazines	$_____
Newspapers	$_____
Furniture	$_____
Appliances	$_____
School expenses	$_____
Health insurance	$_____
Weekend trips	$_____
Vacations	$_____
Housekeepers	$_____
Personal care	$_____
Credit card interest	$_____
Other	$_____
Other	$_____
Other	$_____
Other	$_____
Total	$_____

If you're like most people, once you critically compare your spending to your priorities, you'll find many ways to eliminate expenses you value slightly so you can put more money toward your long-term wealth and well-being: home ownership.

Summing Up

At first glance—especially if you live in a high-cost area—it's sometimes easy to conclude that you can't afford the monthly payments on the home you want. But first consider the tax benefits of owning. Then look for creative ways to increase your income, cut your expenses, or use some type of affordable home finance plan. The successful home-buying experiences of millions of low- to middle-income renters prove that if you can afford to rent, you can afford to buy.

MISTAKE # **4**

No bank will give us a mortgage.

LESSON: Many banks and mortgage lenders have special programs for hard-to-finance buyers. Even better, you may not need bank financing.

When Mary and Joe Cortez filed for bankruptcy, they thought they had lost their chance to become homeowners. They were wrong. Just a little more than a year later, this couple successfully bought their first home with a low-down-payment FHA loan. "We couldn't believe it," says Mary. "Friends told us we wouldn't be able to get credit for years."

No doubt, lenders prefer borrowers whose credit remains unblemished. But the good news is that mortgage lenders do need to make loans. And with thousands of potential mortgage lenders, if you're willing and able to make your mortgage payments on time, you can probably find the loan you need to buy a home.

As long as your past financial difficulties do not carry forward into the present, many lenders will give you a chance. Either convince a lender that your blemished credit occurred for reasons outside your control (plant closing, medical bills, business failure, divorce, unemployment), or show persuasive evidence that you've mended your borrow-and-spend ways. Even homebuyers with terrible *past* credit can qualify for a mortgage—but it does require planning, preparation, and sincere efforts. (Also see Mistake #93.)

Of course, more than likely you haven't filed for bankruptcy or faced other serious credit problems. Nevertheless you may mistakenly believe that other kinds of problems will block you from getting a loan. Maybe you're self-employed or have been in your current job less than two years. Maybe you're a college student who works only part time. Maybe you want to spend 50 percent of your income for a home. Whatever your particular situation, don't assume you can't qualify. Many lenders now specialize in less-than-perfect credit risks with loans graded in B, C, and D categories. Ask around. Talk to knowledgeable Realtors, mortgage brokers, or even other homebuyers who have faced the same kinds of problems you're facing. (Assumable mortgages give you another option. These loans are discussed in Chapter 7.)

Look for Owner Financing

I first started buying houses and small apartment buildings when I was an undergraduate college student. I had no established credit, minimal savings, and only a part-time job as a lab assistant. My strategy was to find older people who had tired of managing their rental properties, yet liked the monthly income their properties provided. These types of sellers proved to be great candidates for owner financing.

By selling their properties to someone who was young and ambitious, they got rid of the hassles of wayward tenants, stopped-up toilets, and furnace breakdowns in January. At the same time, the money they earned in interest on their seller mortgages gave them much better returns than they could have earned from bank savings accounts or certificates of deposit.

The great thing about owner financing is that owners are pretty much free to "lend" to whomever they please on whatever terms seem mutually beneficial.

So, if it turns out you really can't get a bank or savings institution to lend you the money you need to buy a home, look for owner-will-carry (OWC) financing. Or just skip the banks altogether. Many homebuyers and real estate investors don't worry about qualifying for a mortgage with a typical lender. They prefer to finance their properties directly with sellers.

MISTAKE # **5**

Our agent told us to get prequalified by a lender so we would know exactly how much home we could afford.

LESSON: *No lender can tell you exactly how much home you can afford. Affordability depends on you, not just the lender.*

All across the country, mortgage lenders and real estate agents are telling homebuyers to "get prequalified so you know exactly how much home you can afford." It's as if getting prequalified for a mortgage is like being measured for a custom-made suit. It isn't. How much home you can afford depends on you.

Can you increase your income? Can you cut your expenses? What type of home finance plan are you willing to use? Are MCC programs available in your area? Are first-time buyer programs available? What kinds of special financing incentives are new home builders or condo and townhouse developers offering? Do you have friends, relatives, or an employer who can make you a gift or a loan? Are you willing to buy a property that includes an accessory apartment or additional rental unit? How much are you willing to stretch your budget? Would you share your home with housemates? Can you buy jointly with someone else? Can you locate an owner who is willing to carry back financing? Are nonqualifying mortgage assumptions (FHA, VA) available in your area?

Affordability Is Up to You

How much home you can afford depends on answers to these and many other similar questions. When you start looking for a house, find a Realtor or mortgage lender who is skilled in *possibility* analysis. Don't rely on fill-in-the-blank prequalifying calculations or "instant" prequalifying computer programs. You have dozens (even hundreds) of ways to buy and finance your home. Thousands of mortgage lenders and thousands of property owners stand ready to make financing available.

Prequalifying with a specific lender can give you a general idea about how much you can spend based on your current finances and that lender's qualifying standards and loan programs. But it can't reveal all of your possibilities. Only through your own efforts of financial planning and possibility analysis can you really decide how much home you want and are able to afford.

Prequalification versus Preapproval

With prequalification, a lender tells you "how much loan you can qualify for" based upon the information you provide. However, the lender doesn't commit to making you a loan. So, don't assume that a "pre-qual letter" necessarily means your loan approval is guaranteed.

On the other hand, many lenders will go one step further and actually preapprove you for a specific loan amount—even before you've found a home to buy. In fact, getting preapproved is a good idea, because a lender's preapproval letter tells real estate agents and sellers that you are a serious, no-credit-problem buyer. Once you locate the home you want (that's within your preapproved borrowing limit), the agent and sellers need not worry about whether you can actually obtain the financing you need.

Nevertheless, always keep in mind that like prequalifying, your "preapproved" borrowing power will differ among lenders, loan programs, applicable interest rates, and how well you've shaped up your financial fitness and credit record. Preapproval can often work to your advantage. But don't mistake one lender's analysis for a complete inventory of your possibilities.

MISTAKE # **6**

Our agent said not to waste time looking at homes outside our price range.

LESSON: *Learn as much as you can about homes priced above and below your "price range."*

This mistake follows from the "custom-made" suit type of prequalifying that's become so popular. Just as no one can tell you exactly "how much home you can afford," neither do you have a tightly defined "price range." Your price range depends on your possibility analysis. But there's another reason you should look at homes above and below your "price range." You can't know exactly what kind of home and neighborhood you want to aim for until you learn as much about the market as you can. Consider the experience of Sue and Bill Henderson.

Sue and Bill followed their agent's advice and looked only at homes in their "price range" of $110,000 to $120,000. Then after they bought, they were out driving around on a Sunday afternoon and went through some open houses in the $135,000 range.

"Wow," said Sue. "We had no idea $135,000 would buy so much more house than we got for our $116,500. These homes are bigger and a lot nicer. If we had known, we would have stretched our budget and revamped our finances. Maybe we would have switched to an ARM [adjustable-rate mortgage] instead of using a fixed-rate mortgage. We could have even gotten a better school district."

First, Learn What's on the Menu

Don't let someone pigeonhole you into a narrow price range. Look at a wide selection of homes and neighborhoods. Too many real estate agents will ask you, "How much would you like to spend (invest) in a home?" Now imagine walking into a new restaurant and sitting down at a table. The waiter comes up and asks, "What would you like to order?" You would probably say, "I don't know. We haven't seen the menu." Of course, you might also want to know what credit cards the restaurant accepts.

The situation's similar when shopping for a home. Make sure you've thoroughly looked over what's on the menu and what kinds of financing are available. And if you don't see what you want, maybe you should switch to a different neighborhood (just as you might look for another restaurant if you weren't satisfied with the menu or terms of credit). You might find you are willing to pay more than you first thought. Or you might decide to spend less. Maybe the $95,000 to $110,000 price range really gives you what you most need for now. Instead of spending $115,000, you can use the money you save for a more comfortable lifestyle, or perhaps other investments.

Whichever you choose, don't fix on a home, neighborhood, and price range until you've looked at all kinds of properties and neighborhoods (within reason, of course). Learn all your options. Compare *relative* prices and benefits among the available choices. With full knowledge of your choices and trade-offs, you'll make a better home-buying decision—a decision you'll be happy to live with.

MISTAKE # **7**

Sure, we would like to buy our own home someday.

LESSON: *Dreams move on if you wait too long. Put a plan into action now.*

Home buying requires a specific financial plan with specific dates and goals. In my STOP RENTING NOW! seminars, I frequently meet renters in their mid- to late 30s and early 40s who have yet to buy their first home. "Why didn't you buy earlier?" I ask them. "Well, we didn't think we could afford it," they often reply.

But this answer doesn't quite ring true. Why? Because from 20 years of teaching and working in real estate, I know that nearly everyone who wants to own a home can own a home—if they put their minds to it. So I probe further. "What do you mean when you say you couldn't afford to buy? How many mortgage lenders or knowledgeable real estate professionals did you talk to? How many owner-will-carry sellers did you contact? How many books and articles on home buying did you study? How closely and how frequently did you read the real estate and home builder ads in your local newspaper?" By asking them questions, I'm not trying to put them on the spot or make them feel bad. Rather, I want them to recognize the real reason they didn't buy wasn't "unaffordability." It was because they failed to set home buying as a primary goal.

They never educated themselves, planned their finances, or established a time frame to buy. Instead, they procrastinated. Although they knew they wanted to buy, it was always easier to put it off. As long as they told themselves they would buy *someday,* they avoided making the effort and doing the planning that home buying requires.

Sadly, procrastination and limp excuses have cost them tens (sometimes hundreds) of thousands of dollars. Try not to make this same mistake. Learn the lessons of the past. Don't wait for *someday.* Put a home-buying plan into action now. Set up a regular savings routine. Guard your credit record zealously. Don't spend (or borrow) money for things that are less important than owning your own home. Think priorities.

Whether you want to buy this year, or maybe a year or two down the line, plan now to make sure your goals (not dreams) come true.

MISTAKE # **8**

I wanted to wait until I got married.

LESSON: *Don't postpone your plan to buy for some indefinite future.*

Some years back, Megin Silver finished her MBA at the University of Virginia and took a good job in Washington, D.C. With one foot in the future, Megin eagerly accepted the challenge of work and career. But with one foot in the past, Megin was uncertain whether a single woman should embark on home ownership. "Anyway," Megin told herself, "I'll probably be married within a few years. It will be better to wait to buy until then."

Years rolled by. Megin was still single. No marriage plans stood on the horizon. Yet, during the time she lived in D.C., Megin watched Washington home prices more than double. She now wishes she had bought earlier. With a refinance at the low interest rates of several years ago, her mortgage payments would have fallen far below the amount she was paying for rent. Plus, she regrets missing out on years of tax deductions (which in her tax bracket she could certainly have used) and thousands of dollars of equity buildup.

Approximately one of every seven homes sold in the United States is bought by a single person. More than half of these singles are women. Just because you're single is no reason to put off buying. And if you can't get the home you want on your own income, cover your affordability gap by taking in housemates, buying a property with rental units, or bringing in a cobuyer. Still in doubt? Then consider what these singles have said about their successful adventures into home ownership:

- "Most of my friends are getting married and having babies. Home ownership, though, is one milestone that's within my control."

- "With every home-buying challenge I met, I would gain more confidence. Now I feel there's nothing that I can't accomplish."
- "I wanted to move from the suburbs into the city, and it made good financial sense to own. I got a terrific tax break, and if I ever relocated, the place could become an excellent source of rental income."
- "I've lived in apartments all my life and I always wanted to live in a house. When I realized that I could *own* one for just $300 more a month (before tax deductions) than I was paying in rent, I started looking."
- "Owning a home has grounded me. I used to love going out nights and away on weekends. Now I want to go home and have friends spend the weekend with me."
- "It gave me the confidence to make other investments. I actually opened my first IRA and even got into the stock market this year. After buying a home, I feel ready to tackle any major financial matter."

As you can see these remarks, singles who buy homes count many benefits from their experience. So, if you're single, don't postpone home buying until you get married. And if you're married, don't put it off until you have kids. "Waiting until I get married" or "waiting until we have kids" may sound like a plan. But it isn't. As a practical matter, waiting often turns out to be just as indefinite as *someday*. Don't wait for someday.

MISTAKE # **9**
___

We were told not to buy unless we planned to stay put for at least four or five years.

LESSON: *Don't put off buying because you may be moving within a few years. Instead, execute a short-term ownership strategy.*

With recent home appreciation rates slowing to a crawl in some areas of the country, conventional wisdom says, "Don't buy unless you plan to stay put for at least four or five years." On the surface this advice sounds reasonable. When you sell after just two or three years, pay a real estate commission and closing costs, and your home hasn't appreciated much, you could end up losing several thousand dollars.

But what happens if you don't buy? Each year you continue to rent you're losing thousands of dollars in tax deductions (see Mistake #1). As another disadvantage, home prices, mortgage interest rates, or both could jump up quickly, just as they have done in the past. Over time, those increases could cost you tens of thousands of dollars. Although you may incur some risks when you buy, keep in mind that you face even greater risks by not buying.

Develop a Short-Term Ownership Strategy

If you think you might move within a few years, your best bet is to develop a short-term ownership strategy. In her excellent book *Housewise*, Suzanne Brangham tells how she bought and lived in more than a dozen homes in just 15 years. Suzanne says, "There is no wrong time to buy real estate. Regardless of the market, regardless of interest rates, I've turned a profit on my homes through good times and bad for the past 15 years." To achieve her profits, Suzanne buys homes she can improve. With her talents for redecorating and remodeling, Suzanne adds thousands of dollars in value to the homes she buys.

Buying "fixer-uppers" isn't the only way to execute a short-term ownership strategy, though. Reed Povitch boasts, "I make my money when I buy, not when I sell." Reed's strategy is to ferret out bargains. Sometimes he finds highly motivated owners; sometimes he buys at probate or foreclosure sales; on other occasions he buys REOs (real estate owned) from mortgage lenders who have taken back properties from borrowers who haven't made their payments.

Consider a Lease-Option

To Robert Bruss, the highly respected, nationally syndicated real estate columnist, the best short-term buying strategy is the lease-option. "By renting with an option to buy," Bruss advises, "you can establish your credit, build up cash (usually through rent credits) to use as a down payment, and you'll be protected against renewed inflation in housing prices."

A lease-option also gives you another benefit that's often overlooked. If during the option period home prices go up but you choose not to buy, you can sell the option for a profit to someone else. Then that person would be able to take advantage of your lower-than-market price and any rent credits you've earned. (See Resources, also.)

Consider Your Short-Term Options

So, if you don't know how long you might stay in your home, consider one of these short-term strategies:

1. Lease-option a home.
2. Assume a low-interest-rate loan that you can get with low amounts of cash and closing costs.
3. Look for a fixer-upper where you can create value for the home.
4. Buy with a low- or no-down-payment assumable FHA or VA loan. When you sell, your buyer can easily take over your financing.
5. Shop for an underpriced bargain. (See Chapters 2 and 3 for guidelines.)
6. Buy in a neighborhood that's on the cusp of turnaround and revitalization.
7. Buy a home that would make a good and profitable rental property.
8. Buy into a neighborhood, development, or building where "for sale" homes are always in short supply and sell fast.

In today's mobile society, many of us don't know where we're going to live four or five years from now. Yet, this uncertainty may continue for many years. To delay buying because you might move is generally a mistake. As a rule, you're better off to meet uncertainty with a short-term ownership strategy. If you should move in a down market, you don't have to sell. Rent out the home and keep it as an investment until the market heats up again. (For more on the profit potential of rentals, see my book *Investing in Real Estate,* also published by John Wiley & Sons, Inc.)

MISTAKE # **10**

We know exactly what we want.

LESSON: Maybe. But more than likely you will change your mind. Plus, prepare yourself for trade-offs, compromises, and creativity.

To successfully buy a home that meets most of your needs, open your mind to a variety of ideas. Don't commit too early to a specific type of house, price range, or neighborhood. Until you really know the market, don't arbitrarily strike houses and areas off your list of possibilities. Give them a fair chance to prove themselves.

Keeping an open mind is especially important when working with a real estate agent. Before a real estate professional begins to show you homes, he or she should sit down with you, get to know your feelings, and try to understand your concerns, likes, dislikes, and finances. The best real estate agents don't sell real estate. They solve problems.

Likewise, when you go to a doctor, you don't walk into his office and tell him what kind of prescription to write or describe in detail the kind of operation you think you need. Instead, a doctor asks you a battery of questions and takes some tests. Only after he or she gets to know you are potential remedies discussed.

Foremost, both doctors and real estate agents should practice careful listening and "examination." As professionals knowledgeable in their fields, they may be able to suggest solutions you would have overlooked. That's what they're being paid for.

Are Buyers Liars?

On the other hand, among the less successful agents in real estate, there's an old saying, "Buyers are liars." This saying came about because poorer agents see themselves as order takers and chauffeurs, not as problem solvers. When they meet someone who is thinking about buying a home, these agents will ask, "What are you looking for?" or "What price range do you have in mind?"

The buyers might answer, "Well, we'd like a three-bedroom, two-bath ranch, probably in Whitehall or River Ridge." Skipping the preliminaries, this type of agent "takes their order" and starts showing the couple houses. But as likely as not, the buyers don't buy from that agent. They end up with someone else. Then several weeks later the first agent learns the buyers just had their offer accepted on a duplex in Hyde Park. Over coffee at the nearby Dunkin Donuts, the agent mutters, "Well, it's happened again. Those folks were just wasting my time. It just proves 'buyers *are* liars.' "

Knowledge Expands Your Possibilities

Of course, the couple wasn't lying to the agent. They said they wanted a three-bedroom in Whitehall because that's what they thought they wanted. They really hadn't explored their options. After they began to consider the relative advantages and disadvantages of various properties, they changed their minds.

Chances are, you won't buy the type of house you now have in mind. It may not exist. It may cost too much. You might discover other homes you like better. You might decide to trade off some features (property or neighborhood) for other features (fix-up value or investment potential) that you previously hadn't paid much attention to. Maybe through creativity you will overcome the objections to a property (or neighborhood) you originally thought were critical. Or maybe, after all is said and done, you really will find the exact home you know you want. Just don't close your mind too soon to other possibilities.

Features and Goals

Another part of the "we know exactly what we want" mistake is to rank certain home (or neighborhood) features above your most important priorities. Here's what I mean: When you become a homeowner, you are working toward one or more important goals. "Comfortable place to live" or "the best neighborhood" are two possible goals. But at this stage of your life, maybe you should rethink your priorities. In other words, also consider these possible goals:

1. Buy at a bargain price.
2. Buy a home where you can create value through improvements and build equity fast.

3. Buy a home in a neighborhood that is poised to beat the market in appreciation.
4. Buy a home with the price and terms that best match your current budget (better to become a homeowner now than wait until you can afford the home and neighborhood of your dreams).
5. Buy a rental property and live in one of the units.
6. Look for a low-interest-rate assumable mortgage that will minimize your monthly payments.

These goals relate primarily to economics rather than to lifestyle. By pursuing one or more of these goals, you're saying that the chance to make (or save) money ranks above "comfortable place to live" or "the best neighborhood." Yet, by focusing now on economic advantage (as opposed to personal preference), you're really positioning yourself to achieve a much nicer home in the future.

It's Your Decision

By discussing these other types of goals, I'm not encouraging you to substitute profits for preferences. (In fact, maybe you can figure out a way to achieve both.) But, I do warn you not to prematurely tell your agent that you want a three-bedroom, two-bath ranch in Cedar Grove until you have explored all of your possibilities and priorities. Who knows? With several smart buying decisions over the next several years, you might even be able to afford a Bel-Air or River Oaks type of neighborhood within the not-too-distant future.

MISTAKE # **11**

We have to have a pool.

LESSON: Don't let the tail wag the dog.

When Carol and Blair Alsop moved from Michigan to Florida, they decided their new home must have a swimming pool. This was the first priority on their list of features. "We only want to look at homes with pools," the Alsops told their Realtor. Even when their Realtor tried to get the couple to consider other homes that would meet most of their other requirements, they refused. "Nope, we've got to have a pool," they emphasized.

As it turned out, none of the pool homes they could find really hit their hot spots. The homes were either too large or too small. They needed repairs. They were located in the "wrong" neighborhoods or school districts. Sometimes they cost too much. Nothing they saw really seemed to click. Finally, their Realtor was able to persuade the couple to at least look at a home that had just come on the market.

Except for the swimming pool, the home had everything the Alsops could hope for. It was the right size; the right neighborhood; and, best of all, the right price. The sellers were even willing to carry back financing at a point less than current bank mortgage rates. The Alsops were tempted. But they said no. "If we're going to live in Florida, we're going to have a pool."

Eventually the Alsops did buy a home. They paid more than they really wanted. The home needed repairs. It was larger than they needed. And the location wasn't their first choice. But it did have a pool.

Unfortunately, shortly after moving into their new home, the Alsops knew they had made a mistake. They didn't use the pool as much as they thought they would. The pool and the house cost too much for maintenance and repairs; and the commute to work was longer than they liked. Within two years after they had bought it, they sold the house and moved. Their new house didn't have a pool.

Keep Features in Perspective

Now don't misunderstand. By recounting the Alsops' experience, I'm not talking against buying a home with a swimming pool. The Alsops' mistake was not in buying a home with a pool. Their mistake was insisting that one feature of their home should outweigh the importance of all other features. The Alsops really weren't being true to themselves. They had fixated on an idealized image of Florida living—and to their mind that type of living included poolside parties, afterwork swims for exercise and relaxation, and Saturday morning brunch on the patio.

All these things sounded great. But the necessities of career ambitions, running a household, and raising a family put considerable distance between their imagined lifestyle and the reality of their everyday living.

When you shop for a house, put first things first. Align your goals with your priorities. Then, don't insist on a pool, a third or fourth bedroom, a formal dining room, a formal living room, a den, a fireplace, a two-car garage, a big yard, colonial architecture, a view, or any other features that are not critical to the primary benefits your home and neighborhood must provide. Be willing to trade off an idealized image for the way you will actually live.

We all have certain features that we would like in our dream homes. But it's usually a mistake to let these "dream" features override our better judgment. Try to distinguish clearly your wants from your needs. In other words, don't let the tail wag the dog.

MISTAKE # **12**

We liked the house on Elmwood best, but our furniture wouldn't work there.

LESSON: *Buy furniture to fit your new house. Don't buy a new house to fit your old furniture.*

Real estate agents frequently say they can tell when many buyers get really interested in a house. The tape measure is pulled out and the prospective buyers try to figure out whether their furniture will fit in the home. In somewhat similar fashion, some people will flat out reject a house because "there's no way our furniture will work there." Clearly this is putting the cart before the horse. Your present and future needs, not previous decisions you've made about your furniture, should govern your choice of a home.

I confess that I almost made this mistake several years ago. At the time, I owned a 3,000-square-foot house and was planning a move to a new area. Upon learning I was single, the agent I was working with suggested several homes she thought I would like in the 1,800- to 2,000-square-foot range. "Oh, my," I said, "those are much too small. I could never get my furniture to fit in those houses."

Then I began to recall how I had come to acquire a 3,000-square-foot house. I didn't really want or need such a large home. I had bought it because the house had great views of a lake and was located in a very private setting. Naturally, after I bought the house, I filled it with furniture.

So, here I was just about ready to reject smaller (and more sensible) houses because my furniture wouldn't fit. Fortunately, after thinking through the ridiculousness of the situation, I sold some furniture and bought a 1,700-square-foot house that I enjoyed much more than I had the larger home.

Like many other people, I had almost let past decisions set the course for my future decisions. We really are creatures of habit. But a major decision like buying a home should prompt us to reevaluate old habits and old decisions. Whether it's your furniture or some other previous decision, try to distinguish the way you have lived in the past from how you would like to live in the future. Don't unconsciously let your past become prologue.

MISTAKE # **13**

There were so many rules, it was like living under socialism.

LESSON: When going over your possibilities and priorities, don't just think of home features and neighborhoods. Consider also the types of homeowner association rules and regulations you want to live under.

If you buy into a co-op, condo, townhouse, or subdivision development, more than likely you're going to be governed by a homeowners' association. A homeowners' association can require you to live under its rules and regulations; fine you for violations; put a lien against your home if you don't pay your fines, assessments, or monthly dues; and otherwise make your life unpleasant.

After Chuck and Michelle Kane bought their new home, one of the first things they wanted to do was to put in a yard. So Chuck took the first weekend and planted grass seed. Two days later a representative of the homeowners' association stopped by to tell Chuck the bad news. In that subdivision, grass seed was not permitted. To comply with association regulations, the Kanes would have to sod their yard. And to encourage the Kanes to follow all other rules, the association fined the Kanes $400.

Once Chuck and Michelle really started to look over the rules they would have to live under, they learned:

- Their homeowners' association would have to approve any exterior design changes or painting they planned for their home.
- Chuck couldn't park his antique Chevy in his driveway while he worked on it.
- The Kanes couldn't put a Sears storage shed in their backyard.
- No outside clotheslines or television antenna or satellite dishes were permitted.

What Rules Can You Live With?

When Juanita Maertz bought her townhouse, she knew civil rights laws forced the townhouse development to accept her sons, ages four and six. Except for certain housing developments for seniors, neither rental companies nor homeowners' associations may exclude children. But accepting children because of the law and making them welcome are two different issues.

After Juanita moved in, she discovered that kids could not play on the grounds of the development. Parents were supposed to take them to a nearby park. "Sure, we accept kids here," Juanita remembers one disgruntled resident telling her. Then he added, "We just don't tolerate them."

To make her new home livable, Juanita joined her association's board, formed a political coalition with other parents, and eventually got the rules changed to try to create a "children-friendly" environment. "It was a lot of time and effort," Juanita recalled. "But we had no choice. It's our home, too, and our kids should have the right to play here."

Of course, from her viewpoint Juanita is right. But others without children may also feel they have a right to peace and quiet. Unfortunately, there's no easy answer to the question "What rules and regulations should the association enact and enforce?" Whenever people live together in a large complex or development, they undoubtedly will face some difficult choices. For example, how would you judge rules such as these?

- No more than one pet is allowed per unit. Maximum weight of a pet shall not exceed 15 pounds.
- A pet deemed by the Board to be noisy or uncontrollable must be disposed of within three days notice.
- No automobile mechanical work whatsoever will be permitted on the premises.
- Bicycles must be stored in designated areas. They must not be left on the grounds, in hallways, or stored on patios or balconies.
- Personal conduct and attire in the common areas are subject to approval of the Board.
- No signs ("for sale" or "for rent") shall be displayed in any manner whatsoever.
- No owner/occupant shall install drapes or curtains within any unit unless such drapes have a white liner visible from outside the unit.
- No entertaining of more than 10 persons within a given unit shall be permitted.
- Any owner who wants to offer his or her unit for rent must first obtain the approval of the Board. All tenants also must be approved by the Board.
- No leases beyond a duration of one year are permitted.
- The Board retains the right to disapprove a new purchaser in the development for any lawful reason it deems appropriate.
- No driveway basketball hoops and playing areas are permitted.
- No treehouses may be built.

Homeowners' association rules and regulations can touch upon nearly anything you might want to do. So before you choose a development, closely review the "laws" you will have to live under. Even though it's true that homeowners' associations are run democratically and that most rules and regulations operate to enhance the value and livability of the development, for some homeowners democratic rule means "tyranny by the majority." The rules imposed are just too "socialistic."

MISTAKE # **14**

What! Beans for dinner again?

LESSON: *Put as much money as you can into your home. But don't underestimate your other necessary living expenses.*

Smart financial advisors generally recommend that, at least for your first home, you should stretch your budget as far as possible. Buy as much home as you can. This advice is sound. The logic is that as your income goes up over time, your mortgage payments will take a smaller and smaller percentage of your income. Although money might seem tight for a few years, as long as your career progresses on an upward path, you'll soon move into your comfort zone. Plus, a more expensive house often means that you'll build a larger amount of home equity.

What is true generally, however, may not be true specifically. Before you stretch too far to buy, prepare a realistic (even pessimistic) post-purchase budget. If you're borrowing part of your down payment or planning to spend money improving your house, allow for those additional payments. If you are using an adjustable-rate mortgage, figure out how well you could manage financially if the interest rate on your ARM moves up each year to its maximum rate.

Especially after you've been looking for a home for a number of months, it's easy to convince yourself to increase your price range. Or maybe you find the perfect house, but it's $40,000 more than you had in mind. You start thinking, "Well, we can borrow $10,000 from Mom and Dad. We can put next summer's vacation on the Visa card. Plus, we both will probably be getting raises next year. And even though this house means a longer commute, the extra gas won't cost that much." When thoughts like these start running through your mind, you're not making budget decisions. You're rationalizing.

Still, maybe you should stretch to buy. Before you commit, though, write the figures down and (as we would say in business school) run through various financial scenarios. If you feel satisfied with what you see, go for it. If looking at the numbers makes you feel queasy, ask yourself whether you would be happy on a steady diet of rice, spaghetti, and beans. Everyone *should* own a home. But no one should let a home own them.

MISTAKE # **15**

We bought because we were so tired of looking.

LESSON: *Never buy just to "get the decision over with."*

Home buying presents a paradox. Planning to buy can give you one of the most exciting times of your life. Most everyone enjoys getting up early Sunday morning, bringing in the newspaper, reading through the homes-for-sale ads, and then later going out to tour neighborhoods, look at open houses, explore possibilities, and imagine what life will be like in a new home. But searching for the *right* home can also frustrate and depress. At some point, you may reach the let's-forget-the-whole-thing stage. Or you may make a let's-just-buy-something-and-get-it-over-with choice.

If you do begin to feel confused, uncertain, and frustrated, don't let these feelings pull you into an unwise decision. Instead, back up and ask yourself these questions:

- Have we lost touch with our most important feelings, needs, priorities, and goals?
- Do we want to have it all? Are we looking for the perfect home?
- Do we lack confidence in our ability to make a good decision?

- Do our wants or goals lie outside market realities or our financial means?
- Are we buying for ourselves? Or are we worrying about how our friends, relatives, or parents will judge our decision?
- Have we really explored a full range of options and possibilities?
- Have we developed a sensible time schedule for getting to know the market and finding a home?
- Is our ability to choose being unduly influenced by an idealized self-image?
- Can we recast difficulties as opportunities?

By asking these questions, you can probably pinpoint the reasons you're feeling confused, uncertain, or frustrated. More than likely, you're being tugged in different directions because conflicting emotions are pushing and pulling you one way and then another. Decision-making expert Dr. Theodore Rubin calls this type of indecisiveness the chairman-is-missing syndrome. By thinking truthfully about the issues raised by these questions, you can reestablish control over your decision making. You'll pound your gavel. Your inner "chairman" can then bring your internal confusion to order.

MISTAKE # **16**

We feared that discrimination would limit our possibilities for home ownership.

LESSON: Mortgage lenders, Realtors, home builders, and not-for-profit housing groups are reaching out to all potential homebuyers.

No one denies that in the past discrimination has blocked many Americans and immigrants from home ownership. But, to paraphrase Bob Dylan, the times are a changing. Today, as part of the National Home Ownership Strategy, in compliance with fair housing laws, and, most important, in the never-ending pursuit of higher profits, mortgage lenders,

Realtors, and home builders are creating many new home financing programs that reach out to *all* potential homebuyers—regardless of their race, nationality, ethnicity, or marital status.

Yes, in the past, discrimination did block some homebuyers in two possible ways: (1) stereotyping, or (2) "neutral" underwriting standards. So, to better understand the present, let's look at these two types of discrimination.

Stereotyping

Unfortunately, stereotyping people as bad credit risks simply because of irrelevant characteristics such as race, marital status, or occupation has had a long and undistinguished history. Today, though, this type of wide-scale discrimination has virtually been eliminated. No reputable lending institution (realty firm, home builder) willfully discriminates in this way as a matter of company policy.

Undoubtedly, some *individual* loan officers or real estate sales agents do harbor biases that are reflected in their behavior. But if such biased behavior adversely affects your ability to secure a mortgage or to buy a home, the offending individual can suffer civil liability, criminal fines, and loss of professional license. So, even though some stereotypical discrimination does exist, severe penalties are making it increasingly rare.

"Neutral" Underwriting Standards

Far more troubling (and less visible) discriminatory practices are so-called neutral loan underwriting standards. For example, consider "traditional" mortgage credit criteria such as these:

- No home loans for less than $50,000.
- Two years of steady work at the same job.
- A clean credit history and at least four accounts at banks or retail merchants.
- No "mattress money" (cash for a down payment must come from a verifiable, approved source, e.g., a savings account).
- No loans in neighborhoods where more than 40 percent of the homes are occupied by renters (as opposed to homeowners).

- Monthly mortgage payments shall not exceed 28 percent of gross monthly earnings.

On the surface, all of these credit standards (and many others like them) seem neutral. None blatantly discriminate against anyone for any illegitimate reason. Yet, upon statistical analysis, these rules quite frequently create discriminatory effects. And that's where lenders are now directing their attention.

Lenders are reevaluating their "traditional" lending criteria to see why their turndown rates for some minorities are higher than they should be. As a result, most mortgage lenders are pitching out their traditional criteria and rewriting their loan standards to reflect the realities of life as experienced by low- to middle-income borrowers, minorities, single-parent households, immigrants, and other groups that don't fit the cookie-cutter qualifying standards of earlier years.

Reach-out Efforts

Jim Johnson, president of Fannie Mae, the largest and most influential mortgage lender in the country, says that "every American [or legal immigrant] who wants to get a mortgage [to buy a home] will either have their loan approved, or be put on a path that can lead to approval." In putting these words into action, Fannie Mae has pledged $1 trillion in mortgage money and has made a public announcement: "We're looking for millions of missing homeowners. Many are ready now. But they may be intimidated by how the system works; or fearful of discrimination. . . . The housing industry is urgently addressing these problems. And Fannie Mae is taking the lead. We're building partnerships among lenders, real estate agents, credit counselors, and appraisers. . . . Together we've created an outreach program to help everyone who wants to own a home."

These outreach efforts are working. Last year record numbers of blacks, Hispanics, immigrants, singles, single-parent households, and other types of traditionally underserved individuals and families bought their own homes. No longer do lenders arbitrarily rule people out of home ownership. Exclusion through stereotyping and "neutral" underwriting standards is being thrown into the dustbin of history.

So, if you want to own your own home, don't mistakenly believe that discrimination will limit your possibilities. Today, more and more mortgage lenders are reaching out to help all homebuyers either "get their mortgage approved, or be placed on a path that will lead to approval."

CHAPTER 2

Home Ownership: How to Make It Your Best Investment

"High bucks potential of real estate is waning," headlined a recent article in the *San Francisco Examiner.* Quoting economist Charlotte Chamberlain, the *Examiner* story concluded that "housing isn't the sure-fire winner it has been over the past 20 years."

Since the late 1980s up through the present, the media has found naysayers who have warned homebuyers not to consider their homes as good investments. "Buy a home as a comfortable place to live," they say. "But don't expect much appreciation." If you've been influenced by these pessimistic projections, then you need this chapter. For it will give you a much more positive (and accurate) perspective.

On the other hand, if you (like most Americans) realize that home ownership can prove to be your best investment, you, too, need this chapter. For it will not only help you guard against investment mistakes, it will show you how to make sure your home-ownership experience yields the excellent returns you anticipate.

MISTAKE # **17**

We're not planning to buy. Experts say home prices won't appreciate in the future as they have in the past.

LESSON: *"Experts" have been saying that "home prices have reached their peak" for more than 50 years.*

Among all the lessons history teaches, none is more certain than the fact that home prices will go up. Regardless of how high you think prices are today, they will be higher 10 years from now. And much, much higher 20 or 30 years into the future. Don't make the mistake of believing "home prices have reached their peak." Before you put faith in the naysaying of economic "experts," take a quick trip through their faulty predictions of years gone by:

- The prices of houses seem to have reached a plateau, and there is reasonable expectancy that prices will decline. (*Time,* December 1, 1947)

- Houses cost too much for the mass market. Today's average price is around $8,000—out of reach for two-thirds of all buyers. (*Science Digest,* April 1948)

- If you have bought your house since the War . . . you have made your deal at the top of the market. . . . The days when you couldn't lose on a house purchase are no longer with us. (*House Beautiful,* November 1948)

- The goal of owning a home seems to be getting beyond the reach of more and more Americans. The typical new house today costs about $28,000. (*Business Week,* September 4, 1969)

- You might well be suspicious of a "common wisdom" that tells you, "Don't wait, buy now. . . . Continuing inflation will force home prices and rents higher and higher." (*NEA Journal,* December 1970)

- The median price of a home today is approaching $50,000. . . . Housing experts predict price rises in the future won't be that great. (*Nations Business,* June 1977)

- The era of easy profits in real estate may be drawing to a close. (*Money,* January 1981)

- In California . . . for example, it is not unusual to find families of average means buying $100,000 houses. . . . I'm confident prices have passed their peak. (John Wesley English and Gray Emerson Cardiff, *The Coming Real Estate Crash,* 1980)

- The golden-age of risk-free run-ups in home prices is gone. (*Money,* March 1985)

- If you're looking to buy, be careful. Rising home values are not a sure thing anymore. (*Miami Herald,* October 25, 1985)

- Most economists agree . . . [a home] will become little more than a roof and a tax deduction, certainly not the lucrative investment it was through much of the 1980s. (*Money,* April 1986)

- We're starting to go back to the time when you bought a home not for its potential money-making abilities, but rather as a nesting spot. (*Los Angeles Times,* January 31, 1993)

- Financial planners agree that houses will continue to be a poor investment. (*Kiplinger's Personal Financial Magazine,* November 1993)

- A home is where the bad investment is. (*San Francisco Examiner,* November 17, 1996).

Fortunately, the actual history of home prices and real estate investment returns have differed greatly from recurring claims of "the end of real estate" as an investment. During the past 50 years, average home prices have actually multiplied by factors of 5, 10, and in some areas, 20 or more.

So, don't make the mistakes of the so-called economic "experts." Don't confuse slow periods in the real estate cycle with long-term price trends. Since World War II, home prices have frequently jumped by 10 or 20 percent a year. On occasion, they've held steady for as long as three to five years. And when cities experience severe downturns in their local economies, prices sometimes fall temporarily. During the early 1970s, for example, large layoffs at Boeing drove Seattle home prices down by 20 to 30 percent. A local billboard went up with the request, "Will the last person to leave Seattle please turn out the lights?" Yet, Seattle recovered. Now prices there are four times higher than they were in 1971. In fact, a recent article in the *Seattle Post-Intelligence* was headlined, "Through the roof again? Key indicators predict another jump in housing prices." The article opened with this statement: " Yes, once again it appears that we're in for housing price sticker shock. . . . Puget Sound real estate prices will jump 7.2 percent in the next year— and about the same the year after that and the year after that. . . ."

Likewise, as the new century unfolds, we will look back to today's "high" home prices in cities such as Denver, Dallas, Houston, San Diego, Boston, and New York. We'll say, "Boy, those were the days. Can you believe I could have picked up a three-bedroom, two-bath home in Clairemont for just $225,000?" And no doubt, in some future years, we will hear some "experts" tell us, "Home prices can't go any higher. Just since the 1990s the median price of a home has jumped from $135,000 to $210,000. The days are gone when like during the 1990s buying a home for investment was a sure thing."

MISTAKE # **18**

The experts were wrong in the past, but things are different today.

LESSON: *The more things change, the more they remain the same.*

Experts have always put forth plausible reasons to support their predictions that home prices had reached their peak. In 1947 housing economist John Dean wrote that large jumps in home prices in the 1940s had occurred because of "rapid population growth, inflation, and housing shortages." Then he added, "None of these is likely to continue."

In fact, though, what have we seen during the past 50 years? Recurring periods of rapid population growth, inflation, and housing shortages. And what about the future?

Population and Incomes Are Growing

The most recent estimates of the U.S. Bureau of Census show that during the next 10 years, the U.S. population will grow by more than 20 million people. Increasing numbers of births (the echo boom), millions of immigrants, and longer life expectancies are adding record numbers to our population. To house our growing population, people will require around 8 million new homes and apartments. In addition, we'll need between 5 and 10 million homes to replace those that are lost because of fires, abandonment, conversion to commercial uses, and natural disasters (earthquakes, floods, hurricanes, tornadoes).

In contrast to growing demand, a look at supply shows that the number of new homes being built falls far below the numbers that will be needed—especially in the low- to moderate-price ranges. During the decade of the 1990s, fewer apartments were built than at any time since World War II. New home construction was also down. It's almost certain that at some point within the next several years, we are going to experience tight housing markets again. As of early 1997, both apartment vacancy rates and inventories of unsold homes were falling.

Is This the End of Inflation?

Recent economic news regarding inflation has generally been good. "Inflation has been squeezed out of the economy," the headlines tell us. But has it really? Or are we deceiving ourselves? During the past five years, consumer prices have increased, on average, around three percent a year. This rate of inflation does seem low compared to the 10 to 13 percent rates we experienced in the early 1980s. Historically, though, an average annual inflation rate of three percent is not low.

Throughout the 1950s until the mid-1960s, inflation ranged between one and two percent a year. Even between the years 1966 to 1973, annual inflation averaged "only" 4.3 percent. No one at that time, however, thought inflation was low. Most economists were so alarmed about "runaway prices" that in 1973 Herbert Stein, President Nixon's chairman of the Council of Economic Advisors, persuaded the president to impose wage and price controls all across the United States.

Relative to the late 1970s and early 1980s, today's inflation rates are low. Relative to much of our postwar history, they are not low. As Mark Twain might have observed, "The death of inflation has been greatly exaggerated." With a growing population, reduced building of new homes, and continued inflation, the same factors that have pushed up home prices in the past will again push them up in the future. As an additional factor, expanding "growth management" restrictions on land use will continue to push development costs up and limit the number of new homes permitted.

MISTAKE # **19**

Lower rates of inflation mean lower rates of appreciation for homes.

LESSON: *Reduced rates of inflation can actually lead to higher rates of appreciation.*

Conventional wisdom holds that strong rates of appreciation in home prices depend on high rates of inflation. The logic of this argument seems straightforward. It goes like this: With rapidly rising prices for labor and materials, home builders cut back on their new construction and raise their prices. With higher prices for new homes, many homebuyers switch to the resale market and buy existing homes. With more buyers bidding for existing homes, these home prices go up. Increasing demand and a reduced supply of new and existing homes for sale yield strong rates of appreciation for home values.

High Inflation, High Interest Rates

Although this argument is partially true, it doesn't reveal the full picture. Ask any Realtor or home builder who lived through the double-digit rates of inflation of the early 1980s. Contrary to today's recollections, those were not generally good times for real estate. Reporting on the Southern California market of 1982, a leading national newspaper wrote, "Not only are asking prices falling, but in some cases people who have bought homes in the last few years are selling them for less than they paid for them. . . . Now people are buying shelter. . . ." And recall the *Money* magazine article of January 1981 (see Mistake #17). "The era of easy profits in real estate may be drawing to a close," *Money* told its readers.

Although over time higher rates of inflation will jack up building costs, higher inflation also causes interest rates to rise. As interest rates go up, home affordability goes down. People who might like to buy are blocked from the market. Sooner or later, demand for homes falls because with higher interest rates homebuyers can't qualify for financing. Fewer buyers bring price increases to a halt.

Low Inflation, Low Interest Rates

On the other hand, low rates of inflation mean low interest rates. With low mortgage interest, more people can afford to buy. If predictions of low inflation hold true, millions of Americans who would be shut out of the mortgage market with interest rates at 10 to 14 percent—the rates that prevailed throughout most of the 1980s—will be able to own their own homes. More buyers will push prices higher.

In fact, if we look back to the 1980s, it wasn't the high inflation years that brought the steepest home price increases. The greatest rates of appreciation (except for the oil belt; see Mistake #25) occurred between 1985 and 1988.

Then, in 1989, inflation climbed up close to five percent. It was the largest increase in the Consumer Price Index (CPI) since 1982. Mortgage interest rates again went over 10 percent in 1989. Home prices stalled (and even retreated) in many cities. Construction of new homes fell. Defense-related industries suffered cutbacks and layoffs. To become more competitive, firms with large managerial bureaucracies, such as General Motors and IBM, shed employees. The country experienced its seventh post–World War II recession and a slowdown in economic growth.

Now the country is firmly back on its path of rising incomes and employment. Mortgage affordability looks much better than it did during the 1980s and early 1990s. Large firms have dramatically improved their productivity. American steel, auto, and high-technology firms lead the world as low-cost producers of quality products.

Although higher rates of inflation can lead to increased building costs and eventually higher home prices, lower rates of inflation can yield a stronger economy, more jobs, lower mortgage interest rates, and more homebuyers. Don't mistakenly believe that a slower upward drift of the CPI means weak appreciation in home prices. Between 1950 and 1970 average home prices tripled ($10,000 to nearly $30,000). During this same 20 years, increases in the CPI averaged less than three percent a year.

MISTAKE # **20**

We thought we could make higher returns investing in stocks.

LESSON: Even with "low" rates of appreciation, a home will still prove to be your best investment.

Colin and Melinda Stein recently announced proudly to a reporter who was interviewing them, "We earn $80,000 a year and don't own a home. We could buy if we wanted to. But we thought we could do better investing in stocks. At best, we think homes will only appreciate four or five percent a year. We can make a lot higher returns in the market."

Given that the stock market has jumped more than 50 percent during the past five years, no wonder the Steins believe that investment returns from stocks will beat home ownership. But the Steins are mistaken for two reasons:

1. The stock market is not likely to increase during the next five years as much as it has during the past five years. (In fact, by the time you read these words, a stock market "correction" may already have occurred.)

2. When you invest in a home, you gain the magic wealth-building power of leverage. A three or four percent rate of home appreciation yields investment returns far in excess of these "low" rates.

Low Rates of Appreciation Yield High Returns: An Example

Let's say a couple invests $10,000 in a $100,000 home. Assume they finance their purchase with a 30-year, $90,000 mortgage at 7.75 percent. After eight years their outstanding mortgage balance would have been paid down to $81,585. With four percent a year appreciation for eight years, their home's value would have grown to $136,860. If we subtract the couple's mortgage balance ($81,585) from their home's value of $136,860, we find their original $10,000 investment has increased more than fivefold to $55,275 of homeowners' equity. That's the equivalent of an after-tax rate of return of around 24 percent a year (see Table 2.1).

Table 2.1 "Low" Appreciation Yields High Returns

Today

Purchase price	$100,000
Mortgage	90,000
Cash invested	10,000

Eight Years Later

Market Value @ 4% appreciation	$136,860
Mortgage balance	81,585
Home equity	55,275

Equity Growth Rate

$10,000 $55,275

```
 |—|—|—|—|—|—|—|—|
 0  1  2  3  4  5  6  7  8 years
```

Approximate annual growth rate of equity = 24%

Stocks Typically Yield Lower Results

In contrast, depending on whose numbers you use, stocks have yielded an average pretax return of between 9 and 12 percent a year over the longer run. On an after-tax basis, a 10-percent-a-year return on stocks is considered very good. In fact, over the long term, fewer than two percent of professional fund managers have been able to consistently earn after-tax returns on stocks of more than 10 to 15 percent a year.

Consider, for example, that in 1965 the Dow Jones stock index stood at 910.88. By 1982 this index of blue chip companies actually stood slightly lower, at 884.36. During this entire 17-year period, the Dow Jones index went no higher than 974.92. And it fell to as low as 753.19 in 1970.

No doubt, with slower rates of home appreciation—and with the stock market hitting record highs—we've lost our historical perspective. Stock markets and home prices run in cycles. Putting $10,000 into the stock market in 1990 could have yielded better returns by 1997 than a $10,000 investment in an average home in San Diego or Boston. (But not in Seattle, Denver, Chicago, Miami, Austin, or Portland.)

Nevertheless, even in slow housing markets, you still can earn strong returns by shopping for bargains and/or creating value with improvements. Remember, too, that the stock market is far riskier than home ownership. Except in the worst of markets, moderate- to average-priced homes seldom fall in price by any more than 10 to 20 percent, whereas, in the stock market, it's not uncommon to see a company's stock price fall by 50 to 90 percent.

Summing Up

All things considered, an investment in a home can be expected to outperform the stock market. With a home you get the magic benefits of leverage. You invest a relatively small down payment. Yet, you receive returns based on increases in the total value of your home. That's why even a "lowly" four percent annual rate of appreciation will nearly always outperform the returns you could get from stocks or bonds. And not only is home ownership far less risky than stocks or bonds, stocks and bonds won't keep you dry when it rains or warm when the weather is freezing cold.

Certainly, as you grow older, it's best to diversify your wealth into various types of investments. But don't substitute other investments for home ownership.

MISTAKE # **21**

We weren't concerned about our home as an investment; we just wanted a comfortable place to live.

LESSON: *When shopping for a home, you should always factor potential appreciation gains into your decision.*

With talk about "homes no longer being a 'sure-fire' investment," many homebuyers have scratched "investment" off their list of criteria to judge a home. This is a mistake. In both hot and cold markets, you should compare homes and neighborhoods on the basis of your profit potential. Don't adopt the attitude, "Well, if it appreciates, great. If not, we still have gained all the benefits of living in our own home."

No matter how slow your local housing market may appear, good opportunities for profit are always available to those who remain savvy and persistent in their home-buying efforts. Your overall market may not be making headlines with big jumps in prices. But that doesn't mean you can't "beat the market."

Create Your Own Appreciation

Just before California headed into recession in 1989, Beth Rosander got divorced. With two children to raise and no job prospects, Beth decided to make a living buying rundown houses, fixing them up, and then quickly reselling them. If Beth had paid attention to the newspapers, she would have known the California "boom" in housing prices had stalled. No way could she expect to make money buying and selling homes. Couldn't she see? Homes were no longer a good investment.

Fortunately, Beth ignored the steady stream of bad news. Between the years 1988 and 1993, Beth bought, fixed up, and sold six houses. After each sale, she pocketed between $20,000 and $40,000. Remember, too, that Beth bought these houses without income from a job. Bank loans were out of the question. To solve this problem, Beth obtained seller financing. "The deals are not there with a big red flag," Beth points out. "I had to weed through [literally as well as figuratively, I suspect] a lot of properties and get up to speed on the market" (*San Francisco Examiner,* May 2, 1993).

Find a Bargain or "Hot" Neighborhood

Maybe buying a fixer-upper doesn't fit your idea of fun. But that's not the only way to make your home a good investment even in down markets. You also can shop to buy at a bargain price. Make your money when you buy, not when you sell. And you can try to locate neighborhoods that will appreciate faster than average. Nearly every city has "hot" neighborhoods or communities that show far more promise for gains than overall trends in prices would seem to indicate.

How do you locate these promising neighborhoods or communities? Here are eight indicators of emerging hot spots:

1. You can anticipate an upward trend in prices when the number of days it takes to sell a home in a given neighborhood is falling. If last year homes took an average of 120 days to sell, an average time on market this year of 45 days would normally signal that price gains are just around the corner.

2. The gap between listing prices and selling prices is narrowing. Normally, homes sell within 5 to 10 percent of their listing price. If average selling prices climb within less than five percent of their listing prices, sellers are likely to begin boosting their prices.

3. An increasing percentage of the homes are being sold to people moving into the neighborhood from another area of the city or from out of town. This figure shows the "hot" neighborhood or community is gaining in popularity vis-à-vis other areas.

4. The income, education, and occupation levels of the people moving into an area are generally higher than the neighborhood's current residents. (Note: Don't mistakenly assume that changing eth-

nicity of a neighborhood means property values will fall. Such stereotypical views have been proven false. No matter what its ethnic makeup, experience shows that any neighborhood can achieve substantial gains in desirability and value.)

5. New and existing homeowners in the neighborhood are investing in home remodeling and renovations. Home builders are constructing new homes in the area. Typically, increasing investment means increasing values.

6. The percentage of homes in the neighborhood occupied by owners (as opposed to renters) is increasing. Even viewed alone, this statistic is almost a 100 percent indicator of rising home values. It is virtually certain that a neighborhood will appreciate strongly as homeowners displace renters and absentee landlords.

7. Transportation arteries are improving access to the area. Better roads, a new bridge, or extension of a mass transit facility can push property values up dramatically. If your city has any major new (or improved) access routes or facilities planned, figure out which neighborhoods and communities stand to gain much faster commutes to major job centers.

8. The neighborhood has an active community or homeowners' association that zealously works to protect and enhance living conditions in the area. These activities may involve anything from "Take Pride In Your Home" campaigns, to school improvement programs, to crime prevention measures. An active neighborhood association shows that people care about their homes and their property values.

Even in slow markets, opportunities for home-buying profits always exist. Over time, the differences in profit potential among various homes and neighborhoods can mean tens of thousands of dollars to you. When you're choosing your home, don't overlook this potential. In the end, you may still decide to opt for your "preferred place to live." But make this trade-off—if you see it as a trade off—consciously, not unconsciously.

MISTAKE # **22**

We were told to buy in the best neighborhood we could afford. The best neighborhoods always appreciate the fastest.

LESSON: *Compare neighborhoods on the basis of relative prices and benefits. Never assume a "good" neighborhood will appreciate faster than an "inferior" one.*

Few homebuyers investigate and compare neighborhoods for their appreciation potential. Conventional wisdom tells them, "Buy in the best neighborhood you can afford. The best neighborhoods always appreciate fastest." Not true. As a "preferred place to live," you might consider only the "better" neighborhoods, but don't assume these neighborhoods will appreciate faster than "less desirable" ones.

During the California housing recession, the most expensive homes in Beverly Hills fell in value by 20 to 30 percent. Yet, during this same period, homes in Watts and south-central Los Angeles *increased* in value by 30 percent.

Granted, this comparison is extreme. But the general principle holds: Look for the flashing green lights that signal a neighborhood or community is on the move (see Mistake #21). It's highly unlikely that one neighborhood can consistently appreciate faster than an alternative neighborhood for an indefinite period of time. Once you think about it, you can easily see why above-average appreciation rates can't last forever.

Forecasting Appreciation

Say most homebuyers prefer Hidden Valley Estates over the Swampy River subdivision. Homes in Hidden Valley sell for an average price of $150,000. Homes in Swampy River go for about $100,000. Because buyers favor Hidden Valley, its homes have been appreciating at eight percent a year. In contrast, appreciation in Swampy River has been limping along at just two percent a year. Can you count on this trend to continue? Maybe, maybe not.

With five more years of eight percent appreciation, home prices in Hidden Valley Estates would climb from $150,000 to $220,000. Those Swampy River homes—at a yearly appreciation rate of two percent— would be worth $110,000. Hidden Valley homes now cost twice as much as homes in Swampy River. After another five years of similar appreciation, Hidden Valley homes would cost nearly $325,000. Swampy River home prices would come in at $121,000.

Compare Relative Prices and Benefits

More than likely, at some point well before 10 years have passed, most would-be buyers are going to be priced out of Hidden Valley Estates. Instead, they'll meander through Swampy River. "Well, this place has possibilities," they might say. Before long, as homebuyers switch from Hidden Valley to Swampy River, Hidden Valley appreciation rates will begin to fall. Swampy River appreciation rates will begin to rise.

The new Swampy River homeowners will then join with other residents and change the name Swampy River to the River View Plantation. They will spruce up their homes. They will organize a Neighborhood Watch program. And they will pass a bond measure to improve the local schools, libraries, and parks. Within a few years, River View (a.k.a. Swampy River) will emerge as one of the fastest-appreciating neighborhoods in the area.

But fast appreciation can't last forever. After five years (more or less), homes in River View may also become "overpriced" relative to other neighborhoods and subdivisions. Price increases there will settle down. Appreciation rates in other areas will pick up. Savvy home buyers will create another "hot" neighborhood.

Price trends among types of homes, neighborhoods, and communities nearly always run in cycles. Don't assume past appreciation (slow or fast) points to more of the same. Investigate market signals. Compare the *relative* prices, benefits, and features of various homes and areas. "Inferior" neighborhoods often outperform their betters.

MISTAKE # **23**

We were told never to buy the biggest or most expensive house in the neighborhood.

LESSON: *Buy the home that offers the best value as measured against your priorities and possibilities.*

You've probably heard the common advice, "Don't buy the biggest or most expensive house in the neighborhood." Supposedly, the surrounding smaller, lower-priced homes will bring down the value of the more expensive house. As a result, your home's appreciation rate won't perform as well as the other homes in the neighborhood. Once you think about it, though, this advice fails to make sense.

Say the smaller homes in the neighborhood appreciate at six percent a year. The largest homes appreciate at two percent. With the passing of years, the smaller houses would come to sell for more than the larger houses—which, of course, is not likely. In other words, the rules of compound interest work to invalidate this simplistic advice, just as they also prove false the claims that "the best neighborhoods always appreciate the fastest." (see Mistake #22). Table 2.2 illustrates this.

Now, is it likely large houses would sell at $146,462 while small homes sell at $159,380? Not likely. Whether, in fact, the biggest house on the block will provide a good buy for you depends on your needs, your objectives, and the home's price *relative* to houses more typical of the neighborhood. If you're asked to pay 50 percent more for a home

---

Table 2.2 **Simple Comparison of Appreciation Rates**

	Home Values			
Purchase Price	*2 Years*	*4 Years*	*6 Years*	*8 Years*
$100,000 (6% apprec. for smaller homes)	$112,360	$126,250	$141,850	$159,380
$125,000 (2% apprec. for largest homes)	$130,050	$135,300	$140,327	$146,462

---

that's 50 percent larger, you're probably not getting good value. If you can buy the larger home for just 10 percent more, then you're probably getting a great buy.

Don't avoid the most expensive homes. Instead, perform a value comparison. Figure out how much more home you're getting for your money.

Priorities and Possibilities

Just as important, compare the size and features of the larger home to your priorities and possibilities. If you have a large family or need space for a home office or more comfortable living, the most expensive home in a moderate-priced neighborhood might provide an economical way for you to meet these needs.

Also, consider the possibilities side of the ledger. Even if you don't seem to need the extra size or features of the more expensive home, can you think of a use? How about an art studio, library, or work space? Could you rent out a room or two or maybe convert part of the home into an accessory apartment or mother-in-law suite?

Think income potential. Think affordability. You might be looking at a three-bedroom, two-bath house priced at $115,000. With 10 percent down, the mortgage payments on this home would run around $723 a month (7.5 percent, 30 years). Now, say you discover a five-bedroom, three-bath house in the same neighborhood. You can buy this larger house for $135,000. With 10 percent down, payments on the larger house would cost $849 a month.

You may not need this extra space or want to stretch your budget to come up with another $126 a month. But what if the larger home is designed (or remodeled) so you could rent out those extra two bedrooms and a bath for $375 a month? With this income, you'd drop your monthly mortgage payments down to $474. Rather than costing $126 a month more, the larger home would actually cost $249 a month *less* than the smaller house. Yet, you would still enjoy three bedrooms and two baths for your own use.

Don't Build the Biggest and Best

In most instances, you're not wise to *build* the biggest and best home in the neighborhood. The prices of the smaller houses will bring down the value of the more expensive home. Yet, the biggest and best house will still cost you proportionately more to construct. So, building and buying pose two different questions. When *building new,* you'll pay roughly 50 percent more to construct a 50-percent bigger and better house. When *buying an existing* bigger and better house (compared to the neighborhood average), you may be able to pay a premium of only 20 to 30 percent. It's the original builder (or renovator) who will suffer the loss in market value.

MISTAKE # **24**

I'd never buy a condominium. They make poor investments.

LESSON: *Properly selected, condominiums can yield very good returns.*

Several years back, Paul Maglio bought a two-bedroom condominium located near Boston Harbor. He paid $120,500 for the unit. At the time Paul bought, 200 other potential buyers had put their names on the complex's waiting list. Everyone wanted this sure-fire investment opportunity. With appreciation rates running at two percent a *month,* condominiums were the geese laying golden eggs.

Then, the geese died. Throughout Massachusetts, other states in New England, New York City, much of the Southwest, and Southern California, many condominium (and co-op) prices fell 30 to 70 percent off their peaks. Bruce Hopper, another Bostonian who lost a bundle on his condominium, sadly regrets his decision to buy. "It's too bad," Hopper says, "because condos were the ideal situation for a lot of people—first-time homebuyers who wanted the American dream. But it didn't pan out and now we're stuck."

With experiences like these in recent memory, many potential first-time homebuyers hesitate to buy a condominium. They'd rather stay put in their rental apartments than take a chance on getting "stuck" with a condo that can't be sold for anywhere near its purchase price.

Don't Prejudge: Weigh Risks against Potential Rewards

The above fears and concerns are justified. But as with all other investments, you should weigh potential risks against potential rewards. To simply dismiss condos as "poor investments" without looking closely at the specific market opportunities that exist in your area could be a mistake.

It is true that, since the early to mid-1970s, many different condominium markets throughout the United States have seen their prices escalate wildly and then nosedive. Between 1973 and 1975, condo markets crashed in the Southeast, especially South Carolina and Florida. After a steep run-up in condominium prices in Chicago in the late 1970s and early 1980s, condo prices there fell more than the 1987 stock market crash. Between 1978 and 1983, many condos in Dallas and Houston tripled in value. By 1987 these same units were selling for 50 cents on the dollar. From the early to mid-1980s to 1988, Boston condo prices shot up without restraint. By 1989 the market had hit the skids. By 1993 nearly one-half the condominium homeowners' associations in the state of Massachusetts were approaching insolvency. In the Burbank Street complex in Boston, units that originally sold for $50,000 could hardly be sold for $5,000. That's the bad news.

How to Spot a Condo Bargain

Let's now turn to the bright side. First, in nearly every case, the major groups of condo buyers who have lost money have been those who bought within a year or two of the top of the market. Longer-term owners nearly always have come out ahead. Second, condo owners who could see the crash coming and sold out near the top of the market often made tens of thousands of dollars. Third, buyers today who can learn to spot opportunity (and smell potential danger) stand to make good profits.

By learning the lessons of history, you can reasonably judge whether condo prices in your area stand a good chance of going up (or down). To spot opportunity here are the signals to look for:

1. Nearly everyone is pessimistic about future appreciation rates. (Yes, contrarians frequently do make money.)

2. The monthly after-tax payments for principal, interest, property taxes, insurance, and homeowner fees total less than monthly rentals on comparable apartments. In other words, you can own cheaper than you can rent—right now.
3. The market values of the units are substantially below the cost of constructing similar new units (see Mistake #31).
4. Vacancy rates for rental apartments are less than five percent.
5. Local economic indicators (number of people working, retail sales, new car sales, bank deposits, new business starts, etc.) show increasing strength.
6. The units you are considering enjoy some *unique* and *highly desirable* advantages (design, views, location).
7. Very few new apartment or condominium complexes are being built or planned. No major conversions of apartments to condominiums are under way or planned. Government restrictions limit apartment conversions.
8. Compared to single-family homes, condo prices (especially when calculated on a price-per-square-foot basis) sit relatively low.
9. The complex you are looking at is stable: strong financial reserves for repairs and replacements; no pending litigation; very few units occupied by renters (fewer than 20 percent is good, less than 10 percent is excellent); relatively little turnover of owners and residents; well-maintained common areas; and harmonious relations among owners.

On the downside, history shows that, in most cases, a precipitous fall in prices usually is foreshadowed by one or more of these danger signals:

1. A downturn in local employment.
2. Large numbers of apartments being converted to condos, especially when accompanied by very easy qualifier financing.
3. Large amounts of new condo or apartment construction.
4. The current monthly costs of owning greatly exceed the monthly costs of renting.

5. More than 30 to 40 percent of a complex's units are investor owned and are occupied by renters (or even worse, vacant).

6. Everybody "knows" values are going up at least 10 to 15 percent a year. The market is rampant with speculation.

Past experience has taught lenders, investors, and overly optimistic homebuyers that a condominium isn't a printing press for money disguised as a place to live. Nevertheless, with most speculation now squeezed out of the market, condos in many cities once again offer good long-term investment potential. Remember, too, that owning a condominium protects you against future rent increases (see Mistake #1). Even ignoring appreciation, when you can own for less than you can rent, your condominium will yield a good financial return. As you pay down your mortgage balance, you will build up your net worth with home equity. And a condominium can help you escape from renter's jail. Today, in most cities throughout the United States, owning a well-selected condominium definitely beats paying rent to a landlord.

MISTAKE # **25**

IBM never lays anyone off, do they?

LESSON: *Before you buy a home, evaluate the emerging strength (or weakness) of your local economy.*

To understand and forecast the direction of home prices—as well as the prices of all other types of investment—maintain a keen sense of history. When you understand economic cycles, you guard yourself against excessive optimism or undue despair. With a knowledge of the past, you're less likely to lose sight of the fact that markets go through recurring periods of economic boom and retrenchment.

Economic Cycles

Think about these past events: In 1972 the Club of Rome, a group of world "experts," got together in Rome, Italy, and fed a bunch of numbers into a computer. Their output resulted in a study called *The Limits of Growth*. Without zero population growth, this study concluded, the world would soon run out of resources, especially food. Famine was imminent.

Following logically from the conclusions of this study, billions of dollars were invested in U.S. farmland. Within a few years, farm prices jumped from $1,000 to $4,000 an acre. Banks, investors, and farmers rushed in to take advantage of the predicted economic strength of the farm belt states. Profits, it seemed, were there for the taking.

In 1982, after several years of OPEC-induced oil "shortages," the U.S. Department of Energy warned that "at current rates of production, the United States' reserves of petroleum will be used up in eight years—by 1991; natural gas reserves will be used up in 10 years—by 1993." Reacting to the sure profits to be made in the oil belt states, hundreds of billions of dollars flowed into Texas, Oklahoma, and Colorado real estate.

In 1989, as reports of New England's slide into recession caught national attention, homebuyers in Southern California lined up to buy homes as fast as they came on the market. Multiple offers became commonplace. Eager prospects for new homes even camped at development sites while waiting for the kick-off of the sales campaign. "We were afraid that if we didn't buy now, we'd lose our chance forever," said Theresa Nham at the time of her purchase in May 1989. "Forget New England. Southern California's economy is too diversified to suffer a downturn. Home prices here always go up."

In one sense, of course, history proves Theresa right. Home prices have always gone up. But she should have added "over the longer run." In the short run, home prices can weaken. Layoffs and unemployment can bring home prices down. And such a crash is all the more likely when speculation runs amok, as it did in the farm belt, the oil belt, and, more recently, the defense belt. As is now well known, even IBM can hit hard times and lay people off.

Evaluate Your Local Economy

Looking back, it's easy to see that too many homebuyers and real estate investors have focused only on the economic present—or, even worse, carried overly optimistic projections into the future as far as the eye can see. To prevent this mistake, check the strength of your local economy. Is it stable and growing steadily? Does it show signs of weakness? Is it exploding with speculation?

What do the signals indicate?

- Are unemployment claims increasing or decreasing?
- Is help-wanted advertising in the local newspapers expanding or contracting?
- Is credit becoming more, or less, available for local businesses?
- Are office building occupancy rates and rents increasing or decreasing?
- Are used car prices (especially for the luxury or more expensive models) increasing or decreasing?
- Are bankruptcies of local businesses decreasing or increasing?
- Are home prices increasing moderately or have they been going up by 12 percent a year or more for the past two or three years? Are home prices falling?

Within recent history, nearly every area of the country—rust belt, farm belt, oil belt, sun belt, defense belt—experienced some type of economic downturn. Now, as we move toward the year 2000, each of these areas seems to have regained its path of economic growth. Overall, you can expect the future to bring steadily increasing home prices.

But short-term exceptions will occur. So don't simply assume your area's economic future. Investigate the facts. Most areas go through ups and downs. If the short-term economic outlook for jobs in your area seems shaky, you might want to delay buying. Or you might focus on finding a growth neighborhood, a bargain-priced home, or a home where you can create value through improvements.

MISTAKE # **26**

With all the new construction, we thought the economy was really booming. Home prices had to go up.

LESSON: *Large amounts of new construction (homes, apartments, office buildings) often signal boom, then recession.*

When General Motors closed the Buick plant in Flint, Michigan and laid off several thousand auto workers, you didn't need a Ph.D. in economics to know that home prices in Flint would take a plunge. But too much new construction in an area also can temporarily depress home prices. Somewhat deceptively, though, excessive new construction often creates a boom before it creates a downturn. Apart from the contraction or expansion of an area's basic economy, the construction cycle itself can send home prices both up and down.

The Construction Cycle

To see this cycle in action, ask yourself: Why do builders build? To make a profit, right? So as home buying increases and home prices rise, builders start constructing more homes and apartments. This construction and sales activity create more jobs for real estate agents, real estate attorneys, accountants, environmental impact specialists, site engineers, architects, electricians, carpenters, plumbers, suppliers of building materials, loan officers, and all the other people who benefit from home building and home buying.

All this new construction also creates a demand for office space as businesses and professional firms expand. This brings in the developers of office buildings. More construction-related jobs bring in even more demand for housing. Home prices continue to increase. Anticipating higher profits, builders continue to build more homes and offices to meet this growing demand.

But all booms end. Sooner or later, depending on the local levels of wages and employment, builders overshoot their market. Their inventories of unsold homes begin to increase. Office-building vacancies climb. Developers cut back on their building. Workers are laid off. Incomes fall. Demand for homes falls. Builders have to cut prices or offer special buying incentives.

Newspapers take notice. Journalists talk up the weakening market. They find people to interview who are in financial trouble. They quote media experts who say a home is no longer a good investment. Resales of existing homes begin to weaken. Time-on-the-market figures show that homes are taking longer to sell. Prices for existing homes soften. Many potential buyers put their plans on hold. They want to wait and see. They ask themselves, "Why buy today if prices will be lower tomorrow? Besides, maybe our jobs and income aren't as secure as we thought." Both builders and potential buyers begin to fear economic uncertainty.

With the market slowdown, homes can no longer be sold for prices high enough to cover the costs required to build them. Many builders see red ink instead of profits. Lenders shut down their credit lines. Acquisition, development, and construction (ADC) loans become more difficult to get. Lenders also tighten their credit standards for home buyers. The housing boom becomes a bust.

Recovery Begins

Yet, even as this slowdown occurs, the population continues to grow. People get married. Children are born. Workers who have been laid off find new jobs. Recent college graduates begin their careers and start earning a monthly income. Businesses and factories that had closed are reopened by other companies. Entrepreneurs create new businesses. Total employment and wages begin to improve.

These economic changes don't just happen. Nor are they caused primarily by government programs. They occur because people who get hurt by economic downturns figure out ways to get back on their feet. Better circumstances and a more confident outlook means more people buy homes. Prices begin to firm up. Still, builders don't rush into new construction, for as economic recovery takes hold, construction costs tend to rise. Land, lumber, and building materials become more expensive. Cost-increasing safety and environmental regulations are tightened. Cities impose impact fees on new homes to pay the costs of needed roads, schools, parks, and other municipal facilities. Before builders really gear up for large amounts of new construction, they must wait for more homebuyers to continue pushing prices up to higher levels. That's the only way builders are able to cover the now-higher costs of construction.

As recovery takes hold, it's not just new homes that cost more. More upward pressure is placed on the prices of existing homes. As new homes become more expensive to build, the values of existing homes are pulled up along with the higher costs of new construction. When homebuyers, home sellers, and builders regain their confidence in the future, journalists change from pessimists to optimists. They begin to write articles more favorable to home buying. More renters decide to start visiting open houses and calling Realtors for help. Stories of multiple offers are heard. Waiting lists are required for presales of new home developments. Home prices move up by 5 to 10 percent or more. A new cycle is off and running. In response to low inventories of new homes, increasing construction costs, and pent-up demand by wait-and-see buyers home prices ratchet up another notch.

Know the Price Cycle

By understanding how this construction cycle typically works, you avoid the mistake of buying with unrealistic expectations. Absent extraordinary local job growth and land shortages, home prices can't increase at rates of 10, 12, or 15 percent year in and year out. When escalating home prices become the chief topic of conversation at cocktail parties and office get-togethers, you can safely bet builders from throughout your region will be lured into the market with hopes of easy profits. More builders mean more homes for sale. Eventually, more homes for sale means a temporary decline (or leveling off) of home prices.

Buying near the top of the price cycle doesn't mean you've made a mistake. Over time, history shows that "buying now" typically beats buying later.

Too many people who wait for the "best time" to buy end up procrastinating for years while they watch home prices rise to higher and higher levels. In good times they say "prices are too high." In down markets they say "the economy's too uncertain." They always find an excuse to hesitate and avoid commitment. So, "buying at the top" clearly beats perpetual procrastination.

However, if market signals do indicate the market is slowing, develop a cautious buying strategy. Don't use wildly creative (and dangerous) financing. Don't base your purchase on the belief home prices are going to double in four years. The homebuyers who have been hurt most by market downturns are those who have unrealistically stretched their finances and inflated their expectations.

MISTAKE # **27**

The newspapers say home prices are decreasing/increasing.

LESSON: Interpret reports of home price decreases or increases carefully. Often such reports don't mean what they seem to mean.

Have you ever seen newspaper articles headlined something like, "Home Prices Fell 8 Percent Last Year," or maybe, "March–June Home Prices Up 15 Percent Over Same Period a Year Ago." If you have, don't put much faith in them. Chances are, neither of these statistics is right.

In their reporting of home price increases or decreases most newspapers and magazines incorrectly cite median price figures. The median price, however, tells nothing about the actual appreciation (or depreciation) of home values. The median sets a midpoint: Half of the homes sold for more and half the homes sold for less than the median price.

In periods when most homebuyers are buying lower-priced properties, the median will fall. In periods when upscale buyers pour into the market, the median price goes up. Median-price figures can tell you which price segments of the market are most active. But don't conclude that actual home values are moving at the same rate—or even in the same direction—as the median.

"Prince George's County showed the healthiest appreciation of any market," wrote Jacqueline Salmon in the *Washington Post*. "The *median* [emphasis added] price of a single-family house, including townhouses, rose to $133,750." Did homes in Prince George's County actually appreciate? If so, did they appreciate by 15 percent? To answer these questions correctly, you would have to compare sale-resale data for the same (or similar) homes. The median won't tell you.

More First-Time Buyers Mean Lower Reported Prices

By confusing changes in median prices with appreciation/depreciation rates, many reporters like Salmon unwittingly mislead their readers. I've often talked with potential homebuyers who believed home prices were falling, when prices were actually increasing. During the early 1990s downturn in the San Diego market, for example, many renters feared buying because they thought home prices had stumbled. At the higher price levels ($500,000 and up), both prices and sales volume had headed down. Naturally, with slow top end sales and more first-time buyers, the median selling price of homes also fell. At the entry level ($125,000 to $175,000), though, home prices between 1989 and 1993 held steady and maybe even strengthened a bit. With improving mortgage affordability, savvy first-time buyers kept the low-end market strong (as contrasted to San Diego's sagging local economy).

Upscale Buying Pulls Median Prices Up

Likewise, if you don't evaluate price figures carefully, you also could conclude that home prices are appreciating faster than they really are. At some point along the way to full economic recovery, more move-up buyers will come back into the market. As upscale sales increase, the median price could quickly jump 15 to 30 percent. But without looking at sale-resale price data, it would be a mistake to conclude home values had actually jumped that much.

Overall, don't let median prices mislead you. Get the facts about homes, neighborhoods, and price ranges. Ask your Realtor to show you the actual trends in *selling* prices for specific types of homes. With facts instead of averages, you'll develop a better home-buying strategy.

CHAPTER 3

How to Find Good Value

In the old days of home buying, "inflation cures all mistakes" became a popular cliche. The idea was that it didn't really matter how much you paid for your home. With appreciation rates of 10 to 20 percent a year, even if you overpaid by $10,000 or $20,000, who cared? You could get that back in a year or two.

Today, of course, value matters. To make your home pay off as an investment, you should shop for value just as you would shop for neighborhood or property features. The mistakes discussed in this chapter alert you to the most important principles of valuation. When you combine these principles with the knowledge gained from other chapters, you will be able to find a home that offers outstanding value and potential for appreciation.

MISTAKE # **28**

We thought we got a real bargain. Our house was listed $20,000 below other houses we looked at in the neighborhood.

LESSON: *Don't compare homes on the basis of listing price.*

When you start shopping for a home, your natural tendency may be to rank homes as a "good value" or "overpriced" on the basis of their listing prices. Say your real estate agent shows you three similar homes in a neighborhood. One is listed for sale at $172,000, another at $189,000, and the third at $163,000. Based solely on this information, the home priced at $163,000 looks like a bargain. You may tell yourself, "We should grab this one. The sellers are way under the competition." But hold on to your hat. Before you leap for the "bargain," do a little more investigating.

All Homes May Be Overpriced

First, recognize that all the sellers may be asking too much. None of the three homes may actually be priced in line with the current market. In fact, some sales agents have been known to steer eager buyers to three or four greatly overpriced properties and then show the unsuspecting buyers a home that's priced $10,000, $20,000, or even $50,000 less than the others. "I've been saving the best for last," say these agents. "This house just came on the market. You'd be smart to put a contract in on it right away. Several other agents from the office are showing the home later today. This one will probably go fast."

Before you jump at the chance of a lifetime, verify the "bargain" by checking the most recent *selling* prices of homes in the neighborhood. As markets slow down, many home sellers fail to adjust their listing prices with the new market reality. That's one reason for the home seller lament, "Homes aren't selling." It's not that buyers aren't ready to buy. Rather, "homes aren't selling" because sellers have listed their homes with unrealistic expectations.

As a result, houses sit unsold for months. A few sellers who are serious about selling eventually become educated about the market and begin to reduce their listing prices. Others, though, hang on, hoping for a miracle. Although you'll find some homes listed at the owners' dream prices in every market, overpricing almost becomes the norm in slow markets. In those situations, you especially do not want to use list price as a guide to value.

Sellers Will Sell for Less

Listing price can mislead in another way too. You know that most sellers will sell for less than their listing price. But how much less? The owner who is asking $162,500 may hold tight to that figure. The owners who have their home listed for $179,800 may become so panicked about the "slow market" or their need for quick cash that they'll take the first serious offer they get—even when that offer is at $150,000.

Should you find an overpriced home you like, don't write it off. Probe the sellers or your real estate agent to learn how flexible (desperate) the sellers might be. Use market facts about the actual selling prices of neighborhood homes to lead the sellers out of their fantasyland. At first glance, a home listed at $20,000 less than another may appear to be the best buy. But what if you can get the sellers of the overpriced listing to come down $30,000? In that case, the highest priced listing may end up as the real bargain.

MISTAKE # **29**

We thought we got a real bargain. We paid $10,000 less than the appraised value.

LESSON: *Never put blind faith in an appraisal.*

Many prospective home buyers mistakenly believe the end-all of real estate valuation is an appraisal. To the uninitiated, a property is worth what the appraisal says it's worth—no more, no less.

In their book *Getting the Most for Your Home,* Dan Lieberman and Paul Hoffman tell home sellers, "Americans often believe what they see in writing far more than what they are told. A written appraisal for your home, showing its value as higher than your asking price, sitting on the dining room table . . . gives you the edge in the logical part of convincing a buyer of the value of your home. . . . Work the appraisal to your advantage, then sell the house 'below appraised value.' Buyers will feel they are getting a bargain" (p. 242).

On numerous occasions when I've been looking at homes for sale, a seller or real estate agent has used this ploy. "Look at this," the agent might say. "We've got this home priced $15,000 below its appraised value. The sellers are moving out of town. To get a quick sale, they're willing to practically give their house away."

Maybe they are. But maybe, too, they've "worked the appraisal" to their advantage to make "buyers feel like they are getting a bargain."

Should you run into this type of sales presentation, here are several things you should know about appraisals and appraisers.

Appraisals Have Time-Limited Value

Appraisals are like a no-refund airline ticket. At best, they're good for one date only. So, one of the first things you need to do is look at the date the appraisal was performed. If home prices are changing (up or down), an appraisal that's even a month or two old could already be out of sync with the market. (A sample appraisal form is reproduced in the "Resources" section of this book.)

Consider the Comp Dates

Even more important than the date of the appraisal are the sale dates of the comparable homes listed in the appraisal, or "comps." Every home appraisal is based on the recent selling prices of similar homes in the neighborhoods. Ideally, these sales should have taken place within the past 90 days. Often, though, in slow markets no comp sales have occurred recently. In these cases, appraisers sometimes go back six months or a year for their sales data. Obviously, "stale" comps may not indicate today's value.

If appraisers do go back in time for sales price data, they are supposed to bring the figures up to date with a time adjustment. But without recent sales data, how are they to know how much to adjust the past figures? As a result, they don't. They simply use a p.f.a. (pulled-from-the-air) adjustment. Because of these appraisal difficulties, you should seriously question any appraisal that's derived from out-of-date or time-adjusted market data.

Appraisers Don't Measure Value

An appraisal is not a certificate of value. Nor do appraisers measure or determine a home's worth. An appraisal is one person's opinion of the price buyers are likely to pay for a home. Naturally, then, since appraisals reflect opinions, the appraisal process leaves wide room for subjective judgments. As a buyer who is informed about the market, you should feel perfectly free to refute an appraisal. Don't let a seller, sales agent, or appraiser intimidate you. You need not accept an appraiser's estimate. Use an appraisal as one source of market information—not as "the answer."

Many Conditions Limit Appraisals

Appraisals include many limiting conditions. Although we won't go into most of them here, one that I will point out reads as follows: "The appraiser assumes there are no hidden or unapparent conditions of the property, subsoil, or structures which would render it more or less valuable. The appraiser assumes no responsibility for such conditions, or for engineering which might be required to discover such factors."

In other words, except for patently obvious defects, the appraiser values the home as if it were problem-free. If the appraiser can't see the defect, then for the purpose of the appraisal, the defect doesn't exist.

Or sometimes, even when the appraiser can see the defect, he or she may assume it doesn't exist. Several years ago I was interested in buying a house in Gainesville, Florida. I was dealing directly with the owner because she was a friend of a friend and hadn't yet formally listed the home for sale. The house was only four or five years old, well designed, located in a good neighborhood, and only a 10-minute walk from the University of Florida campus. The owner showed me an appraisal on the property that estimated its value as $85,000 to $88,000. Those figures were typical of the neighborhood.

The Appraisal Ignored Property Defects

However, there was one problem with the house. The lower level, which consisted of a three-car garage and an unfinished home office, had several long (18-foot) cracks running through it. The cement floor had buckled up much like large tree roots can buckle a sidewalk. I asked the owner, "What caused those cracks?"

"Oh, those are settling cracks," she said.

Settling cracks? Not likely. I called a home inspector to take a look at the problem. He knew the cause of the cracks right away. "This house is built on clay with an improper foundation," he told me. "Every time it rains heavy, the clay absorbs the water, expands, and literally pushes the house upward. Then, when the clay dries out, it contracts, and the house falls."

That didn't sound too good. So I called several soil engineers and building contractors. Repairing the problem would cost anywhere from $10,000 to $40,000. And those costs didn't include any warranty or guarantee that the work would be successful.

I'm a bit of a risk taker, so I told the owner about the problem. (Later, I found out she already knew the real cause of the cracks.) I said, "Let's talk price. Given the serious and indeterminate nature of the necessary repairs, I'm willing to pay $60,000."

She balked. "Sixty thousand dollars? The appraisal says $85,000 to $88,000," she pointed out.

"Yes, but that's not considering the foundation and soil problem," I countered.

"Yes, it does," the owner argued. She then showed me in the small print where the appraiser had commented that the cracks in the floor could cause some buyer resistance. Therefore, a probable selling price would sit closer to $85,000 than $88,000.

I said, "That's nonsense. No one's going to pay $85,000 for this house." I then called the appraiser. "How could you discount the value of a house just $3,000 or so when the repairs could cost $10,000 to $40,000?"

The appraiser said repair estimates weren't a part of her job. "Besides," she added, "that home inspector you used is always too critical." To make an even longer story shorter, I got nowhere with the appraiser. The owner eventually came down in price to $80,000. But she did that only reluctantly. Again and again she referred to the "appraised value" of the house of $85,000 (or more). "At $80,000," she said, "you're really getting a bargain. Plus, I'm willing to offer good terms on the financing. (Of course, she had to carry back financing on the property because no financial institution would have touched it with its foundation defects so obvious.)

As you can guess, I passed on the deal. I'm not that much of a risk taker. But this experience shows how appraisers can pretend problems don't exist, even when they know about them. Just as important, it shows how an owner would mistakenly ignore the common sense of the matter in favor of wishful thinking. The owner had an appraisal that said the house was worth $85,000. To her way of thinking, any price less than that would be giving the house away. (I just hope the seller didn't find a naive buyer who failed to understand the limitations of an appraisal and the need to get a home's physical condition checked out by a professional inspector.)

Verify the Facts and Figures

To be safe, you should check the arithmetic of the appraiser's calculations and the factual description of the appraised property. With the use of computer-prepared appraisals, appraisers have been able to cut down on their errors of addition, subtraction, and multiplication. Still, mistakes do occur. So, taking a few minutes to verify the appraiser's arithmetic can be time well spent.

Beyond mathematical errors, though, appraisals all too often fall into the "garbage in, garbage out" trap. When appraisers are busy, they might go through 8 to 12 houses a day. Also, some appraisal firms operate "factory appraisal shops." They use untrained, low-wage employees or appraisal trainees to perform property inspections. Then back at the office a licensed appraiser fills in the appraisal forms and signs off on the report.

No matter what appraisal procedures are used, though, there are many ways errors can slip into the process. I recently saw an appraisal that included errors in the following areas: the square footage of the home, the size of the site, neighborhood zoning, the floor plan of the house, and the arithmetic. That was truly a "garbage in, garbage out" appraisal.

By cautioning you to verify the facts and figures in an appraisal, I'm not implying that most home appraisals are prepared incompetently. Just recognize that checking both the accuracy and reasonableness of an appraiser's estimates is good insurance. If you naively accept an appraisal without carefully looking at it, you are making a mistake. And these words of warning apply especially when an appraisal is presented as part of a homeowner's selling effort.

Beware of Lowball Appraisals

Although most often you must guard against sellers' appraisals that come in too high, sometimes you also might face a lender's appraisal that comes in too low to justify your mortgage loan. Consider the experience of Phil Tortellori.

"We had spent almost a year looking at houses," says Phil. "We liked a lot of them, but for one reason or other nothing quite excited our fancy. Then one Saturday we drove by a house we knew we had to have. It was priced right—or I should say, we thought it was priced right. Unfortunately, less than 10 days before closing, we learned the lender's appraiser had reported a different opinion. Her estimate of the home's value came in $10,000 less than our purchase price.

"To offset this lower appraised value, the lender said we'd have to increase our down payment by $8,000. Or, instead, we could ask the sellers to reduce their price. We had bargained hard as it was, so we didn't think the sellers would agree to come down more. And they wouldn't. As for raising our down payment by $8,000, no way could we do that. So, the financing fell through and we had to begin our home search all over again."

Both homebuyers and home sellers have complained of lowball appraisals that killed home sales. In some instances lenders have used low appraisals to turn down loans they didn't want to make. At other times lender appraisers have given low appraisals in response to tightened government appraisal regulations. Either way, a lowball appraisal can definitely spoil your home-buying plans.

How to Prevent Deal-Killer Appraisals

To help prevent this problem, you can do several different things. First, before you offer to buy a home, make sure your agent shows you recent sales prices (and terms) of similar homes in the neighborhood. Use those prices as a guide for your purchase offer. Second, if possible, learn the name of the appraiser your lender plans to use. Have your agent tell the appraiser the comp sales you relied on to figure your offer. Third, once the appraisal is complete, get a copy from the lender. (You are entitled to a copy of your appraisal under the 1991 Equal Credit Opportunity Act as well as various state laws and the rules and regulations of the Federal Reserve Board.) Examine the appraisal according to the checks we are discussing in this chapter.

If your lender doesn't approve your loan because of the appraisal, you can legitimately back out of the transaction and recover your earnest money deposit. On the other hand, if you think the appraiser has low-balled you, schedule a meeting with the appraiser, or write out your objections to the appraisal and give them to your lender.

In response, the appraiser can either accept or reject your comments. If he or she rejects them, you can ask the lender to send out another appraiser. If the lender wants your business, it will probably agree to obtain a second opinion. But if the lender doesn't oblige, you will have to increase your down payment, ask the sellers to reduce their price, or apply for your mortgage somewhere else. (To appease your frustrations with the appraiser, you could write a complaint to the state licensing board. But that won't help you get the financing you need.)

Lowball appraisals don't seem to be a major problem right now; but it is a practice you need to stay alert for. On the other hand, in sharply rising markets—at least in the past—you have to watch out for "over-appraising." With rapid rates of appreciation, lenders, appraisers, and homebuyers alike can get careless. With eyes focused on the future, no one worries much about the price today, because it's sure to be even higher tomorrow.

Appraisals Don't Include Personal Property

Keep in mind one more thing. Appraisers limit their value estimates to the house and lot (real estate). If your purchase agreement includes any expensive personal property (antique Oriental rugs, custom-made draperies, furniture), or if the seller is paying all or a large part of your mortgage points and closing costs, the lender's appraiser can legitimately exclude these amounts from his or her value estimate. In cases like this, there's a good chance you won't be able to borrow the full 80, 90, or 95 percent of your purchase price. So, before you write seller concessions directly into your contract, learn your lender's rules on concessions and ask your real estate agent (or attorney) to figure out the best way to handle them. Sometimes it's to your advantage to write up a separate agreement to cover these items (see also Mistake #78).

MISTAKE # **30**

The appraiser didn't tell us home values were going to fall.

LESSON: More than likely, your appraiser, your lender, and your real estate agent will not warn you that home prices may be weakening in your area.

Maria and Jorge Olson were sitting in the living room of the home they were hoping to buy. Five other hopeful buyers were also present. The home was listed for sale at $290,000. The sales agent for the owners came into the room. Nervous tension hung in the air. "We're going to start the bidding now," the agent said. Offers started flying. Pandemonium broke lose.

"It was really wild," Maria recalled. "Then, after everyone had had their say and written up their offers, the agent and the owners left the room. When they came back, we just knew we'd won. We were right. The owners accepted our offer of $310,000. We celebrated that evening by going out to dinner at the most expensive restaurant in town. With home values increasing 30 percent a year, even at $310,000 we got such a great deal we felt rich."

Sadly, three years later Maria and Jorge were in divorce court. They needed to sell their home and hired an appraiser. His value estimate came in at $260,000—just about the same as the listing price that several real estate agents had suggested to the Olsons. (Several other agents had estimated much higher.)

Lawsuits against Appraisers Require Proof of Negligence

To say the least, the Olsons were distressed and angry. They wanted someone to blame. So, they decided to sue their lender and the appraisal firm the lender had employed to appraise the home when they had bought it. That appraisal showed a value for the home of $325,000. The Olsons knew the current market was weak. But surely prices couldn't have fallen that much. The first appraiser must have overvalued the home. Or, if prices were really going to fall that much, the Olsons argued, the lender and the appraiser had a duty to warn them.

The Olsons lost the court case for two reasons. First, expert testimony showed that the original $325,000 value estimate fit within a reasonable price range for the home at that time. Although one could question the appraiser's judgment on several points, the appraisal itself contained no egregious errors. Second, the court ruled that appraisers weren't hired to predict the future. Estimates of market value apply only to the date of the appraisal. Neither the Olsons nor any other homebuyers should expect an appraiser, their mortgage lender, or even their real estate agent to tell them whether home prices are headed up or down.

Appraisers Don't Forecast Values

Throughout the United States, the ruling in this case generally holds. With limited exceptions, homebuyers must make their own forecasts. Appraisers only describe the current market. Appraisers might believe, "The market is wild with speculation. Buyers are crazy. Within a year prices are going to fall faster than the stock market crash of '87." But unless asked, appraisers aren't likely to put these comments in their appraisal reports.

Likewise, in performing a market value appraisal, an appraiser wouldn't comment, "This is the best market for homebuyers we've had in years. Home prices are sure to double within the next five years." You could ask an appraiser (or real estate agent) to give you his or her opinion about where the market is headed over the coming years. But for you to see the future as clearly as possible, look to the market signals that are discussed in Chapter 2.

Many homebuyers think they are getting a great buy if they purchase their home for less than its current market value. However, that's not all you need to consider. Ask yourself these two questions before you buy: (1) What market signals (or property features) indicate this home will be worth more tomorrow than it is today? And (2) what market signals spell D-A-N-G-E-R? (See Mistakes #24, #25, and #26.)

MISTAKE # **31**

We didn't think to calculate replacement costs.

LESSON: The cost to reconstruct a home at today's prices can give you a good idea where market values are headed.

If you look on the back side of an appraisal form toward the upper left-hand corner of the page, you'll typically find a box for calculations called "Estimated Reproduction Cost New of Improvements." By completing this section of the appraisal report an appraiser tries to figure out how much it would cost to build the subject home (house or apartment) at today's prices. After subtracting for depreciation on the home and adding in the value of the lot, the final result is supposed to reflect the current market value of the house.

Very few homebuyers, however, pay much attention to these types of cost calculations. Like appraisers, most homebuyers prefer to rely heavily on the comparable sales method of estimating a home's value: A house is worth about the same amount as other homes in the neighborhood that have sold recently. In fact, most appraisers simply fiddle with numbers in the cost-approach-to-value section of an appraisal report. They try to make the numbers agree with the comp/sales value estimate. Most appraisers believe a home is worth what someone is willing to pay. How much it costs to build doesn't matter.

Use Replacement Costs to Help Forecast Values

For purposes of estimating today's market value, the appraisers are right. Reproduction costs don't matter much. But for predicting whether home prices are going up or down, construction costs matter a great deal.

When Suzy Wilson and Carrie Sloan bought their townhouse in an overheated Dallas market, they paid $123,000 for a 1,100-square-foot, two-bedroom, three-year-old unit. That price works out to about $112 per square foot. Since the market was booming, Suzy and Carrie's real estate agent had found quite a few comparable townhouse units that had sold recently. Based on the selling price of similar units, these young accountants got a good price.

But Suzy and Carrie focused too much on current and rapidly escalating home prices of the past year. In doing so, they missed two critical market signals: (1) The Texas oil economy was showing signs of slipping; (2) more to the point for our purpose here, townhouses similar to the unit these women bought could be newly built at a total cost of approximately $85 a square foot (including land). That meant condo developers could expect to construct new units, sell them at their market prices (over $100 per square foot), and make a profit (killing) of $20,000 to $30,000 a unit. Naturally, this fact did not escape the attention of condo developers. With banks and savings and loans shoveling money out to developers (who frequently owned the S&Ls), the condo market became glutted with new units. As the oversupply of condos ran head-on into the weakening Texas economy, what had been a severe shortage of homes for sale quickly became a surplus. Condo prices crashed.

Single-Family Homes Also Were Overbuilt

At the same time, similar cost-value imbalances were felt in the markets for new and existing single-family homes. First, market values rose far in excess of land and construction costs. Then, fueled by the optimism of rising prices and increasing profits, builders rushed in to build more homes.

You know the end of the story: billion-dollar bailouts for banks and S&Ls.

This particular experience was extreme. Nevertheless, similar episodes of overbuilding run throughout our economic history. And they will again. But you can protect yourself against value losses by talking to builders, contractors, or knowledgeable real estate agents. Ask them what it would cost per square foot to construct the type of home you're thinking about buying. Then do some rough calculations. If, after allowing for land (lot) value and depreciation, your home-to-be is priced too high relative to its construction costs, don't count on short-term appreciation. When home prices are, say, 25 to 40 percent higher than construction costs, home values can't be expected to continue increasing.

On the other hand, if market values are too low to cover new construction costs, then builders won't build new homes and apartments. As the local economy strengthens, growth in incomes, employment, and population will push existing home prices up.

At any specific time, market values can rise above or fall below a home's building costs. Over time, though, home prices nearly always keep pace with the costs of new construction. Today's costs of construction may not tell you much about today's home values. But, more than likely, they will signal whether home prices are headed up or down. When builders can't build at a profit, they won't build. When excessive profits are expected, too many builders enter the market. Then, increasing numbers of new homes drive prices lower.

MISTAKE # 32

We didn't pay attention to lot value. We wasted $22,000 on remodeling.

LESSON: *Before you buy a home, separate the value of the house from the value of the lot.*

When Jeri and Rod Craig bought their older, slightly rundown home, they had great plans for it. The home was located in a neighborhood where larger and newer homes were valued at $450,000. The Craigs paid just $145,000 for their house.

After moving in, the Craigs undertook a top-to-bottom remake of their home. Doing much of the work themselves, they refinished the hardwood floors, installed tile and fixtures in the bathrooms and kitchen, added a deck, enclosed a porch, and gutted the kitchen's out-of-date cabinets and appliances. Through their renovation, they transformed the kitchen into a chef's delight. Indeed, throughout the home, their pride of workmanship displayed itself in every detail. Admiring the fruits of their labor, the Craigs were confident their six months of toil and $22,000 of expenses would enhance their home's value by at least

$50,000 to $75,000. At a price of, say, $200,000, their home's value still came in near the low end of the price range for the neighborhood.

Unexpectedly, the Craigs got to test their value-added theory sooner than they wanted. Within a year of completing their home's makeover, Jeri received a great job offer from a firm in another city. The Craigs decided to move. They knew the housing market had done well. Sales activity was high. Values were up. Compared to the other (and relatively few) lower-priced homes in the neighborhood, the Craigs' home stood out as the best. Since several of these lesser homes had recently sold for $165,000 to $175,000, the Craigs decided to list their house at $200,000 and go for a quick sale.

But 30 days passed, then 60 days, then 90 days. Several offers came in at around $170,000, but the Craigs felt insulted. They kept pointing to the high quality of their renovation work. Potential buyers agreed but wouldn't increase their bids. Eventually, when the Craigs could delay their sale no longer, they reluctantly accepted an offer of $175,000— hardly enough to cover the cost of the home and their out-of-pocket expenses, not to mention all the work they had put into it.

Beware of Over (or Under) Improving Your House

Why couldn't the Craigs fully profit from their home improvements? Because prior to their renovation work, they didn't think about the value of their lot. When they paid $145,000, they didn't really pay for a house. That came free. They paid for the land. Three weeks after they moved out of their perfectly modernized 1,400-square-foot bungalow, a bulldozer came in and leveled it. In its place, the new owners began construction of their five-bedroom, four-bath, 4,200-square-foot home. The Craigs had misspent their time and effort on a house that was obsolete for the neighborhood.

In one sense, Jeri and Rod had underimproved their lot. A small remodeled house was not the highest and best use of the site. In another sense, they had overimproved their house. Since the house no longer fit the neighborhood, remodeling it wasted time and money.

Before you buy a home with the idea of remodeling, figure out whether your remodeled home will fit the neighborhood. You can put too much money into a home if you try to increase its value well beyond other nearby homes. And you can also put too much money into a home that's *undervalued* for its location.

Site Value Is Critical

When a site's value exceeds 60 or 70 percent of the total value of the total property, be careful. More than likely, the house is functionally obsolete for its site. Most (or all) of the appreciation potential for the "home" lies in its lot value. That's not bad from an investment standpoint. But in such cases, you should improve the house primarily for personal reasons. At some point in the future (depending on the strength of the housing market), the house may become a "teardown," regardless of its physical condition. In the Kerrisdale section of Vancouver, British Columbia, for example, perfectly good three-bedroom, two-bath houses of 1,600 to 1,800 square feet have been sold for $350,000 to $400,000. Within a year of sale, the "small" homes have been torn down and replaced by new houses of 4,000 to 5,000 square feet with values approaching $1,000,000 or more.

Finding a "low"-priced house in an upscale neighborhood can be a great way to get started in home ownership. But go cautiously with your plans for improvements. In many instances, it's your lot that's going to appreciate—not your remodeled house.

MISTAKE # **33**

Those "comps" weren't really comps.

LESSON: *When relying on an appraisal, verify that the comp houses are really very similar.*

"When I bought my home," says Sergio Cabila, "I looked at the appraisal the owner showed me. I didn't know much about it. It looked okay. The other houses listed on the form sold for about the same price the owner was asking. I offered $10,000 less and eventually we compromised. He cut his price by $5,000."

"It was only after I moved in," Sergio continued, "that I learned the other houses shown in the appraisal were in a better school district. That didn't bother me because I don't have kids. What did make me mad was that houses in the better school district typically sell at a \$15,000 to \$20,000 premium. I paid the premium but didn't get the school district."

Sergio's experience illustrates a specific instance of a more general home-buyer (and appraisal) mistake: The comp houses shown in the appraisal weren't really similar in all important respects. As a result, the appraised value of his home was misleading.

In theory, the comparable sales approach to value tells appraisers (or homebuyers) to estimate the value of one home by looking at the sales prices of other "comparable" homes that have sold recently. In practice, defining "comparable" and discovering recent sales can prove difficult. So, whether you're using the comparable sales approach yourself, or are relying on an appraisal, look for differences among homes that can make a difference.

1. Make sure the comparable homes really are located in the same neighborhood. When you're unfamiliar with an area, it's easy to overlook subtle differences in location such as school district, zoning laws, prestige, accessibility, noise level, proposed or planned changes (e.g., street widening, airport expansion, new commercial development), crime rates, insurance costs, or property tax rates. (See Chapter 4 for more on these points.)

2. The homes should be similar in size, architectural style, floor plan, amenities, and condition.

3. The lots of comparable homes should be about the same size, configuration, and value.

4. Ideally, you (or the appraiser) should find several sales of similar homes slightly inferior to the home you're looking at, and several slightly superior. If you can say "This house is clearly worth more than these two houses, and clearly worth less than these other three houses," then you've bracketed a minimum and a maximum value for your home. Avoid using comp sales that all sit on either the high side or the low side. By bracketing, you can get a much clearer picture of a home's value. Be wary of appraisals that don't bracket the "subject" property between higher- and lower-priced comparables.

Now you can see why choosing comp sales requires judgment and knowledge. Often it's not easy to say definitely that one house is "inferior" and another "superior." When it comes to homes, subjective feelings, tastes, lifestyles, and personal preferences all play a part. In addition, what if no truly comparable homes have sold recently?

All of these difficulties make it prudent for you to examine and carefully review any "appraised" values you make or rely on. There is plenty of room for error as well as for reasonable differences in opinion. Looking at the sales prices of similar homes can help you (or an appraiser) make more informed estimates of value. But since ideal comps seldom exist, you need to address these three questions:

1. How do these homes differ in size, features, quality, condition, or location?
2. How much are these differences worth?
3. Do these homes differ to such a large degree that they really shouldn't count as comparables?

If you can't answer these questions with satisfaction and confidence, gather more (and better) market data. Put your agent to work. Get him or her to comb through more past sales. Go out and look at more properties. Until you come up with the market sales data you need, you can't accurately estimate the market values of the homes you're interested in buying.

MISTAKE # **34**

We figured the swimming pool added more to the home's value than it really did.

LESSON: Beware of costly extras, room additions, and other special features.

When you start looking at houses, you'll soon begin to notice many differences that make a difference. One house has an oversized swimming pool and patio, another a hot tub, and another a paddleball court. The home in Oakridge has a remodeled kitchen, the Fairfield house is larger because the owners converted the garage to a den. The Pine Meadows house includes new Berber carpeting throughout the entire home.

How do you figure how much these differences add to the value of these houses? Unfortunately, no hard-and-fast rules apply. And that exposes you to the mistake of overpaying. If you find a home with a feature (or features) that really hits your hot button, you may get so excited about the pool, the big yard, the great room, the hot tub, or the remodeled country kitchen that you overestimate how much that feature is worth. Or even worse, you "buy the feature" more than you buy the home. In that case, you may end up with a great room you love and a house you don't like.

Guidelines for Pricing Features

Although you can't simply plug numbers into a calculator to price a house's features, the following guidelines can help you estimate how much to pay for costly extras such as room additions or special amenities:

1. Learn how much it would cost to replace the feature, and then subtract for depreciation. If a swimming pool and patio could be built for $12,000 and are 10 years old, the pool should add no more than $5,000 or $6,000 to the home's value (assuming 50 percent or so depreciation).

2. How easily could the feature be added to the home? Adding a swimming pool is a lot of trouble. Adding a hot tub or new wall-to-wall carpeting throughout the house is relatively easy. You should pay less for features that anyone could duplicate easily in nearly any home.

3. What is the cost of the feature relative to the price range of the house? Expensive features (such as Berber carpeting or Poggenpohl kitchens) don't add much value to low- to moderate-priced homes. "The owner just spent $18,000 for these new custom-made cabinets and SubZero appliances," says the real estate agent. "Yes, they're very nice," you respond. "But I'd have to pay to have them removed. They're too rich for me."

4. Does the feature preserve the basic style and integrity of the home? Or does it seem out of character? I recently looked at a well-kept late of 1940s Craftsman bungalow. The owner (a single man) had remodeled the kitchen along the lines of a 1970s suburban tract home. To make matters worse, he had decorated and designed the master bedroom with mirrors and lighting that suited it more for the exploits of Heidi Fleiss. Although costly, no sensible homebuyer should pay more than 10 or 20 cents on the dollar for out-of-place or excessive cost features. (In fact, such features often decrease the home's value.)

5. Does the feature appeal to most homebuyers in that neighborhood or price range? If not, you probably won't have to pay much for it. Without wide-based popularity, it's not a selling feature—and may even detract. In other words, you're fortunate if the features you like are in high supply (e.g., most houses have small yards, and you prefer a small yard, while most other buyers want large yards).

6. Don't forget to account for land value. Remember the Craigs (Mistake #32). If the present house on the site isn't the best use for that location, don't pay much extra for special features or a tip-top condition. You could be wasting your money.

In valuing "differences that make a difference" here's something else you should know: Appraisers may drive by the comp houses listed in an appraisal report, but they don't typically go inside them—or even walk around the house and the yard. When an appraiser says one house is worth $8,000 more than another home because it's in better condition, that figure's a guess.

Be Wary of PFA Adjustments

The same thing is true for all the "adjustment" figures used in the comp sales approach to value that are shown on an appraisal report. These numbers don't come from the appraiser's informed judgment. They're either pulled from the air (PFA), based on rule-of-thumb estimates, or derived from second- or third-hand sources (multiple listing data, property tax records, talks with real estate agents).

This standard operating procedure of appraisers introduces considerable potential for error into the appraisal process. How can an appraiser know one home is in $8,000 better condition if he's never been inside it? He can't.

On occasion, when faced with an appraisal that lists large and numerous dollar adjustments for differences, I've actually gone out and inspected the comp houses. I've knocked on the doors, told the owners what I would like to do, and in most cases I've found them cooperative. In fact, they're usually interested to learn what information the appraisal includes about their home and the other houses valued in the appraisal report. As often as not, I've found the appraisal rife with serious errors.

Although you might feel uncomfortable asking strangers to let you in their homes, at least drive by the comps. Get an impression of the homes and the surrounding neighborhood. You might even talk to the real estate agent(s) who handled the transaction. (Remember, comp houses are homes that have sold recently.) Whatever you do, don't casually accept an appraiser's adjustment figures. They're seldom based on his or her firsthand knowledge.

MISTAKE # **35**

We looked at selling prices but still overpaid.

LESSON: Discover the facts behind the selling prices.

"We thought we were getting a really good deal on the house we bought," says Steve Rizzoli. "My brother and I knew the house three doors down had sold for $98,200 six weeks before. Our house was about the same size and looked nicer on the outside. In addition, our house had a fireplace and a peek-a-boo view of the mountains from the upstairs front bedrooms. Based on these things, we were really happy to get ours for $100,000."

Later, though, Steve and his brother learned not all selling prices are created equal. The house three doors down did sell for $98,200. But to get that price the sellers: (1) paid most of the buyers' loan closing costs,

(2) contributed $2,000 toward an interest-rate buy-down, and (3) escrowed money for roof repairs. Together, these seller concessions were worth around $7,700.

In transactions more typical of the Rizzolis' area, seller concessions ranged between $1,500 and $2,000. So, here, the sellers paid around $6,000 more than normal. Although the purchase contract showed a price of $98,200, the buyers actually got the house for a real price of around $92,000. When the Rizzolis compared their home's cost of $100,000 to the $92,000 price their neighbors actually paid, they no longer felt they had gotten a bargain. In fact, they felt they had overpaid.

Recent selling prices of comparable nearby homes can give you a good idea of the value of your home. But don't accept these numbers without question. Sometimes there's a story behind a home's sale that has pushed the selling (contract) price above or below the home's market value. Consider these questions:

1. Has either the buyer or seller been pressured by time or other circumstances? Sellers who need money fast may sell below market value. Buyers who need a quick move-in date may pay more than market value.

2. Does the sale price include any of the seller's personal property or home furnishings? The sellers may not be willing to part with the $2,500 crystal chandelier in the dining room—unless the buyers up their price accordingly. The same thing is true for the custom-made draperies, the kitchen and laundry appliances, the antique grandfather clock, or the basement workshop fully stocked with tools and equipment. If any of these items becomes a part of the sale, it also may become a part of the price.

3. Was the sale at arm's length? Whenever parties to a transaction are friends or relatives, the selling price may not tell the full story. More than likely, parents selling to their kids won't insist on top dollar.

4. Was the transaction handled by real estate agents? Buyers and sellers who rely on real estate agents tend to be better informed about the market. Their transaction prices are more likely to re-

flect market values. On the other hand, sellers or buyers acting on their own are more likely to sell for too little or pay too much.

5. Does the sale involve owner financing or other seller concessions? Cash-short buyers may agree to pay more for a house if the sellers help with the financing or pay the buyer's loan closing costs.

6. When did the sale occur? Often, the sale date recorded in public records or multiple listing files is the date of closing. That's the date money changed hands and the home's title transferred to the new owners. But for purposes of setting sales price and terms, the actual date that the purchase agreement was signed by the buyers and sellers could have taken place months earlier.

In stable markets, time differences of several months needn't cause much concern. In changing markets, however, a difference of several months can mislead you. As a check, ask your Realtor to tell you the date the contracts were signed for the comparable home prices you're evaluating. Then ask whether the market seems to be changing. Are the inventories of unsold homes growing? Are homes taking longer to sell? Is there an increasing gap between listing price and offering prices? Has buyer traffic been dropping off at open houses?

When you ask these questions, you guard against buying into a slowing market with unrealistic expectations. When markets are changing, look beyond past selling prices. They won't necessarily tell you where prices are headed. Remember, keep track of other market signals.

MISTAKE # **36**

The sellers named the price, we named the terms.

LESSON: Never agree to pay more than market value for a home—unless you weigh the risks.

In crazy housing markets of earlier years, buyers and sellers were doing nearly anything they could to make a sale work. With mortgage rates at

12 to 16 percent, few buyers could qualify for bank financing. That left buyers and sellers to work out their own terms. "Creative financing" became the norm. There were seller seconds, wraparounds, balloons, third and fourth deeds of trust, lease-options, and land contracts.

The commonplace rule of home buying was "You name the price, we'll name the terms." As long as buyers could handle the cash-down and monthly payments, they didn't care about the price. Anticipating high inflation, buyers figured that even if they overpaid, tomorrow's appreciation would bail them out and still leave room for a healthy profit.

Unexpectedly, though, the tide turned. Home prices stopped their upward spiral. Homeowners who tried to refinance to pay off short-term seller financing found they owed more than their homes were worth. Others who had relied on creative financing and lost their jobs also fell between a rock and a hard place. They couldn't afford to make their monthly payments and they couldn't afford to sell and pay off a mortgage that exceeded their home's market value.

Cash-Short Buyers Meet Overpriced Sellers

Here's how these and thousands of other homebuyers made this mistake: In most (but not all) instances, the buyers were cash short or for some other reason couldn't qualify for bank financing. The would-be sellers frequently had priced their home too high. This combination offered opportunity for a match. The buyers say, "Okay, we will accept your price of $149,000 if you will accept $5,000 down and monthly payments at six percent interest. After the first three years, we'll refinance and pay off the balance we owe you."

The sellers accept. They receive their $149,000 price (for a home actually valued around $130,000). The buyers receive the terms they want. Unfortunately, three years later the home's value has risen to just $140,000 and the buyers can't come up with the money to pay off the sellers. The buyers face foreclosure. The thrill of owning their first home turns into worry, fear, and sleepless nights.

Does this mean that you should never trade price for terms? Not necessarily. But if you do, think about the downside. Don't expect unrealistic appreciation; don't expect mortgage interest rates to fall; don't figure you're going to save more money from your paycheck than you normally save. Do put a clause in your contract with the sellers that extends your payoff date should the housing market or mortgage market go against you.

Most important, know the cash sale value of the home you're buying. Especially in hot markets, some homebuyers have jumped into a deal so eagerly, they didn't even stop to think how much premium they were paying for the sellers' liberal finance plan. Whenever you offer (or a seller offers you) easy terms, know what those terms are costing you. How much of a price premium are you paying?

MISTAKE # **37**

Everything looked like a bargain.

LESSON: *When moving from a high-cost area to a low-cost area, recalibrate your sights. Avoid overpaying.*

If you are moving from, say, San Francisco or Boston to Memphis or Orlando, get set for a great surprise. When you first start looking at houses, you won't believe your eyes. "Four bedrooms, three baths, pool, den, and a half-acre lot—all for $199,900. Unbelievable!" You'll begin to think all the sellers have gone crazy. "Better act quick, this house is a steal. The owners must not know what they are doing."

Filled with excitement about the bargains everywhere, you may lose your critical awareness. You'll mentally compare the houses you're looking at to the prices of the houses back in your previous hometown. Compared to your last city, all the houses seem to be priced low. So, you run the danger of overpaying.

Avoid this mistake. Get good local market information. Check selling prices, terms of sale, market conditions, and neighborhoods. Put the home prices of Boston or San Francisco out of your mind. Recalibrate your sights. Stay focused on Memphis or Orlando. Work with a real estate agent who's smart, savvy, and motivated—an agent who will educate you into the local market. Avoid agents who want to urge you to make a quick and uninformed buying decision.

MISTAKE # **38**

I didn't buy anything. All the houses were grossly overpriced.

LESSON: When moving from a low-cost area to a high-cost area, recalibrate your sights. Don't pass up a bargain.

If you move to (or live in) a high-priced housing market, you may tell yourself, "Home prices are outrageous. Everything is overpriced." You talk with other people. You read newspaper articles lamenting the housing crisis. You see articles quoting experts who say homes are no longer a good investment. You hear politicians proclaim something must be done: "Only 18 percent of our young families can afford to buy their own home." Even more depressing, you know friends or family in Des Moines who just bought a nice three-bedroom, two-bath ranch for $99,500.

With all these influences telling you homes are overpriced, it's easy to develop a negative mind-set. Sure you would like to own. You might even (sort of) plan to own. Yet each time you meet the high housing costs face to face, you walk away. You keep thinking about those housing bargains in Des Moines.

You're Surrounded by "Acres of Diamonds"

Around the turn of the century, Russell Conwell, the founder of Temple University, became famous for his speech "Acres of Diamonds." His speech was so powerful, so enduring, and yet so simple that, throughout the country and throughout his life, Conwell was called upon to deliver it more than 25,000 times.

Conwell would say, "My friends, that mistake is very universally made . . . I say to you that you do have 'acres of diamonds' right where you now live."

By "mistake" Conwell meant focusing on the "better" advantages or conditions that are thought to exist in other places, while passing up the possibilities (acres of diamonds) that you can find in your own "backyard."

A Missed Opportunity

I confess to this mistake myself—and I've seen it made countless times by others. In 1977, I moved from South Carolina to Vancouver, British Columbia. In South Carolina, I owned a new, custom-built brick home in a very nice professional neighborhood. I sold the house for $51,000 (a fair price). In Vancouver, that $51,000 would buy a 650-square-foot one-bedroom condominium. To buy a small, single-family older home would cost around $90,000. Rather than focus on what Vancouver had to offer, my mind kept drifting back to South Carolina, where one could get twice the house for half the money. "These prices in Vancouver are ridiculous," I thought. And it was no trouble at all to find others who agreed. I did prefer to own, but everything simply looked too expensive. So, by default, I rented.

One year later, the owner of the house I was renting approached with an offer. "I've decided to sell," he told me. "If you'd like to buy before I list the house with a real estate agent, I'll give you a good price."

"I don't know. What kind of price do you have in mind?"

"Eighty-seven thousand," he said.

"Eighty-seven thousand!" I choked. "No thanks."

To this day, I can recall then laughing with a friend about the price the owner had proposed. My friend and I agreed that $87,000 for a one-bedroom house was ridiculous. Someone would be a fool to pay that much.

Well, that "fool" was shortly found. The house sold several weeks later at a price of $91,000. The new owners completely rebuilt the house into a four-bedroom, three-bath home. Today that home would sell for around $750,000. The lot value alone would run around $450,000.

In misjudging this opportunity, my friend (also new to British Columbia) and I had compared the price of the one-bedroom house (instead of focusing on lot value) in Vancouver to home prices in the relatively low-priced cities where we had previously lived. By that yardstick, Vancouver prices looked ridiculous.

The family who bought the home, though, enjoyed a different perspective. They were from Hong Kong. They realized Vancouver ranked highly as a world-class city. Compared to Hong Kong, Tokyo, San Francisco, New York, or London, Vancouver prices (at the time) were a bargain. Even better, the house was located just a 5-minute walk to the beach, a 5-minute walk to shopping and restaurants, a 20-minute walk to the campus of the University of British Columbia, and a 10-minute drive to downtown Vancouver and Stanley Park. In addition, the house enjoyed a panoramic daytime view of the mountains and English Bay and a nighttime view of the city lights of downtown Vancouver.

Yet, if asked at the time, I'm sure most people in Vancouver (not just newcomers) would have believed Vancouver home prices in general (and that home in particular) were overpriced. The press and nearly everyone else complained about the "housing crisis." No one spoke of great opportunities.

But great opportunities existed then, and they exist today. No matter how high home prices have climbed in your area (or the area you're moving to), relative bargains can be found. Compared to major cities throughout the world, most American and Canadian home prices still look cheap. In every metro area, you can find homes and neighborhoods well priced relative to others. Most important, in the future, today's home (and lot) prices will be viewed as the good old days.

For the past six decades, our population has grown, our economy has grown, our exports have grown, total employment has grown, and home prices have grown. The coming decade will yield the same types of increases.

Just remember: Get accurate sales data that applies to a wide variety of homes and neighborhoods. Compare prices, sizes, condition, features, amenities, and locations. Then choose from among those that offer the best values *relative* to the others. As Russell Conwell would tell you, "Keep an open mind. Explore your possibilities. You're sure to discover acres of diamonds in your own backyard."

CHAPTER 4

Locate a Great Neighborhood

If you're like most homebuyers, you'll want to own a home in a great (or at least a good) neighborhood. But the concept of neighborhood includes many different elements—such as school district, appreciation potential, affordability, resident demographics, resident lifestyles, government services, convenience to shopping, jobs, and recreation, zoning, aesthetics, and many other features.

Naturally, you're going to have to make choices and trade-offs. Which elements do you value most highly? In addition, many neighborhood characteristics don't jump out and announce themselves. To get the facts, you must think like a private investigator. Don't assume that what you see is what you get.

Read through the mistakes in this chapter. The experiences of these homebuyers will surely lead you to think more clearly about your own neighborhood preferences and comparisons.

MISTAKE # **39**

My agent told me this was a good school district.

LESSON: Never accept a real estate agent's opinions at face value. Concentrate on verifiable facts.

"When I started looking for a home," says Lori Pines, "I wanted the Richmond neighborhood. My sister has two kids in Richmond Elementary, and she thinks it's great. Since my own children were age four and six, a good elementary school was very important to me. Besides, it would have been nice to live near Sandy and Rick.

"But the problem was I really couldn't find a house I liked at a price I wanted to pay. So my agent suggested I look in Brookview. She said I could get more house for the money and that the schools there were just as good as Richmond's.

"Well, the agent was right about one thing. I found a house I loved in Brookview for about $25,000 less than it would have cost in Richmond. But I got so excited about the house, I forgot to check out the schools.

What Is a Good School District?

"I just accepted my agent's opinions at face value. What a mistake that was. I'm now having to drive Lisa and Sean halfway across town every morning to a private school. The money I saved on the house I'm spending for gas and tuition."

Did Lori's agent really mislead her about the quality of the schools in Brookview? Maybe. Maybe not. Could Lori have easily avoided her mistake? Definitely yes. Lori should have followed this rule: Don't ask your real estate agent for opinions. Ask for facts. Then verify.

When working with an agent—especially an agent with whom you've developed rapport—it's easy to rapid-fire questions about the neighborhood: "Is this a good location? Is there much crime? How long does it take to get to downtown from here? Is this a good school district?"

Now think for a moment about these questions. What do you mean when you say "good" school district? What is "too much" crime? Going downtown? By what route? To which building? At what time of the day? For answers you can rely on, you need to ask more concrete questions. And you need to push your real estate agent to answer with facts.

Telling you the commute to downtown is a "breeze" doesn't give quite the same information as, "Between 7:30 and 9:00 A.M. the commute will normally range between 25 and 35 minutes." To an executive used to a 6:00 A.M., 90-minute drive from Long Island to Manhattan, a 25- to 35-minute commute might easily qualify as a "breeze." To an Indiana University professor who can walk to her office in less than 10 minutes, a 25- to 35-minute hassle with traffic everyday could bring on ulcers.

As to crime, consider a divorced mother with two children. She's in residency at a hospital. She'll be working long hours at all times of night and day. She plans to ride her bike to work. Compare her likely definition of "too much" crime to a 34-year-old single man who is 6'4", a triathlete, and an ex-Golden Gloves boxer. "Let 'em try something with me" might be his attitude.

Facts! Not Opinions

By asking your agent for facts, not opinions, you'll significantly reduce the chance the two of you are talking on different wavelengths. Remember, career real estate agents want to do the best job they can for their homebuyers and sellers. To earn a living, they need referrals from satisfied clients. You can help them help you by asking concrete questions they can answer with verifiable facts. "The mean SAT score of college-bound seniors last year at Lincoln High was 1,150," tells you much more than "I believe Lincoln High enjoys a very good reputation." Knowing there were 27 house break-ins in the neighborhood during the past six months tells you much more than the subjective report, "This is a relatively safe neighborhood."

All of these opinion statements may be "true." But the factual statements convey more useful information and leave less room for ambiguity and later disappointment.

MISTAKE # **40**

We never saw the railroad tracks.

LESSON: *Ask the sellers and your sales agent to disclose any disturbing noises in the neighborhood.*

"When we bought our house," says Amy Lee, "all we saw in the back-yard was an eight-foot-high wooden fence with tall bamboo growing in front of it. We liked the fence and the bamboo because it gave us so much privacy. We never thought to ask what was on the other side. After we moved in, though, we soon found out.

"Twice a night, every night, a loud house-shaking freight train comes roaring through at 2:00 A.M. and 4:00 A.M. The railroad tracks—we now know—lay just on the other side of our backyard fence."

Before she bought, Amy Lee forgot to inquire about noise pollution in the neighborhood. Hundreds of thousands of homebuyers have made the same mistake because it's so easy to make. Even if you should visit a house three or four times before you buy it, how much time are you likely to spend in the home? Three hours? Four hours? At most, per-haps, five hours. You can't learn much about neighborhood noise pollu-tion—trains, buses, trucks, aircraft flight patterns—in such a short amount of time. You must do some research. Ask the sellers. Ask your Realtor. Talk to neighbors.

The (Un)Quiet Street

I once bought a house located on a small road removed from noisy traf-fic. At least that's what I thought. As I soon learned, though, the small road was a major shortcut teenagers used to travel to and from their high school. Since my house was near an intersection with a stop sign, during the morning, lunch, and after-school hours, it often sounded like race trials for the Daytona 500 were being held outside my door.

Like many other homebuyers, I looked at houses primarily on the weekends. On Saturday morning the home was perfectly quiet. And this brings us to another reason it's easy to miss noise pollution. Quite often visits to a house occur at the very times noise pollution is least likely to create a noticeable bother.

You can physically inspect a house at nearly any time of the day or week. Its physical condition won't change. The neighborhood presents a separate issue. The timing of your visit can make all the difference. So before you buy, if you can't camp out near the home for 24 hours a day for a week or two, do the next best thing. Vary the times and days you visit the home; and ask the sellers, neighbors, and your Realtor to fully describe and disclose any disturbing noises that may plague the neighborhood.

MISTAKE # 41

We bought into an upscale development that's moving downscale.

LESSON: *Before buying into a new development, find out what type of homes the developer has planned for later phases.*

"Several years ago we bought our first home in an upscale new development," says Dorthea Washington "We paid $250,000 and put five years of savings into our down payment. Now we've learned the developer plans to build townhouses and smaller homes right next to ours. He intends to sell them for $125,000 to $160,000. We're afraid this will change the character of the development and make our home less valuable. We wouldn't have bought here had we known the subdivision was going downscale."

Dorthea is describing a not-uncommon complaint. Sometimes developers build the most expensive phase of a development first. The upscale homes create a prestige image for the project that makes it easier for the developer to sell the more modest homes that are built later. Naturally, buyers of these later phases are attracted to a development that's already noted for its fine homes, manicured lawns, safe streets, and driveways stocked with BMWs, Volvos, and new SUVs (sport utility vehicles). Just as naturally, though, the BMW crowd's not too enthusiastic about the "cheapening" of their neighborhood.

So this creates a problem: How can prospective buyers of early-phase homes guard against surprises that could "downscale" the neighborhood?

Ask the Developer

The first line of defense is to ask the developer. Usually, later phases of the development are planned before phase I sales begin. Also, try to determine whether the developer plans to "merge" the stages of the development. Will all homeowners share the same common area amenities (tennis courts, pools, parks, trails), or will each area enjoy exclusive use of its own facilities? Will the separate phases share a common entrance to the development? Will the lower-priced units be marketed under their own names, or will the total development go by the same name, or perhaps Windwood I, Windwood II, and Windwood III? Will the separate phases be organized into one combined homeowners' association, or will each community have its own membership roster? Will the phases be visually and physically separated from each other by natural or artificial boundaries such as parks, lakes, creeks, trees, and major streets?

However, even though development plans may be *proposed* for later phases, seldom are they etched in stone. Over time, housing markets change. Move-up homes may sell fast for several years and then the market might slow. Starter homes might gain more popularity. In a changing market, plans for $300,000 homes may be scrapped in favor of $150,000 townhouses and maybe even some rental apartments.

Look for Legal Restrictions

As a second line of prevention, determine whether the developer's plans for later stages are subject to market changes. Or are the developer's options and prerogatives limited by zoning laws, deed restrictions, or a vote by members of the phase I homeowners' association?

For example, in many developments, deed restrictions prohibit lot sizes of less than, say, one acre, or homes of less than 2,400 square feet. Laws or restrictions also limit housing densities—usually stated as so many units to the acre. Developers of condominiums, townhouses, and apartments typically push for densities as high as they can get them. On the other hand, homebuyers in early phases prefer low densities in later stages.

As a rule, when you investigate a development, you'll find your best protection against downscaling lies with the deed restrictions. Deed restrictions are very difficult to weaken without a majority vote of all affected homeowners. Zoning and other land use laws give you some protection. But they're subject to change depending on the direction of the political winds. Warranties and representations from the developer concerning future plans suffer in effect because most developers won't make written promises—and you should *never* rely on the oral promises of the developer's marketing staff.

The builder's sales reps may give you a color brochure and show you scale models of how the development will look in 5 or 10 years, but don't pay much attention to this type of promotion unless it's backed up with guarantees. Too many homebuyers have relied on glowing visions painted by an enthusiastic sales staff. Then, later, they have met with disappointment. In recalling oral promises or promotional brochures, disgruntled homebuyers have on occasion won lawsuits against developers to prevent downscaling. But litigation is a last-ditch effort. It costs years of frustration and hundreds of thousands of dollars in legal fees. And your lawyer still might lose your case.

It's far better to avoid this mistake in the first place: Don't assume later phases of a development will fully complement and enhance the value of earlier phases. Investigate what legal protections the developer (or government) has put into place.

MISTAKE # **42**

When we bought our house, the land across the street from the subdivision was a cornfield. Now it's a parking lot and shopping center.

LESSON: *Always envision the future within your neighborhood.*

"I remember when we bought," says Aaron Vasko. "The neighborhood was quiet and you had no trouble pulling in and out of the subdivision entrance. Now, since the shopping center's come in, you might have to wait through two or three light changes, especially at the commute times or on Saturday when it seems like everybody in the world's out shopping."

No one can anticipate all the changes that might affect a neighborhood. Some changes, though, are easier to spot than others—if you know what to look for. As a starting point, look around for vacant or "underutilized" land. Are croplands beginning to seem out of place? Are there wooded areas of private property near other tracts that are already being developed? Are roads or streets being widened?

If you're buying into a city neighborhood, find out whether rates of home ownership in the neighborhood are increasing or decreasing. Are growing numbers of property owners renting out rooms or cutting up single-family homes into apartments? Are any of the single-family homes being converted to offices or retail use? Does the government own any nearby land? Does the federal, state, or local government plan to put up any public low-income housing nearby? Are the parks deteriorating? Is graffiti spreading? Are the number of vacant buildings increasing?

When you buy a home, you're also buying the future of the neighborhood and the surrounding areas. As the neighborhood goes, so goes your home's value. But investigating a neighborhood doesn't just mean looking at what exists today. It means trying to imagine what it will look like 5 or 10 years down the road.

Imagine How the Coming Years Will Bring Change to the Neighborhood

Close your eyes and let your imagination carry forward from the present into the future. What types of buildings will sit on those vacant tracts? Will the streets and roads become more congested? Will property owners have improved their homes and landscaping? Have property owners and neighborhood residents joined together to work for revitalization? Or have they been indifferent (or even destructive) to the character and appearance of the area? Relative to other neighborhoods and communities, will this one have moved up or down the scale of desirability?

Especially think about traffic congestion. Will it get worse? Can the present roads accommodate all the new development? Will other areas or neighborhoods become more (or less) convenient?

Congestion Can Create Opportunity

Some years back, in metro Columbia, South Carolina, the northwest corridor of the city running out along Interstate 26 became the most popular area for new development. Homebuyers were scrambling to get their children out of city schools and into the suburban school districts. Relative to most other areas of Columbia, the northwest corridor was hot.

But each new subdivision created more traffic. Several of the key interstate exits would back up for half an hour. To many potential homebuyers, the traffic congestion looked intolerable. So they started searching for other developments in less congested sections of the metro area. Within two years home appreciation in the northwest subdivision slowed. Appreciation rates in the less congested northeast and southeast areas picked up speed. In fact, within two years, home values in one southeast development that found particular favor jumped by 40 percent.

When evaluating neighborhoods, subdivisions, and communities, remember that change is a fact of life. Never assume the future will look like the present. The chances are it won't. By trying to anticipate and envision the changes that seem imminent, you're more likely to avoid unpleasant "surprises"—and you might even be able to pick a star performer.

MISTAKE # **43**

It didn't occur to me that on weekends the place could turn into a zoo of wild kids and party animals.

LESSON: *Try to find out if your neighbors' lifestyles are compatible with your own.*

Like many first-time homebuyers, Ann Hennig had thought about investing in a home off and on over a period of years. Yet, indecision and procrastination conspired to keep her renting. Then, when Ann's landlord gave her a 30-day notice that he wanted to move back into the home where she had been living, Ann decided the time was right. She would buy a home of her own.

Pushing herself to act quickly, Ann found a townhouse that was priced right, spacious, and located only five minutes from her office, and it could be bought with a low-down-payment VA mortgage assumption. Best of all, her mortgage payments (after tax deductions) would cost her less than she'd been paying in rent. Those were the good points.

Finding Unpleasant Surprises

After moving in, Ann discovered a few things she had overlooked: "Children screaming and riding their Hot Wheels, everyone blasting their boom boxes and car stereos, barking dogs, and late-night parties—all these things came as a big surprise to me," says Ann.

How did Ann get herself into this kind of situation? Here's her account. "First of all," Ann continues, "I have to explain my own ignorance. I came from the neighborhood I had grown up in. I had known my neighbors all my life, and, except for an occasional outburst, the neighbors were pretty set in their ways and were generally quiet and considerate. You could always count on peaceful afternoons and quiet evenings. Since I had never been faced with the problem of constant noise, it was not something I consciously thought about. It didn't occur to me the place could turn into a zoo of wild kids and party animals.

"Also, I moved into my townhouse in October when the children were in school, most of the neighborhood was working, the weather was cold, and not many people were outside. The few times I visited the unit before I purchased it, I didn't stay long and didn't hear any of the neighbors, or maybe I just came on relatively quiet days. Anyway, I didn't pay much attention.

"But something else aggravated the problem. It seemed like we had a Gresham's law of neighborhoods. Bad residents were driving out good ones. Since I came from a neighborhood where people rarely moved, I had naively assumed that the neighbors I had when I moved in would be my neighbors for many years. At least in the beginning I had relatively quiet neighbors beside me and in back. Within a year they were both gone. In their place came a divorced man who partied constantly indoors and out on his patio, and a young single woman behind me who played her stereo from 8:00 A.M. to 10:00 P.M.—I think to accompany her barking dogs.

"On top of all of this, parking was another problem. Each unit had its own assigned parking space. When I visited the units before buying, many of the spaces were empty so it looked like parking was plentiful. But, of course, most people had been at work. On the weekends and in the evenings it was a different story. Since most units had more than one car, parking was clearly inadequate. I was also soon to learn that most residents totally disregarded the parking rules. Sometimes cars were even abandoned. Repeated calls to the police were all in vain.

Apathy Prevails

"Later, when some of us tried to reform our homeowners' association to develop and enforce stricter rules, we ran into a brick wall. Too many of the units were owned by absentee investors. Since they didn't live there, they couldn't have cared less about unruly neighbors. And they certainly didn't want to put more money into maintenance and upkeep of the property."

No doubt, Ann's negative experience sounds extreme. Nevertheless, it can't be emphasized too strongly: Determine as well as you can the compatibility, stability, and cooperativeness of your future neighbors.

Ann's mistake is very common. She assumed her new neighbors would behave with the same consideration and friendliness that she had known in the neighborhood where she grew up. As she learned to her regret the facts contradicted her assumptions.

MISTAKE # **44**

Those people were a bunch of snobs.

LESSON: *Want to socialize with neighbors? Then first find out whether you'll fit in.*

In today's world of hectic schedules, easy transportation, and instant communication, our chief socializing may take place on a catch-as-catch-can basis with friends and relatives located across town or across the country. Unlike the past, today many of us seldom get together with neighbors—we may not even know their names. The old notion of sipping morning coffee at the neighbors' kitchen table seems as outdated as the TV reruns of a 1950s family sitcom.

To Abe and Lucille Hoskins, though, the very idea of neighborhood meant neighborliness. That's the type of neighborhood they each had grown up in and had become accustomed to while raising their own children. Abe and Lucille were also a living example of the American Dream. Starting life poor, and lacking a college education, by their mid-forties Abe and Lucille had achieved an income of $90,000 a year and a net worth (primarily equities in rental houses) of nearly $500,000. Their level of income and wealth placed them near the top two or three percent on the income scale in their midwestern town. In economic terms, they were among the town's "well-to-do."

But Abe still worked at the steel plant, and whenever their tenants moved, Lucille personally cleaned their rental houses. Following the model of Sam Walton, Abe drove an old pickup truck. Lucille bought her clothes at Kmart. The one extravagance they both wanted (and could certainly afford) was a home in Woodshire, the best upper-middle-income neighborhood in their city.

After much searching, the Hoskins found a Woodshire home they fell in love with. They put an offer in the first time they saw it. The house was exactly what they wanted.

Sadly, though, as Abe and Lucille soon discovered, the neighborhood disappointed them greatly. Although in appearance and convenience it left nothing to be desired, in neighborliness it failed on every count. Not only did the neighbors seldom socialize with each other, they overtly snubbed the Hoskins with an unspoken attitude: "Since you're not professionals and don't have a college degree, you're not as good as us. We choose not to acknowledge your existence."

Neighbors Make the Neighborhood

Many homebuyers could ignore this nasty attitude and go on with their lives. Not Abe and Lucille. They did not want to merely own a house, they wanted to feel like they were part of a community. That didn't happen. Within two years the Hoskins sold their "dream house" in Woodshire and moved back to their old home on South 14th Street (which they had kept as a rental). "Those people in Woodshire were a bunch of snobs," Lucille told her friends. "We didn't fit in."

Houses and lawns, trees and shrubs, streets and sidewalks, parks and playgrounds, schools and libraries, shops and restaurants; these are the parts of a neighborhood you can see. But look beyond the physical characteristics. Before you buy a home, find out who lives in the neighborhood. Is there a feeling of community? Where do the people work? What are their educational backgrounds? What are their ages? Are they primarily married or single? Do they have children? What are their lifestyles and attitudes? Are they neighborly? Do you think you will fit in? Does it matter? Had the Hoskins investigated these questions, they would have prevented their home-buying mistake.

MISTAKE # **45**

You're saying we can't build a fence around our yard! Isn't that unconstitutional?

LESSON: *State and local governments can regulate the use of your property down to the smallest detail.*

The Fifth Amendment to the U.S. Constitution declares that no person shall be "deprived of life, liberty, or property, without due process of law; nor shall private property be taken for public use without just compensation." In addition, nearly all state constitutions include clauses similarly written to stop governments from encroaching on an individual's property rights.

In interpreting these protective clauses, though, courts have defined a "taking" very, very narrowly. In effect, courts have said governments may squeeze an owner's rights as tightly as they want—so long as an owner still enjoys some minimal use of the property. As Nicole and Brett Gates learned to their dismay, a neighborhood prohibition against backyard fences by the Village of Inverness did not even come close to testing the "takings" clause.

Government Restrictions: For and Against

Of course, government regulations can work for you or against you. If your neighbor is planning to build a second story onto his home that will block your view of the bay, you'll be more than eager to remind him that the added height of his remodeled home will violate the zoning and building regulations. On the other hand, when you learn you aren't allowed to rent out the room above your garage to a local college student, you're very likely to feel government has gone too far. After all, isn't a "man's home his castle"?

In real life, there's nothing objective about government restrictions on property rights. Whether you're for or against them all depends on what you intend to do with your property and what you want to prevent your neighbors from doing. Nor are property rights and restrictions uniform among neighborhoods and communities. One neighborhood might encourage accessory apartments, another might prevent them. Jackson Heights might permit in-home businesses, Fairview may outlaw them. All this means that before you buy a home or a lot, investigate the types of government restrictions that will apply to you and your neighbors.

Allan Funt's Surprise

Consider what happened to Allan Funt, best known for his *Candid Camera* movies and television shows. Mr. Funt bought 1,200 acres of land near Monterey, California. He intended to build four buildings on the site: a house, a visitor's guest house, a barn, and a stable. The California Coastal Commission (the "zoning" authority over the 1,200 acres) refused permission. Instead, the commission allowed Mr. Funt to build just two structures and ordered him to grant the public a 300-acre scenic easement through the site. To top that, the commission further specified that Mr. Funt situate and landscape his home such that after dark, no passersby would be able to see the home's lights.

More than likely, government won't regulate you to the same degree that the California Coastal Commission has regulated millions of Californians. But here are the types of restrictions you might face:

- *Height restrictions:* Most homes are limited in height. You may not be able to add a second or third story.
- *Side yard, front yard, and backyard restrictions:* Land-use laws typically require a home to be set back a certain distance from each of the site's boundaries. You may not be able to build onto the house or garage.
- *Floor area ratios:* These regulations limit the maximum square footage of your home.
- *Use restrictions:* These laws may prevent you from operating an office or business from your home.
- *Occupancy laws:* These regulations may limit the number of people who can live in your home. On occasion, they also may prevent more than three or four singles from sharing a home.
- *Rental unit prohibitions:* You may not be permitted to rent out a basement suite or add on an accessory apartment.

- *Energy conservation:* These laws may apply to anything from window size and placement to retrofitting your toilets with water-saving devices.
- *Nuisance ordinances:* These include virtually anything you do that annoys your neighbors or vice versa. Fence heights, barking dogs, overhanging trees, car parking, practicing musical instruments, public nudity (sunbathing au natural in your backyard)—the list goes on.
- *Remodeling and renovation:* Nearly any serious remodeling or renovation will require a permit and government approval.
- *Historic preservation:* Should you buy a historically significant home or a home located in a designated historical district, any changes you make to the home will have to conform to prescribed historical aesthetic and architectural standards.

Your Realtor Won't, and Shouldn't, Advise You About Regulations

Jason Shields, an Ohio Realtor, says that far too many homebuyers pay too little attention to zoning and building regulations. "They buy a home with big plans. Then they find out they can't do what they want to do. Because I can't give legal advice," Jason points out, "I tell them to talk over their intentions with a lawyer, a reputable contractor, or the city planner's office. But they forget or let it slide and end up disappointed.

"Sometimes it also works the opposite way," Jason adds. "By failing to check neighborhood zoning, they get all upset when an apartment building starts to go up two blocks over. Or maybe they don't like the idea of their neighbor operating a workshop out of his garage and parking four or five cars along the street. Either way, I try to emphasize that the laws will help determine the character of the neighborhood. So they ought to make sure they get the protection they want, yet not so restrictive as to interfere with their own plans. It really is a matter of finding the neighborhood with the right balance."

MISTAKE # **46**

No need to worry, those laws are never enforced.

LESSON: *Be wary of nonconforming and illegal property uses.*

More than likely, some of the homes you look at will not conform to the neighborhood's existing zoning laws or building regulations. It's not uncommon to walk into a home and find a built-on den that sits too close to the property line, an illegal basement rental suite, or maybe outdated (but not hazardous) wiring. If you question the real estate agent or sellers about the violation, they may say something like, "Don't be concerned, those laws are never enforced." Cy Torre, though, found out differently.

Cy bought a four-unit flat in Waukegan, Illinois. It was his way of getting over the affordability hurdle to home ownership. Cy lived in one of the units and collected rents from the other three apartments to cover a big part of his mortgage payments. At the time Cy bought the fourplex, the neighborhood was zoned single family and duplex. Cy knew his fourplex violated the law, but so did a number of triplexes and fourplexes in the area. The seller told Cy, "There's nothing to worry about. It's been this way for years and no one's ever said anything." So Cy bought the flats without investigating further.

Beware of Neighbor Complaints

Cy had chosen this neighborhood because it was being revitalized. Recent buyers had begun to spruce up their homes, clean up the nearby park, and establish a neighborhood crime watch program. They also began to complain about parking.

Since this was an older neighborhood, many homes lacked garages, and few had enough on-site space to park two cars. As a result, these younger recent homebuyers (who owned more cars than the previous homeowners) often found themselves driving around the block several times before they could find a parking space. Joining with other neighbors, they put pressure on the mayor to solve the problem.

Whenever some neighborhood group complains about inadequate parking, the first casualties are owners of homes with illegal suites or flats. "Get rid of these tenants and there would be enough parking spaces for us homeowners."

So that's how the mayor solved the problem. He sent investigators out to count mailboxes at all properties in the neighborhood. Owners with more than two boxes were cited for violating the zoning ordinance and ordered to bring their properties into compliance within 60 days. Cy not only had to spend $2,200 to remove kitchens and take out several walls, his rental revenues went down. Over the long run, Cy will probably benefit from these changes through increased property values in the neighborhood. In the short run, though, he suffered a near-fatal cash crunch.

In Cy's case, his building violations were illegal. Whenever you own a property that *illegally* fails to conform to existing zoning or building regulations, you run the risk that an enforcement campaign will require you to make costly repairs or renovations. (Another, more costly, example is Lawrence Ginsburg, a New York City developer, who was forced to remove the illegal top 12 stories of a 31-story apartment building he had constructed five years earlier. In addition to losing the rental income of 12 stories, Mr. Ginsburg had to pay $1 million for their demolition.)

Nonconforming Uses

Sometimes zoning or building regulations are changed and existing uses are "grandfathered." Once grandfathered, they become "nonconforming" uses, but not illegal. Still nonconforming uses do pose two risks.

First, the governing powers may change their minds. If they choose, they usually can take away or phase out a grandfathered use. So, political winds blowing from a different direction, or "offended" neighbors who raise a fuss, can lead a nonconforming use to a premature death. (In Palo Alto, California, for example, complaining neighbors forced the political powers to get rid of a nearby office building. In compromise, the owners of the office building were permitted a 15-year phase-out.)

As a second risk, you might lose permission for a nonconforming use if you suspend or discontinue it. Say you operate a home business that doesn't conform to existing laws but has been grandfathered. If you shut down your business for several months, you may not be allowed to re-open it.

Small Fire, Big Repairs

I once owned a rental house that had a 60-amp electrical system that was grandfathered. Current building codes specified a minimum of 100-amp service. Unfortunately, the home suffered a small fire in which some of the wiring was damaged. But the building inspector wouldn't permit a small repair. Instead, he pointed out the law required me to completely rewire the entire house to comply with present standards. A $200 fire cost me $2,000 to repair.

Throughout the United States, as many as 50 percent of houses and small apartment buildings may violate some neighborhood zoning ordinance, building regulation, or environmental restriction. Especially if you're buying an older home, you may not be able to avoid these kinds of properties. Just don't buy blind. Try to discover the violations. Learn whether they're illegal or merely nonconforming. And think through what risks they might present.

As the risks grow bigger, your offering price should drop. If you're expected to bear the risk of noncompliance, then the sellers should discount their price to make up for it.

MISTAKE # **47**

We live in Naperville, but our kids can't go to Naperville schools.

LESSON: *Your address doesn't necessarily tell you where you live or the services you are entitled to.*

The address of my current home is in Berkeley, California, and I receive mail service through the Berkeley post office. But for purposes of zoning, building codes, school district, and property tax rates, the house falls within the jurisdiction of Oakland, California. Highland Park, Texas, a self-contained high-income community within the city of Dallas, is well known for its high-quality schools. But if you live on the wrong side of the freeway that slices through Highland Park, your kids must attend the Dallas public schools.

In Naperville, a prosperous and growing suburb of Chicago, home-buyers have flocked to the new subdivisions being built south of town. Homes typically cost $150,000 to $300,000; but some of the buyers have been surprised to learn they are not located in the Naperville school dis-trict. Rather, they're within the Wheatland school district. Although Wheatland's schools are good, many families prefer the acclaimed pro-grams of Naperville.

Do You Live Where You Think You Live?

Throughout the country, city addresses, school districts, and governing jurisdictions do not necessarily follow the same boundaries. You can't as-sume your address gives all the information you need. What is true for school districts also stands true for services such as fire and police pro-tection, trash pickup, water, sewage and utility hookups, and cable tele-vision. Before you buy, and verify the school district, property tax rates, and municipal services that will apply to your home-to-be.

Also, when you're talking to the secretary or clerk at the school dis-trict headquarters, the planning agency, or the tax assessor's office, de-scribe specifically where the house is located.

In Urbana, Illinois, Marlene Watts asked school personnel whether her home-to-be on Florida Avenue would put her kids in Wilson Junior High, which is the school she wanted. The secretary Marlene talked to replied yes. The correct answer was no. True, residents on the south side of Florida were within the Wilson Junior High school district. But homes on the north side of the street, where Marlene had moved, were not. Florida Avenue was the dividing line. It wasn't enough to live on Florida. You had to live on the south side of the road.

Remember Marlene's mistake: Verify municipal boundaries, school districts, taxes, and services as specifically as you can. As odd as it sounds, your house might not be located where you think it is located.

MISTAKE # **48**

We didn't know there were stables nearby. The wind was blowing from a different direction the day we looked.

LESSON: Find out if any foul odors periodically intrude into the neighborhood.

In the town where I was raised, relatively few homebuyers wanted to live in the southwest part of town. Six or eight days a month a local chemical plant released huge volumes of what smelled like hydrogen sulfide (which smells worse than rotten eggs). This foul odor just hung in the air. Fortunately today, with much tougher environmental laws, industrial emissions don't cause quite the problem they used to. Still, not all noxious industrial odors have been eliminated. So if you are relocating to an area you don't know well, do some investigating.

Industrial odors aren't all you need to think about. Kevin Conroy remembers the day he and his wife looked at the suburban development where they bought a lot to build their new home. "It was a crisp cool afternoon in early November," says Kevin. "We were looking forward to getting out of the city into the clean fresh country air. And that's what we found.

"Then, one day during the following spring when we were pretty well along with our construction, we were almost knocked over by the strong odor of horse manure. We didn't know it at the time, but we soon found out. There were riding stables and a large horse farm less than a half-mile in back of our development. Overall, we were lucky, I guess, because the wind doesn't come in from that direction very often. But when it does . . ."

MISTAKE # **49**

No one told us we had bought in a flood plain.

LESSON: Ask your real estate agent or mortgage lender if your home is located in a flood plain. Then buy flood insurance.

Every year throughout the United States, thousands of homeowners suffer heavy financial losses due to floods. All too frequently these losses could have been prevented. A case in point is Emily and Dennis Bruner. Emily and Dennis bought their home in a flood plain. In and of itself, there's nothing unusual about that. Millions of American homes are located in flood plains. But (according to the Bruners), no one—not the previous homeowners (the sellers), the real estate agent, or their mortgage lender—explained to them the area's flood potential.

Consequently, the Bruners didn't buy flood insurance. Sure enough, several years after Emily and Dennis bought their home, the Des Plaines River overran its banks. The torrent rushed through their home at depths of five feet and more. Their home's foundation was destroyed, as was its interior, all of their furniture, and their personal belongings. Not counting the drowning of their Yorkshire terrier and the emotional trauma of losing their life's possessions, the Bruners' direct dollar losses totaled $60,000.

If this wasn't bad enough, their mortgage lender pushed the Bruners for full payment of their outstanding mortgage balance. The Bruners were without a home, without personal belongings, and saddled with a mortgage debt of $91,381. Bankruptcy looked like their only solution.

Eventually, when threatened with a lawsuit for failing to advise the Bruners to buy flood insurance, the mortgage lender backed off and forgave their debt. Still, even with debt forgiveness, the Bruners were out their direct losses and their accumulated home equity. They avoided bankruptcy, but the lack of flood insurance cost them their life's savings.

Flooding is a real risk that many homeowners face. But you can't adequately judge the flood potential of a neighborhood by driving through it. You need historical data. That's why the federal government has drawn up flood maps and designated certain areas as flood zones.

Of course, just because a home is located in a flood zone doesn't mean a flood is likely, or even imminent. In fact, some critics complain the government has defined flood zones much too broadly. But would you rather be safe or sorry? To be safe, buy flood insurance. (In fact, your lender may require it.) Your homeowners insurance policy will not pay for flood losses.

MISTAKE # **50**

After a downpour, we can't drive down these roads.

LESSON: *Think bad weather. Will you be able to get to and from your home?*

More than likely, you won't shop for homes when it's raining so hard you have to hunch over the steering wheel to see where you're driving. Likewise, on days when ice and snow cover the ground, you'd probably rather stretch out on the sofa, read a book, or watch a football game. For the great majority of homebuyers, bad weather is not the best time to go out looking at houses. Rather, the best time to look at houses is when the sun is shining, the days are nice, and you feel like getting out and driving around.

But think for a moment. On reasonably nice days, you won't be able to see whether snow or rain makes the roads leading to and from your home inaccessible. "We wanted to move out to the country so bad," says Stevie Rankin, "we didn't even consider what it would be like driving in during the winter snows or spring rains. But we found out. After a downpour or heavy snows, you can't drive down these roads. Sometimes it takes a couple of days for the snow plows to clear the roads. Then, if we're dumped on again, we're stuck for another couple of days.

"When it rains hard, the dirt road leading out to the county highway becomes so muddy, you can only use it as a last resort. We had to buy a four-wheel-drive."

Of course, dirt roads aren't the only potential source of trouble. More than a few cities and suburban developments have improperly graded streets and inadequate sewers for water runoff. I've seen neighborhoods where, after a heavy rain, the kids get out and go "swimming" in the streets.

Also, it's not uncommon for houses situated below grade to receive a flood of water flowing from the streets into their driveway, garage, or basement in heavy rains. (Remember, water does run downhill.) If you live where it sleets and snows, look at the grade of your driveway. Is it so steep you will have trouble pulling in or out of it?

Yes, go out and shop for your home on those nicer days. But at least think bad weather. When it's raining or snowing, will you be able to travel easily to and from your home?

MISTAKE # **51**

We hardly ever see the sun here.

LESSON: *Discover your metro area's microclimates.*

Does your metro area have "microclimates"? In and around some cities, within commuting distance of a central business district, a July day might bring fog and 60 degree temperatures in one neighborhood, 70 degrees and rain in another, and 90 degrees and sunshine elsewhere. Oceans, lakes, rivers, hills, mountains, bays, and even tall buildings can affect weather patterns.

Within a 15-mile radius of downtown Vancouver, British Columbia, rainfall varies from 15 inches to more than 100 inches a year. In San

Francisco, the Cow Hollow and Marina District neighborhoods enjoy noticeably less fog and more sunshine than other neighborhoods located near the zoo and the Pacific Ocean. If you live in Walnut Creek (20 minutes from the San Francisco Bay Bridge), you'll find many summer days over 80 degrees. To city residents, though, 80 degrees feels like a heat wave. In the Los Angeles metro area, Ventura residents breathe (relatively) clean air, while in Palmdale residents suffer 150 smog-day warnings a year. Skyscraper office and apartment buildings not only block sunlight, they can dramatically affect wind velocity. (Don't try walking near the Sears Tower in Chicago or the World Trade Center in Manhattan on windy days.)

If you now live in a metro area with microclimates, you may know how weather differs among local neighborhoods and communities. On the other hand, if you are moving to a new area, talk to Realtors or perhaps call a government weather station. To avoid unwelcome surprises, it pays to know the weather patterns before you choose a neighborhood.

MISTAKE # **52**

We bought in the country to avoid the city's high property tax rates.

LESSON: Property taxes are only one side of the coin. Also compare government services.

Many homebuyers flee the cities to locate in rural or suburban areas where they can find lower property tax rates. That's what motivated Jack Byers and his family. "We wanted to buy a home in the country," says Jack. "We knew that once we moved outside the city limits, our tax rates would drop 30 percent. But I forgot about services. Out here in the country, we pay for our own trash collection; we are assessed separately by the fire district; and the city's water and sewage lines don't run out this far. That means we have to maintain a well and septic tank.

"We don't have gas lines either," Jack continued. "So our energy costs for drying clothes, home heating, water heating, and cooking are higher. Nor are we connected yet to cable television. And because the closest fire station is a partly volunteer outfit three miles away, we pay more for homeowners insurance than people in the city.

"I don't want to complain," Jack added. "I'm just saying, we didn't look at homes in the city because we wanted lower taxes. Now it looks like after we consider everything, living in the country's actually costing us more."

Sometimes it's easy to get so concerned about cutting taxes you forget that cities do provide services. So, when shopping locations, compare tax rates. But also compare what your taxes buy.

MISTAKE # **53**

After we bought, the city cut our services and raised our taxes.

LESSON: *Determine whether your community is solvent.*

Everybody would like more services, better schools, and lower taxes. But many Americans are getting the opposite. Cities, counties, and states throughout the United States have fallen into a financial black hole. What we used to call financial irresponsibility now goes by the name revenue shortfall. But regardless of political semantics, the results are usually the same: higher taxes and cutbacks in education, libraries, street repairs, police protection, and social services. "The month after we moved in," says Shannon Brown, "they jacked up tax rates, canceled the bus service, and raised the tolls for the bridge."

If you're thinking about buying a home in a community that's running a large deficit, beware. Since state and local governments can't borrow with the same reckless abandon as the federal government, at some point—sooner rather than later—someone's got to pay the piper. And as likely as not, that someone will be the homeowners. Property tax rates will probably be headed up. You'll be paying more for less.

Look to the Future

Before you buy, don't just look at current tax rates. Find out the financial condition of the community. Does it balance its books? Or is it headed toward insolvency?

As an added precaution, ask your Realtor or the city treasurer's office about the level of the community's bonded indebtedness. Sometimes communities that expect rapid growth float bonds (borrow money) to pay for new streets, roads, sewage facilities, parks, libraries, schools, fire stations, and other types of infrastructure necessary to support housing development and an increasing population. (In California, these are called Mello Roos bonds.) Over time the bonds will be paid off by taxing all the residents in the new developments. As long as growth occurs as expected, financing infrastructure this way generally doesn't create a problem.

However, if growth stalls, or the local economy collapses, then early residents may end up with a serious problem. After the Colorado oil bust stalled growth in that state, for example, new developments and communities went bankrupt. Some owners of $100,000 houses were getting property tax bills for as much as $12,000 a year. Of course, most owners didn't pay these taxes. They just walked away from their houses. Lawyers for the tax authorities, mortgage lenders, and bond holders were left to litigate over the remains.

The Colorado experience was extreme. But it does illustrate an easily avoided mistake: Understand the risks of owning a home in a community that spends dangerously more than it takes in.

MISTAKE # **54**

Everyone around here seems apathetic. They've accepted decline.

LESSON: Look for communities and neighborhoods with an entrepreneurial let-us-make-things-better spirit.

No law of the universe says a city, community, or neighborhood must decline. Or if down, that it must stay down. Communities improve when they look at their strengths, search for ways to overcome problems, and develop a can-do attitude. They decline when people overlook their resources and advantages. As he watched the for-sale sign go up in his front yard, Paul Dillon says, "We didn't want to move, but everyone around here is so apathetic. They've accepted decline. We just don't want to be here as it happens."

More than 100 years ago, Henry Grady, editor of the *Atlanta Constitution,* used the funeral of a man to describe the dying of nearby Pickens County, Georgia:

> The grave was dug through solid marble, but the marble headstone came from Vermont. It was in a pine wilderness but the pine coffin came from Cincinnati. An iron mountain overshadowed it, but the coffin nails and the screws and the shovel came from Pittsburgh. With hard wood and metal abounding, the corpse was hauled on a wagon from South Bend, Indiana. A hickory grove grew near by, but the pick and shovel handles came from New York. The cotton shirt on the dead man came from Cincinnati, the coat and breeches from Chicago, the shoes from Boston; the folded hands were encased in white gloves from New York, and round the poor neck, which had worn all its living days the bondage of lost opportunity, was twisted a cheap cravat from Philadelphia. Pickens County, so rich in undeveloped resources, furnished nothing for the funeral except the corpse and the hole in the ground and would probably have imported both of those if it could have done so. And as the poor dead fellow was lowered to his rest, on coffin bands from Lowell, he carried nothing

into the next world as a reminder of his home in this, save the halted blood in his veins, the chilled marrow in his bones, and the echo of the dull clods that fell on his coffin lid.

The residents of Pickens County could not see their own opportunities and potential. Is this the type of community or neighborhood you're considering? Or is there an active entrepreneurial spirit that declares, "We can make things better. We can and will determine our own future." It was this spirit that lifted Pittsburgh, Denver, Austin, and Houston from their economic fall. It's this spirit that is bringing back neighborhoods like south-central Los Angeles, Candler Park (Atlanta), Mt. Rainier (Washington, D.C.), South of Market (San Francisco), and North End (Boston).

MISTAKE # **55**

The sellers said it was only 25 minutes to downtown by train.

LESSON: *Commuting to work? Test travel the route before you buy.*

"True, it was only 25 minutes to downtown by train," recalls Andrew Ho. "But that was if you arrived at the platform on Saturday afternoon just as the train was about to pull out.

"On the other hand, if you're leaving our house to get to work by 9:00 A.M., you better be out the door by 7:30 at the latest. With the morning traffic backup at 95th, it can take 20 to 30 minutes just to get to the Sommerville station. Then parking (when you can find it) and walking to the platform takes another 5 to 10 minutes. And at commuter hours, the train takes 40 minutes, not 25. Next comes an eight-minute walk to the office. So that's about an hour and a half if everything goes without a hitch—which you can't always count on.

"We liked the house so much," Andrew adds, "I wanted to believe I could get to work in 30 to 40 minutes. I don't really blame the sellers for misleading me as much as I blame myself. Rather than discover the facts, I preferred to be blinded by illusion."

As Andrew now recognizes, when buying a home, it's easy to accept an illusion. You tell yourself what you want to believe. To avoid this mistake, test travel your commute *during the hours you will be commuting.* Whether driving or taking public transportation, you might find an assumed 30-minute trip actually puts you on the road for an hour and a half.

MISTAKE # **56**

We didn't walk the neighborhood.

LESSON: *Walk and talk the streets where you plan to locate.*

Several months ago Carol and Wendy Tabor bought their first home. It was located in a San Francisco neighborhood that looked pleasant enough when they discovered it on one of their weekend neighborhood excursions. But as the Tabors soon learned after they moved in, the neighborhood was infested with drug dealers. Even worse, a crack house was located just two doors down from their home. Shocked and hurt by what they now know, the Tabors are suing their real estate agent and the sellers of the property. Carol and Wendy complain that the agent and the former homeowners should have told them about the neighborhood drug problem.

Without prejudging the case, my inclination is that Carol and Wendy are right. Yet, to some degree they must share responsibility for this mistake. Before making an offer to buy their home, they should have walked the neighborhood and talked to the people who lived there— not just to get the facts on crime but to discover other information that could help them decide whether it met their priorities. For example:

- Are the residents friendly? Do they welcome newcomers, or are they stand-offish?

- Where are most people in the neighborhood employed? What are their occupations? Are their jobs and employers solid or unstable?
- Are there any recent or planned zoning changes? Street widenings? Commercial or apartment construction?
- Do the streets flood when it rains hard? Are the streets cleared promptly after a snowfall?
- Is the neighborhood plagued with noisy neighbors or other disturbances?
- What types of people are moving in and out of the neighborhood? Is it heading upscale, downscale, or holding its own?
- Is there an action-oriented homeowners' association that's working to improve the neighborhood?
- If residents could change three things in the neighborhood, what would they list?
- Do residents think they receive good public services for the taxes they pay?
- What schools do neighborhood children attend? What are their strengths and weaknesses? Who's doing what to improve them?

In addition to talking with residents, walking the neighborhood can help you sharpen and focus your observations:

- Look closely at the houses. Do they show signs of neglect and disrepair? Or do nearly all people show pride of ownership?
- Are the yards well landscaped? Have residents accented their homes with flowers, shrubs, and other attractive plantings?
- Do you hear any disturbances or detect unpleasant odors?
- Are the parks and public spaces well kept? Or are they littered with sacks from McDonald's, marred by graffiti, and populated by derelicts?
- Do any (or many) of the houses show multiple mailboxes or cars lined up in driveways?
- Do you see signs of home remodeling, improvements, or renovation?

Your real estate agent and the sellers *should tell* you about the neighborhood. But you can learn even more by *experiencing* it for yourself.

CHAPTER 5

Is This Home for You?

Just as with neighborhoods, no one "best" home exists. When you choose a home, you're really answering these questions: "Based upon a carefully thought-out list of possibilities and priorities, does this home feel right? Based on where you are now in life—and where you plan to be in the future—will this house meet your most important goals? Does it fit within the amounts you want to spend (invest)? Does the home offer good value?"

To answer these questions, get a savvy agent to help you. Then, examine your house closely. Envision its livability for your family. Estimate maintenance and repair costs. Overall, don't leave anything to chance. Read through the experiences and the mistakes of the homebuyers in this chapter. You'll discover that with careful inspection, you will make a good home-buying decision.

MISTAKE # *57*

Our agent said it was a lot of house for the money.

LESSON: *"A lot of house for the money" can sometimes mean "a lot of money for the house."*

"We had been looking for a two- or three-bedroom, two-bath house," recalled Tyrone Jones. "That size was all we needed or wanted. But our agent alerted us to a great bargain that had just come on the market. The house had four bedrooms, three baths, and a total of 2,400 square feet. At a price of $139,500, our agent told us it was really a lot of house for the money.

"Since I can't pass up a bargain," Tyrone continued, "we decided to take a look. Based on the price information our agent gave us, I figured we would buy this house for less than $60 per square foot [p.s.f.]. Other houses we had considered were priced around $120,000 for 1,600 to 1,800 square feet. That works out roughly to $70 p.s.f. Compared to these other houses, the bigger one seemed cheap.

"And even though other houses were more in line with what we were hoping for, we didn't want to miss this deal. So we bought it. Looking back, I think that was the wrong decision. To buy the house, we pushed ourselves financially. Yet, the house didn't give us the warmth and comfort we wanted. Besides, it costs too much time and money for upkeep. Instead of getting a lot of house for the money, we feel like we're paying a lot of money for the house."

Tyrone and his wife fell into the "bargain trap." They sacrificed their basic goals for a "good deal." When someone needs a good buy just to afford a house, shopping for a bargain makes sense. Or if you find a home that fills your most important needs and you buy it at a bargain price, that's even better. But think twice before you commit yourself. Don't simply grab a great deal unless you have placed "great deal" as your top priority.

Sometimes a Bargain Is Not a Bargain

Whether an apparently "bargain-priced" home actually will save you money is a separate issue. To Tyrone, going for a price of $58 p.s.f. as compared to $70 p.s.f. seemed like a moneywise decision. But Tyrone later realized the larger home required higher property taxes, insurance, utilities, mortgage payments, and maintenance expenses. As his experience shows, you don't want to think just in terms of "a lot of house for the money." You need to figure the extra costs of owning the house over the years. Do you want to spend money for rarely used unnecessary space? (Of course, before you answer this question, be sure to consider whether through creativity you might turn wasted space into productive uses.)

Just as important, be careful when you compare the per-square-foot costs of homes of different sizes, quality, and design.

- Smaller homes nearly always cost more per square foot than larger homes of the same quality. The expensive components of a house (baths, kitchen, heat and air, plumbing) generally don't increase proportionately as a home increases in size. In comparing large to small, the question should be whether the difference in price and operating costs makes the larger home a better buy than a smaller home.

- Dollars-per-square-foot works best when you're comparing homes of the same size, amenities, and quality. Tyrone should have compared the p.s.f. price of the large home he bought to more similar homes. If he found that other comparable large homes typically sold for, say, $65 p.s.f., only then could he have reasonably concluded that his home (at $58 p.s.f.) *may* present a bargain.

- Nonetheless, before coming to a final decision, Tyrone should have compared the homes according to their livability, energy efficiency, architectural style, and condition. Price per square foot can serve as one important standard of value. But it doesn't tell the whole story.

MISTAKE # **58**

Our agent was part order taker, part chauffeur, and part narrator—but she didn't give us the service we needed.

LESSON: *Know what services you expect from your agent, then work with an agent who delivers.*

"Since this was our first home," Peter Chen reflects, "we didn't really know what to expect from a real estate agent. Ours was friendly enough. But she hardly did anything that we couldn't have done for ourselves.

She seemed like she just wanted to take our order, chauffeur us around, and then act as a narrator or announcer.

"She'd say things like 'What kind of home are you looking for? What neighborhood do you want? What price range fits your budget?'

"The problem," says Peter, "is that we weren't sure what, where, or how much. That seemed to frustrate her. When she did drive us around to look at houses, she didn't seem to know very much. Once inside a house, her major contribution to helping us evaluate the house was 'This is the living room. This is the kitchen. This is the master bedroom.' Even with us being first-timers, we know a kitchen when we see one.

"But, as I said," Peter continued, "she was nice, so we didn't want to hurt her feelings and switch agents. In the end, though, we realized we made a mistake by sticking with her. I think that with a better agent we could have explored more options and made a better choice. In fact, after it was over, we laughed because we realized how silly it was for us to stick with an agent we would not recommend to our friends."

A Good Agent Does More Than "Show" Houses

Peter Chen and his wife fell into the same trap that catches many first-time homebuyers. They called a real estate office about a listing, got hooked up with an agent who wanted to show them some houses, and then stayed with the agent more or less by default. You can prevent this mistake by learning what service to expect from an agent and then working only with an agent who delivers.

Here are many of the ways a real estate professional should be willing and able to help you make a better home-buying decision:

- Talk through your housing possibilities and priorities. Help you clarify and rank your potential choices.

- Review your finances; help you improve your "borrower profile," and suggest finance plans and lenders that can maximize your affordability (see Chapter 7).

- Suggest trade-offs and compromises that will help you satisfy your most critical needs and priorities.

- Inform you about neighborhoods, communities, and developments that seem right for you.

- Provide you with market facts, such as recent sales prices and time-on-the-market data for homes similar to the ones you're interested in.

- Alert you to good buys as soon as (sometimes even before) they come on the market.

- Get the sellers of homes you're interested in to prepare a "Seller Disclosures Statement." A disclosure statement should warn you of deficiencies or defects that can mar the desirability of a home or its neighborhood.

- Point out ways you might improve (redecorate, remodel, renovate) a home to enhance its market value or better meet the needs of your family (preferably both).

- Stay in tune with your home-buying efforts from beginning to end. Make sure everything gets taken care of that needs to be taken care of.

- Anticipate, prevent, or overcome roadblocks or problems that may arise. Keep you fully informed. Pave the way for as smooth and successful a home-buying experience as possible.

You may not want all of the services mentioned above. But you do require more service than order taker, chauffeur, and narrator. Successful real estate agents have worked with dozens (often hundreds) of homebuyers. They've run up against all types of home-buyer problems, obstacles, and goals. By expecting and requiring agents to deliver a variety of services, you gain the benefit of their expertise, insight, and experience. Remember: The best real estate professionals don't *sell* real estate. They help people become homeowners. A good agent works with you until you're sure you've found the right home.

MISTAKE # **59**

Our agent never mentioned . . .

LESSON: Always ask sales agents (or sellers) for specific factual disclosures that list the defects or problems of a home and its neighborhood.

One of the most misunderstood topics in real estate is the legal concept of "disclosure." Because the laws and practices of disclosure are constantly changing, many home sellers, buyers, and even sales agents have become confused.

From the early 1900s up to the 1960s, real estate agents represented sellers. Legally, agents were required to work exclusively for the interests of the property owners. In contrast, with respect to homebuyers, the rule was *caveat emptor,* "let the buyer beware." In most home purchases, the law required neither sellers nor their agents to reveal a home's defects. If you didn't discover a home's crumbling foundation or inadequate wiring until after you bought it, that was your tough luck. You had little recourse to the sellers and even less to the agent. Unless the sellers or their agent gave explicitly false warranties or representations—"That foundation could support a 12-story building"—you were assumed to have bought the home in as-is condition.

Today, however, the doctrine of *caveat emptor* is dead. From the late 1960s and still evolving up through the present, innumerable court decisions, federal and state laws and regulations, and real estate licensing standards have sealed the coffin lid on "let the buyer beware." The general rule has become "let the sellers and their agents beware." The consumer is king.

Today the law gives little comfort to sellers or agents who fail to disclose a property's serious defects. Regardless of whether you're working with a "seller's" agent, a "buyer's" agent, or a "dual" agent, any agent who doesn't mention a property's serious defects can be held liable for that omission. Yet, even with the death of *caveat emptor,* plenty of room still exists for confusion, misunderstanding, and deception.

Serious Defects

First, consider the term "serious." What kinds of defects actually qualify as "serious"? At one extreme is a recent Massachusetts case. A house had a dangerously defective gas heater. On several occasions the heater had malfunctioned. The soon-to-be seller was told by the repairman the heater could easily start a fire. Even with this warning, though, the seller did not replace or adequately repair the heater. Nor did he inform the eventual buyers of the home.

Shortly after the buyers took possession, the heater exploded. The results were fatal: Two members of the family died. The court held the seller criminally liable. He was convicted of involuntary manslaughter and sentenced to 15 years in prison.

Defects in a home that could likely lead to extensive property damage, injury, or death are serious. Both sellers and agents must disclose them or suffer the consequences. But what about substandard wiring that is in good condition and has never created a problem? That's a gray area. What about several light switches and electrical outlets that don't work? Those are probably not serious.

Due to these gray areas of liability and uncertainties—not to mention potential injury or loss of life—you must explicitly insist that sellers and agents list all of a home's problems. Many sellers, and some agents, have not adjusted to the demise of *caveat emptor.*

To illustrate: Consider this question from a would-be seller. In a letter to Q&A columnist Nina Groskind, a homeowner writes that he knows his home has "several flaws, some minor, some more significant." He then asks (evidently fully prepared to hide as much as possible), "What obligation do I have to 'tell all' to people interested in purchasing my home?"

Ms. Groskind answers that the homeowner might be able to get away with "nondisclosure." But (1) he'd better not tell his real estate agent, because the agent would have to pass the information along to the buyer; and (2) the owner should not make any explicit false statement that could mislead any prospective new owners of the home.

It's sellers like these that you must guard against.

"Known" or "Suspected" Defects

As you try to get as much information as you can about a prospective home and neighborhood, another type of problem arises. What if the seller or the agent doesn't know about the termites in the foundation or the wood rot under the roof? What if they don't "know" but only "suspect" a defect might exist? In the case of no knowledge, courts generally rule that sellers or agents can't be expected to disclose what they don't know. However, ignorance doesn't offer an airtight defense.

Laws in many states require owners or agents to make certain kinds of property investigations. In Massachusetts sellers must test their homes for urea formaldehyde foam insulation. In California real estate agents must visually inspect most homes they list for sale. Even further, some judges and juries have held sellers or agents liable for not disclosing defects they should have known about or reasonably suspected might exist—even though they claimed no direct knowledge.

In a far-reaching California case, a realty firm was held liable for not disclosing that a home's hillside location made it susceptible to damage from mudslides. The agent claimed no knowledge or expertise on the topic of mudslides. The court said "too bad." Even if the agent didn't know, he should have reasonably suspected there might be a problem.

As you can see, the entire area of inspections and disclosures can confuse everyone involved in a home-buying transaction. In so many ways the "law" is ambiguous or simply not well understood. That's why the area of "disclosure" and "nondisclosure" contributes to so many home-buying mistakes. Of course, the traditional tendency and practice of sellers to hide or understate defects adds to the potential for error.

But there's also another long-standing practice in home buying that can divert you from getting the information you need to make a good decision. It's called "puffery."

Beware of Puffery

"This is a great neighborhood. You're really getting a bargain. This home's in superb condition. You'll just love the people here. Oh yes, it's very quiet." Often homebuyers who don't get the information they need fail because they unconsciously accept puffery in lieu of facts (see Mistake #39). None of these statements actually includes any factual information.

Some unethical agents (or sellers), though, purposely use puffery to mask their lack of knowledge—or as an explicit attempt to avoid disclosure. These agents have learned to couch their comments in terms of puffery or opinions because opinions permit them to escape liability for misleading you.

"You said this was a great neighborhood," complain the angry homebuyers to the agent who sold them their home.

"Well, it is a great neighborhood," responds the agent. "Sure there's a crack house several doors down and I know the drive-by shootings can be annoying. But the neighborhood association is working hard to turn things around. All this community spirit really does make this a great neighborhood. You just can't find that spirit and feeling of togetherness in many neighborhoods these days."

By the agent's definition, the neighborhood is "great." Can you prove that your definition of "great" outweighs the agent's? Did the agent misrepresent the neighborhood? Or were his comments merely sales puffery and a matter of opinion? If you took a case like this to court, you would probably stand a better chance of winning today than in years past. But in most states you'd still be better off spending your money on lottery tickets than on lawyers.

Exceptions to the Laws of Disclosure

Although society is moving away from the doctrine of *caveat emptor,* the evolving laws still exclude some types of sellers, properties, and transactions. For example, government agencies, financial institutions, auctioneers, and court-appointed trustees may not be covered under some disclosure laws. Buyers of commercial and investment real estate receive less protection than homebuyers. And if you're buying at a foreclosure sale or through probate, you will probably be buying "as is." Also, in some states, FSBOs (owners who sell their homes without an agent) need not meet the same high standards of disclosure required of real estate agents.

Rules to Follow

When you shop for a home, you want to get the best information you can. In general, today's laws of disclosure make this job somewhat easier than it has been in the past. Yet, disclosure laws aren't the full answer to the difficult task of information gathering. They scatter into many gray areas; they may be circumvented by puffery; they may not be understood adequately by agents or sellers; and these laws frequently carve out exceptions for certain types of persons, properties, or transactions.

As a result, your home-buying efforts must be proactive. To prevent mistakes, don't depend on others to reveal all they know or should know about a home and its neighborhood. Take the initiative. Protect yourself by following these guidelines:

- Ask your real estate agent (or lawyer) to explain fully the laws of disclosure that apply to home buying in your area. Learn where disclosure laws may not apply; learn the types of nondisclosure problems that are prone to arise in the homes or neighborhoods you're looking at.

- Always ask your agent specific questions that require factual answers. Don't settle for opinions. Probe for facts.

- Ask the sellers to prepare a written list of every defect, problem, or shortcoming of their home and neighborhood. If something's not 100 percent right, tell them you want to know about it.

- Don't accept agent or seller evasions such as, "I believe," "I think," or "As far as we know." If the sellers or their agent don't truly know, then make a note to follow up with further inquiry or investigation. Too many homebuyers mistakenly accept these kinds of seller or agent "hedges."

- Hire professional inspectors to examine critically the condition of the house, its component systems (heating, air conditioning, electrical, ventilation), and built-in appliances.

- Closely inspect the home and neighborhood yourself. In the end, it's going to be your house. Successful homebuyers take charge of the inspection process.

- Assume everyone you're working with is acting in good faith. But take precautions as if they aren't.

MISTAKE # **60**

We didn't hire a professional inspector. My dad knows all about houses.

LESSON: *Ask your dad, brother-in-law, or Uncle Harry to inspect your home as an additional safeguard. But don't substitute family members or friends for a professional inspection.*

If a friend or family member "knows all about houses," you may be tempted to skip a professional inspection and save yourself $200 or $300. Don't do it. Marci Alvarez tells why.

"When we bought, we were short of cash. So I asked my dad to inspect our house for us. He has worked as a painter, a carpenter, and even built a den and an extra bath for my parents' house. With all that experience, I figured he would be able to discover any trouble spots. Unfortunately for all of us, he missed some type of problem with the fuse box and the wiring. After we moved in, we must have blown a dozen fuses, and several wall outlets kept getting really hot everytime we plugged something in and turned it on.

"When I told my dad about the problem, he tried to fix it, but I think he just made it worse. Eventually, we did get an electrician out to the house. By the time he finished his rewiring, his bill was over $900.

"If that wasn't bad enough, my husband first blamed me and next blamed my dad. They argued over it for several weeks. Let me tell you, it was not fun. Spending $900 for circuit breakers and whatever else it was the electrician charged us for was bad enough. But the family turmoil was even worse.

"Then, after I thought the whole episode was behind us, my dad insisted on giving us a check for $900. We didn't want it. But there was no way we could refuse without more arguing. So, now we have the $900, but I feel guilty about accepting the money and regret ever getting my dad involved in the first place."

Don't Burden Parents or Friends

When it comes time to get your home inspected, hire a professional house inspector. Professional inspectors evaluate dozens of houses a month. They know what to look for. They own the necessary tools of their trade. They learn to recognize signs of problems in their early stages so they can caution you about what to expect in the future. Moreover, professional home inspectors take on financial liability for any mistakes they do make.

Ask your family and friends to join with you to celebrate the joy and achievement of your becoming a homeowner. Don't ask them to shoulder the full responsibilities of inspecting a home. If tempted, remember Marci's experience.

MISTAKE # **61**

We didn't think a new home needed to be professionally inspected.

LESSON: *Even when you're 100 percent sure of your builder's reputation, buy some peace of mind. Secure a professional inspection.*

"Christine Estep is weary—weary of paying for a home she can't live in," opened a front-page article in the *Miami Herald*. Christine Estep is one of the tens of thousands of homeowners whose homes were damaged by Hurricane Andrew. But instead of having her home repaired, Christine and the other 343 homeowners in her Village Homes condominium complex are about to see their homes demolished. The relatively new complex was "so riddled with construction defects" that engineers have recommended tearing down all the units and rebuilding from scratch.

To make matters worse, the developer of the complex was the well-known Florida development company, Arvida. And at the time of the first phase of construction, Arvida was a subsidiary of the Walt Disney Company. After Disney, another company of high standing, JMB Realty of Chicago, became Arvida's parent. In a multimillion-dollar case like this, accusations fly among homeowners, architects, lawyers, engineers, and contractors. Yet, no one disputes the engineers' basic conclusion that the construction quality of the units in the Village Homes complex failed to meet even minimum standards of safety.

Engineers, as well as a government investigators, say the homes had undersized foundations, inadequately designed roof trusses, masonry walls without necessary steel reinforcement, unanchored support posts, and missing hurricane straps. Now you might wonder, aren't newly constructed homes supposed to be inspected and approved by government building inspectors? How could major defects slip by? A lot of other people are asking the same questions. But it's not the first time.

Government Inspectors Sometimes Fail to Do Their Jobs

Over the years most cities throughout the United States have been rocked by various types of permits-for-sale bribery and payoff scandals. In fact, Janet Reno, now attorney general of the United States, previously worked as Florida's prosecuting attorney for Dade County (Miami). In that capacity she spearheaded a drive to investigate the government building inspection process. Ms. Reno never charged anyone with a crime, but her office investigation did result in charges of lax enforcement of building codes.

One building inspector who was followed by an investigator somehow managed to inspect and approve seven homes in five minutes. A former building inspector in Dade was quoted by the *Miami Herald* as saying, "It was a farce. The building and zoning department for years pushed quantity, not quality."

My purpose here is not to point the finger at anybody. It will be years (if ever) before a complete accounting of errors and responsibilities are tallied up and assigned to the various parties involved in Christine Estep's case. But you should know the construction defects and lax inspection practices that contributed to Christine's emotional and financial worries are all too common. Just because a home is new (or nearly new) does not mean it's defect free. A few builders and developers are crooks; others are careless; some need to cut corners "temporarily" to stay solvent; and others just plain make mistakes. Any way you look at it, new does not necessarily mean perfect.

Avoid unpleasant surprises. Employ a professional inspector even when you're buying a new or recently built house or condominium.

MISTAKE # **62**

I thought lead paint had been outlawed years ago.

LESSON: *Environmental concerns have come home.*

When your concerns turn to the environment, you may think of disappearing habitat for the spotted owls, mass illegal killings of elephants for their ivory tusks, or perhaps clear-cutting the African and Amazonian rain forests. But some of the most dangerous environmental problems may actually lie right where you live.

Jackie Shattuck and her husband, Mike, recently bought a home. Their inspection report showed the house to be nearly defect free. The wiring, plumbing, roof, foundation, and appliances were all found to be in good condition. Unfortunately, the Shattucks thought only of the physical condition of their home. They forgot to check its environmental quality. That mistake cost them nearly $5,000.

"Lead paint," Jackie recalls saying when she heard the bad news. "I thought it had been outlawed years ago."

As a matter of law, Jackie was right. Once it was learned that lead-based paints could cause serious illnesses, including brain damage (especially to children), this toxic metal was phased out of use in household paints. Prior to 1977, though, lead was a common ingredient. Although no one knows exactly how many older homes still have layers of lead-based paint lurking under less toxic (and more recent) paint layers, estimates place the number somewhere between 20 and 40 million houses.

"If you're buying a home built before the late 1970s," advises lead specialist Stephanie Pollack, "assume there's lead until proven otherwise."

To remove the danger of lead-based paint (which is called deleading) requires trained specialists with special equipment and protective gear. Depending on the size of the house and the number of rooms affected, deleading a home can easily cost $3,500 and may run up to $6,000 or more. Without deleading, paint chipping and flaking through natural wear can create a health hazard. Should you begin sanding, tearing out walls, or other particle-disturbing remodeling efforts, lead-based paint becomes a clear and present danger. Inhaling lead paint dust can cause permanent respiratory or neurological damage.

Other Environmental Concerns

Lead-based paint isn't the only potential contaminate you need to have checked before you buy. San Francisco Board of Supervisors member Angela Alioto, an outspoken environmentalist, discovered an old, long-out-of-use buried oil tank in her home's yard. To remove the tank and clean up the soil cost her $9,000. When journalists questioned the councilwoman, she admitted she had not had her home inspected for environmental dangers before she bought it.

Don't make the same mistake. Environmental dangers can threaten health and sometimes cost thousands of dollars to remedy. This is one instance where "better safe than sorry" really applies. The exact type of environmental dangers you confront will vary by where you live, the age of the home you're planning to buy, and the type of building materials used in your area.

Talk with local or state environmental agencies. Many of these agencies have published environmental booklets that are written especially for homebuyers and homeowners. You might also pick up an environmental booklet from your local Realtor. After due consideration, you may decide against a full environmental inspection of your home-to-be. But stay alert at least for the following types of potential problems:

- Lead-based paint
- Lead pipes or lead solder

- Asbestos (commonly found in many types of building supplies, materials, and floor tiles)
- Formaldehyde, especially urea formaldehyde foam insulation
- Contaminated ground water
- Volatile organic compounds (VOCs are found in most household chemicals, adhesives used with wall-to-wall carpeting, and pesticides)
- Radon (a gas released by radioactive decay that rises up from the ground especially into the lower levels of a home)
- Underground heating oil tanks
- High-power electrical lines and transformers

In our industrial world, no one can escape all contaminants. Still, at least identify risks, assess their relative dangers, and estimate the cost of cleanup. Many state, federal, and local laws now apply to environmental hazards. Some of these laws mandate seller disclosures. Others require that you be given various forms or booklets. Whatever the case may be in your area, actively investigate. The environmental quality of a home ranks just as important as the condition of its roof or foundation.

MISTAKE # **63**

We now know why the sellers put up paneling in the downstairs den.

LESSON: Be cautious of recent redecorating, repairs, or remodeling by sellers. They may be hiding a problem.

"If you want to get top dollar for your house when you sell, put it in tip-top condition." Over the years, this frequent advice from books and real estate agents has encouraged millions of homeowners to clean up, paint, wallpaper, panel, or otherwise redecorate and repair their homes before they place them on the market. "Package your home for profit," writes

Peter Percelay in his book by the same title. "By effectively packaging your home, rather than just putting it on the market, you can reap thousands of additional dollars on your sale."

Percelay then goes on to tell his readers, "Your goal is to give buyers confidence in your product. . . . But you should never use packaging techniques as a way of hiding serious problems or defects in your home." Yes, and you should never inflate your resume, pad your expense account, or bring pens and pencils home from the office. But some people do.

Within our society, there are dishonest practices that, if perhaps not widely accepted, are at least widely practiced. Hiding a home's defects through redecorating or remodeling seems to be one of them.

When you're shopping for a home, stay alert to this possibility. Many people who consider themselves honest have nevertheless imbibed too much of the spirit of *caveat emptor.* More than 200 years of this attitude hasn't been eradicated by two decades of consumerism. Sally Roth knows from experience.

Sally bought a home that was built into a hillside and had a lower-level den. Not long before the sellers had put their home up for sale, they had "packaged it for profit" by installing wood paneling on the walls of the den. Not only did the paneling add a nice aesthetic touch, it perfectly hid the permanent waterstain marks that showed where water poured through during the rainy season. Since Sally moved into the home in July, she didn't learn of the problem until the wet months of December and January.

Most people who prepare a home for sale simply want to enhance its appeal. They're not trying to hide anything. But some people are. So if you find a home that has been freshly painted, plastered, paneled, wall-papered, repaired, or redecorated, closely inspect the improvements. As diplomatically as you can, secure written disclosures and warranties that pertain specifically to the condition of the property before the improvements were made. As I said before, assume the sellers are honest, but inspect the home as if they weren't.

MISTAKE # **64**

After we moved in, the sellers' remodeling contractor put a lien against our home. And we had to pay it!

LESSON: Ask to see the sellers' receipts to verify that all recent work on the home has been paid in full.

Every state allows contractors to place a lien against a home for unpaid work or materials. The exact nature of these laws differ, but they generally give firms and tradesmen at least 90 and sometimes up to 180 days after they have completed their work to file a lien.

In Rob Shoo's case, his sellers had remodeled a back porch into a sunroom at a cost of $2,700. The work was completed in late February. In March the sellers placed their house up for sale. In early April Rob put in his contract and the owners accepted. The transaction closed in mid-May. On May 27 the Dependable Construction Company filed a mechanic's lien for unpaid wages and materials.

As a matter of law, the sellers were financially liable for the charges. But the mechanic's lien establishes a valid claim by Dependable Construction against the house—regardless of who now owns it. The lien sits in the public records as a cloud on the home's title. Unless Rob can somehow get the sellers to write a check for the amount they owe, at some point he will have to write a check himself. As long as the mechanic's lien remains valid, Rob cannot sell or refinance his home.

To avoid this potential mistake, check the sellers' receipts for any work that has been performed recently on the house. As further precaution, you might ask the sellers to sign an affidavit stating (1) all work performed has been paid in full; or (2) no work to the home has been performed within the past 90 days (or whatever other statute of limitation for filing liens applies). Should you buy a home with recent improvements, don't assume the contractors have been paid. If you do, you run the risk of paying for them twice—first when you buy the home, then once again when you need to pay the mechanic's lien to clear the home's title.

MISTAKE # **65**

We should have looked at the sellers' utility bills.

LESSON: Energy audit a home before you buy it.

"We were renting a house just about the same size as the one we bought," says Patty Snyder, "so we thought we had a pretty good fix on how much our utility bills would run in our new home. Boy, were we mistaken! Believe it or not, our heat and air-conditioning bills nearly doubled. Our utilities now average $330 a month. We should have examined the sellers' utility bills."

Most energy rates have stabilized since their run-up after the OPEC oil crisis. Nevertheless, the total utility costs of operating a household can still amount to $3,000 to $5,000 a year. With utility bills at these levels, an energy-efficient house can save you $750 to $2,000 a year—or even more. I've talked with some homeowners in Maine and Vermont who, after installing super-energy-efficient improvements, have reduced their *total* winter heating bill to as low as $900 a year.

Check the Home's Energy Usage

One simple way to check a home's energy usage is to examine the sellers' utility bills. That won't tell you everything you need to know because you'll have to adjust for their family size, lifestyle, and comfort zones. But if you find their winter heating or summer cooling bills top say $300 or $400 a month, you may want to find out why.

Besides looking at utility bills, examine the windows, doors, appliances, water heater, furnace, and air conditioner. Do these promote energy conservation? What about the site placement and exterior design of the house? Is the home situated to protect against north winter winds as it brings in sunlight from the south? What about water usage? Fresh water for households is becoming a more expensive resource. Does the yard require heavy watering? Are the showers and toilets equipped with water-saving devices? What's the political climate? Is it likely your local or state government will require an "energy retrofit" for the home at some time in the future?

In many parts of the country, utility costs rank right after mortgage payments as the largest household cost—higher than property insurance, maintenance, or property taxes. Because energy-efficient houses save you thousands of dollars, don't mistakenly leave this factor out when you're comparing homes.

MISTAKE # **66**

We underestimated how much all of those little repairs and renovations would add up.

LESSON: *Little things can mean a lot.*

If you buy an existing home you may want to paint and wallpaper, lay new carpeting, repair wood rot around the eaves, enclose a porch, put in a skylight or two, restore the hardwood floors, strip the white paint and refurbish those natural oak doors, patch the roof, and maybe remodel a bath and kitchen.

How much money, time, and effort will these repairs and renovations add up to? Well, if you make what seems like a reasonable estimate, double it, then add a 25 percent contingency factor. You may come close to an accurate answer. Some unwritten law of the universe states that everything costs more and takes longer than you originally think. This law certainly applies to putting a house into shape.

Compare it to paying bills. You sit down to write a few checks for $50, $100, maybe $200, and, all of a sudden, the checking account balance drops $1,650. How do all those little checks add up to such a large amount? I don't know, but they do.

When you evaluate a home, don't forget that little things do add up. As you think about the repairs, redecorating, and renovation you'd like to do, make a list. Make it comprehensive. Check figures with qualified contractors or suppliers. Most important, don't simply keep a bunch of little numbers running around in your head. Total them.

Redecorating and renovation can boost your home's value by thousands of dollars. But the amount of your *profit* depends on how accurately you anticipate your costs.

MISTAKE # **67**

Before we could add central heat and air, we had to spend $1,800 for new wiring and ductwork.

LESSON: *Often, repairs and renovations can't be made without incurring other necessary costs.*

You may find out a new roof costs $3,500. But if the sheets of plywood under the shingles that have been leaking have suffered wood rot (water + wood = rotten wood), your costs could climb to $4,500 or more. If interior ceilings and supports also have been water-damaged, the costs could go higher.

When Jagdish and Carrie Sheth bought their Galveston, Texas, home, they planned to spend $2,800 to add central heat and air conditioning. Their actual bill totaled $4,600. Although Jagdish and Carrie figured right about the cost of the heat and air unit, they forgot to add the cost of upgrading the 100-amp electrical system to 200 amps. The upgrade was necessary to power the heat and AC system safely. Also, because the previous heating in the house had been gas floor heaters, the home lacked ductwork. Together, the electrical upgrades and new ductwork pushed up their costs beyond their original estimates.

One Thing Leads to Another

Often, planned repairs and renovations will cost more than you originally figure because the work you want can't be performed by itself. To do this, you must first do that. In home repair and renovation, one thing often leads to another.

Unfortunately, many contractors calculate their estimates only for the basic work. Some purposely lowball their bids to get you committed to the job. Then they "discover" other work that they must (or should) perform. In other instances, it really is impossible to know the full extent of necessary repairs until well into the work. For example, all competent heating and air-conditioning contractors know the necessary electrical upgrade their heat and air units will require. However, roofing contractors may not know how much wood damage a house has suffered until they rip off the old roof.

There is no perfect way to handle this problem. But you can try to get a "no-surprises" estimate. As a matter of good communication, make sure your contractor (or other cost estimator) understands that you want to know the costs (or at least the nature) of all labor and materials necessary for a total repair or renovation. Also ask for a worst-case/best-case range of estimates. At least then you have a lower and an upper limit. None of these solutions is perfect, because even the best "no-surprises" estimate can miss the mark. (The construction budget for the world-famous Sydney, Australia, opera house began at $6 million. Total costs at completion were over $100 million.)

Keep in mind that repairs and renovations may require additional, and often unanticipated, expenses. So if you buy a home that needs work, keep the risk of cost overruns in mind. Use this fact to help negotiate a lower price. You can reduce this risk through good planning and communication, but it's a mistake to think you can eliminate it entirely.

MISTAKE # **68**

The house *looked* great. I just didn't like cold showers, listening to my son's favorite radio station, or lugging groceries up the stairs from the garage.

LESSON: *Looks aren't everything. Evaluate a home's livability.*

The feeling's great when you see a house you fall in love with. High ceilings, hardwood floors, lots of natural light, a large country kitchen, a big stone fireplace, beautifully finished woodwork: The house could work as a photo feature for *Architectural Digest*. Before you jump to make an offer, though, evaluate whether the house will work for you. Don't mistake great looks for livability.

Walk the Floor Plan

As a start, walk the floor plan—not for the purpose of viewing the rooms, but to judge internal accessibility and convenience. In your daily living patterns, what rooms will require frequent travel between them? How many steps is it from the master bedroom to the kitchen, the laundry facilities, or the main living area? How convenient is the parking (garage, carport, street) to the kitchen? Imagine yourself carrying several bags of groceries from your car to the kitchen.

Now enter the kitchen. Ideally, you should be able to work efficiently between the stove (oven), the sink, and the refrigerator. This area is called the work triangle. A poorly designed work triangle can add hundreds of steps a day to food preparation and cleanup. Next measure the kitchen counter space, cabinet space, and placement. Are cabinets and counters situated to provide enough room to work, prepare, and store food and kitchen supplies conveniently?

Before leaving the kitchen, turn on the dishwasher. How loud is it? Can you hear it as you walk to other rooms of the house? What about televisions, radios, and stereos? Where will you place them? Take a radio from room to room. Can you play it without hearing the sound elsewhere in the house? Problems with noise rankle many homeowners and family members. Do you really want to hear heavy metal blasting from your son's bedroom at 10:00 at night?

What about privacy? Does the floor plan of the home provide enough private space? Can family members retreat from each other when they want to?

Next, check the bathrooms. How convenient are they? How long must the water run before you get hot water? How strong is the water pressure in the showers? Does the pressure ebb when someone flushes a toilet or turns on a faucet or another shower elsewhere? Does the water temperature hold constant? Can you hear a running shower or flushing toilet throughout the house? Do the bathrooms have enough natural or artificial light?

From the Outside In

Once you've completed a livability inspection of a home's interior, go outside. Admire the azaleas, the hedges, the flowers, the expansive yard. Now think. How much care and expense will this greenery require? Do you want to spend weekends pulling weeds, trimming bushes, and cutting grass? Can you afford to pay someone else to do it for you? Cast your eyes around the exterior of the home. Will it require frequent painting or staining? How much time and money will you spend to maintain the appearance and condition of the home?

Winding up your exterior inspection, go to the main entrance. Will future visitors stand in the rain until you let them in? Or is there an area that protects from the weather? Step inside the house; is there a coat closet nearby? Imagine living in the house. What would incoming visitors see? Piled-up dirty dishes in the kitchen? Children's toys scattered about? A pristine formal reception area and living room? Do you even care what visitors will see?

Sum Up Your Thoughts

Consider the house as a whole. Does the home reflect a sense of scale and proportion? Are some rooms too large, others too small? Does it have enough closet and storage space? Will the home heat and cool evenly? Or will it develop hot spots and cold spots? Is differential zone heating and cooling possible?

Now evaluate. Bring your thoughts together. Are the good looks superficial? Or are they integral to your needs and to the design, function, and livability of the home?

Real estate agents love to show homes with "curb appeal." They like homes they can advertise as a "decorator's dream." Agents know most homebuyers prefer a home that looks good, a home they can show off to friends and relatives, a home they can be proud of. All perfectly reasonable. Few buyers want a home that's considered the ugly duckling of the neighborhood. But when comparing houses, stay somewhat detached.

Don't fall head over heels in love with appearance. First, figure out whether the home could live well for you and your family.

MISTAKE # **69**

We *had* such great views.

LESSON: *Before buying a house with a view, determine whether the view is "protected."*

Heather Caldwell loved the townhouse she bought. It was close to the city center, yet the development was surrounded by trees. "We felt like we were living in a forest," Heather remembered. "At least for a while, that is," she added.

One year after Heather bought her new unit, the townhouse developer began phase two of the project. The bulldozers arrived, down went the trees, and that was the end of Heather's view of the woods. But her disappointment didn't end there. Once the second phase of the project was sold out, trees along the road leading into the complex were cut. In their place, the developer built a strip shopping center topped off by an orange roof. "Within less than four years," Heather said, "we lost our wooded views and tranquil setting."

In Chicago, Fred Poynter bought his one-bedroom condominium at Lake Point Towers because it offered spectacular panoramic views of the city from both his living room and bedroom. Three years later Fred's view had changed. Instead of city lights, Fred looked straight into another high-rise. Not only had Fred lost his view, he had lost his privacy.

On the outskirts of Orlando, Florida, Mindy and Ron Lange bought their home because its lot bordered a grove of orange trees. Then Central Florida was hit with back-to-back winter freezes. The orange trees were killed. Instead of replanting, the grower sold his land and moved his business farther south to Homestead. The Langes' property now backs up to another subdivision. Gone forever are the views and privacy the orange groves provided.

Only Pay for "Protected" Views

Before you buy a home with a view, check to see how well that view is legally protected. Do zoning laws, building regulations, or environmental restrictions keep someone from blocking or destroying your view? Too many homebuyers pay a premium price for a view home, only then to lose not only the view but also thousands of dollars of value from their homes. Although you can't get 100 percent protection since the government might change the protection laws, at least know what chance you're taking.

Both Heather Caldwell and Fred Poynter mistakenly believed their views were permanent. Had they checked the zoning laws or developer's plans, they would have discovered the views were temporary. Naturally, the Langes couldn't have forecast back-to-back record-setting winter freezes. But, had they investigated the area, they would have discovered that even before the killer freezes, many orange growers were selling their groves to subdivision developers. With this knowledge, the Langes may have decided to look for better protection elsewhere; or they may have chosen to offer a lower price for the home.

Never *assume* your view will last. Before you buy, look into the future. Then, adjust your price accordingly.

MISTAKE # **70**

I didn't notice that the house was situated on two lots.

LESSON: *An extra lot can mean extra value.*

Ralph Wozniak tells how he missed out on several hundred thousand dollars. "Some years back," says Ralph, "I was looking at houses in the well-established Point Grey neighborhood. My choice came down to two houses. One was sitting on a normal 33-foot lot. The other was built on a 50-foot site that included two 25-foot buildable lots. To my way of thinking, the houses were about equal in pros and cons. Both were priced at a little over $100,000. In the end, I bought the house with the 33-foot lot because I preferred its kitchen. The fact the other house was sitting on two buildable lots didn't affect my decision one way or the other. That was my mistake."

Lots Appreciate More than Houses

Here's why Ralph should have noticed the profit potential offered by two lots. Four or five years after Ralph bought, home prices in Point Grey started spiraling upward. They went from an entry level of around $90,000 up to around $200,000. Ralph recalls that at the time he was feeling pretty happy with himself. His home had grown in value to around $225,000. Then he heard the two-lot house he had passed up just sold. The price was $395,000.

It wasn't the homes in Point Grey that were appreciating, it was the lots. This time around, the two-lot house was not sold to a homeowner. It was sold to a builder, who promptly tore down the house. In its place she built two houses—one on each lot. These two new homes sold for $475,000 each.

When Ralph considered his home to be worth around $225,000, he was wrong. His home was worth $25,000 to $35,000. His lot was worth $190,000 to $200,000. Remember: Homes seldom appreciate. Only in times of rapid inflation in construction costs will a house increase in (nominal) value. In most instances, it's the land value that's going up. When you own two (buildable) lots, you double your chance for gain.

Find Bargains in Slow Markets

In hot markets, smart homebuyers quickly learn that a home with two lots means extra profit potential. They bid up its price. In slow markets, though, buyers don't give it much value. Since they don't expect appreciation, they're not willing to pay a premium for a two-lot house. To them, an extra-large site just means a bigger yard. So if you're buying in a slow (or uninformed) market, there's a good chance you can "buy" a second lot for a relatively small amount of money. Generally, the best places to look are older neighborhoods (especially neighborhoods that show strong potential for turnaround or even well-kept neighborhoods that are moving upscale).

Depending how a home is situated on a two-lot site, you might put the extra lot to immediate use. If the size is big enough, you might subdivide the site. This would permit you to sell the extra lot by itself. Or you might build another unit (house, cottage, carriage house) that you could rent out and hold as an investment. Given these possibilities, think carefully before you reject a house with two or more (buildable) lots. You might be passing up substantial hidden value.

MISTAKE # 71

We focused on problems, not possibilities.

LESSON: Don't reject a home without thinking through its possibilities.

To some homebuyers, shopping for a home amounts to one frustration after another. If a house isn't too large, it's too small; or maybe it's a long commute to work, located in a less-desirable school district, needs too much work, lacks enough light, is too expensive, or has the wrong floor plan or architectural style. Whatever the home's features, these homebuyers can easily point out problems. They reject everything they look at because no house seems quite right.

Tom and Joan Search in Vain for the Perfect House

Past friends of mine went through this stage. Tom and Joan wanted to own their own home for more than two years. They earned good incomes and had saved a down payment. They worked with good real estate agents. They diligently pored over the real estate classified ads. And during two years of looking, they must have inspected 80 to 100 houses, maybe more. Yet, they never bought.

Why? Because to them every home they inspected had some problem, defect, or flaw. Tom and Joan said they knew exactly what they wanted and wouldn't settle for anything less.

Although at the time my friends didn't realize it, the difficulty of their home search was not what they thought it was. They described their

problem as "We just can't find what we're looking for." But their real difficulty was attitude. When they walked into a house, they immediately
began to find fault. In their mind's eye, they thought they could imagine
exactly what they wanted; and if the house they were inspecting in some
way violated their wish list, they rejected it—no ifs, ands, or buts.

No Perfect Spouse, No Perfect House

Then one day when Tom was talking with me about the couple's "inabil-
ity" to find a home, I abruptly changed the subject and asked, "Tom,
why did you marry Joan? You've complained that she's overweight, and
she hates football. And you know she's always trying to get you to stop
fishing and hunting."

As I finished, Tom immediately began to defend Joan, list her good
points, and emphasize how well they got along together (which of
course I knew). Then the lightbulb went on in his mind. He stopped his
praise of Joan and said, "All right, I see what you're getting at. I may not
be perfect, and Joan may not be perfect, but we've still got a very good
marriage. So why not stop insisting on the perfect house and find one
that will work for us?"

"You got it," I answered.

Several months later, Tom and Joan bought a triplex, renovated it,
lived in it several years, sold it at a profit, and then built a custom-
designed house. After they moved in, I asked Tom, "Well, now that you've
custom built your own house, do you have everything you wanted?"

Tom smiled and said, "Do we have the perfect marriage? No. Do we
have the perfect house? No. We love each other and we love the house,
but nothing's perfect."

Are you frustrated shopping and comparing homes? Then think of
Tom and Joan. Shift your sights from what's wrong with a house to
what's right—or could be made right. Much of this chapter describes
mistakes in home buying that commonly result from failing to spot a
home's defects, flaws, or features that don't suit your priorities. But you
can also become too critical and reject houses too quickly. Strike a profitable balance. Don't just list problems. Look for ways to make a less-
than-perfect house work for you. You can always trade up later.

CHAPTER 6

Negotiate Win-Win

Negotiators typically fit into one of three types of negotiating styles: (1) adversarial, (2) accommodating, and (3) win-win. The adversarial style is typically practiced by lawyers. Such negotiators make outrageous demands. Then they push, pull, or threaten to move you as close as possible to their position. Adversarial negotiators care not whether their "opponents" end up satisfied. All they care about is "winning" for themselves.

In contrast to the adversarial approach, the accommodating negotiator tends to give in to every request or demand. Accommodators feel powerless to effect the outcome they really want. They often feel helpless due to lack of money, time, information, knowledge, or experience. Often, accommodators detest conflict. They would rather "lose" than stand their ground. When negotiating through a real estate agent (or other third party), accommodators typically delegate too much responsibility. "Oh, just do what you think is best" or "Let's just agree and get the whole thing over" are two common responses of accommodators.

Negotiate Win-Win

When you negotiate win-win (as you should), you adopt a little of the adversarial style, and a little of the accommodating style. Most important you adopt a different perspective. Win-win negotiators recognize that every negotiation brings forth multiple issues, priorities, and possibilities. They also recognize and respect the other party's (not oppo-

nent's) concerns, feelings, and needs. Win-win negotiators do not operate along a single line of contention (e.g., price).

Win-win negotiators primarily work to secure a strong, mutually beneficial agreement that everyone is committed to seeing to completion.
By reading through the home-buyer experiences and mistakes in this
chapter, you will see how to shape a win-win agreement. In addition,
you won't fall prey to the win-lose transactions of the adversarial "hard-
ballers" or the "passive-accommodators."

MISTAKE # **72**

We thought our agent represented us.

LESSON: *Before you begin to work with a real estate agent,
set ground rules for your relationship.*

Since you will probably negotiate your home purchase through a real estate agent, you should understand how agents can work for you—or
against you. During the past several years, "who represents whom" has
ranked as one of the most controversial issues in home buying. Until recent years, nearly all real estate agents were employed by sellers to find
buyers for their homes. Under this traditional system, you may have
worked with an agent who advised, counseled, and helped you negotiate
your home purchase. But as a matter of law, that agent was most likely a
subagent of the sellers—not "your" agent. Here's how the traditional
system worked and why it has sparked so much confusion.

Under the traditional system, a home seller might sign a listing contract with Fox Realty. In turn, Fox Realty would forward this listing to a
multiple listing service (MLS). The MLS probably included dozens of
other real estate agencies who employed hundreds, maybe thousands, of
real estate agents. Let's say one of these other cooperating realty firms is
Hoosier Realty, and Joe Salesman works for Hoosier Realty as a sales
agent. You've met Joe through your local church, or maybe a friend recommended him.

You call Joe. He sets up a meeting where you discuss your housing needs, finances, how much you're willing to invest in a home, and the neighborhoods you prefer. With this information, Joe suggests some homes to show you. If all goes well, you find a home you like and tell Joe to make an offer. Joe advises you about the price, terms, conditions, and contingencies and then helps you negotiate a purchase agreement with the sellers through their listing agent, Sally Saleswoman, who's employed by Fox Realty. After some give and take, you and the sellers strike a deal. Everyone seems satisfied.

What's Wrong with This Picture?

Now what's wrong with the way this transaction was handled? Your agent, Joe, was representing you and looking out for your interests. Sally was representing the sellers and advising them about their interests. Or at least that's the way it may seem.

But, in fact, under the traditional sales system, Joe didn't represent you. As a salesman with Hoosier Realty, a firm that had joined with Fox Realty as a cooperating broker, Joe owed his allegiance to the sellers— not to you.

As a matter of law, Joe was required to relay to the sellers your statements like, "We just have to have the house. It's the best one we've looked at by far." Or, "Let's try an offer of $175,000, but we'll go to $195,000 if we have to." Or perhaps the sellers learned you had told Joe, "We're really pressed for time. Our apartment lease is ending and this is the only house we've looked at where the sellers are willing to give early possession." Or maybe from the opposite direction, you believed Joe when he told you "the sellers won't budge. Their absolute low dollar is $195,000." So, thinking you had no choice, you paid $195,000.

The Traditional System Upsets Many Homebuyers

How would you feel if you later learned the sellers were really experiencing a cash crunch and were so eager to sell they would have accepted a price of $170,000 for their home? Yet, your agent, Joe, the man you trusted enough to share your confidences, never mentioned this fact to you. In effect, Joe's silence kept you from learning this choice bit of information that would have greatly increased your negotiating power. How would you feel? You would probably feel angry and cheated. After all, Joe led you to believe he was representing you, but in reality he was working as an agent of the "enemy." You might even think about suing Joe for deception.

And that's exactly what Sheila and Jeff Buck did. The Bucks sued their agent because, "We thought our agent represented us, when she really was working for the sellers. Had Diane told us she was duty bound to the sellers, we never would have told her our top dollar. We're sure she used the information against us."

States Enact New Agency Disclosure Laws

To help you and other homebuyers prevent the mistake of the Bucks (and their agent), nearly all states have recently enacted some type of agency disclosure laws. In addition to agency disclosure, state laws and the National Association of Realtors are making it easier for you to use a "buyer's broker" or "buyer's agent" when you shop for a home or negotiate a purchase agreement.

Under these new laws, real estate agents disclose to you the types of agency relationships that are legal in your state, explain their meaning, and then give you a choice. Although state laws differ, in general, you have three or four choices:

1. You can elect the traditional system where you work with an agent or subagent of the sellers.
2. You can choose dual agency. Here the agent helps both sellers and buyers but agrees not to divulge confidential information that could give one party an unfair advantage over the other.
3. You may employ a facilitator. A facilitator owes no fiduciary responsibility to either you or the sellers. He or she would act more as a mediator. The idea is to find agreement, not to represent either buyer or sellers.
4. As a fourth and growing option, you might use a buyer's agent who should represent your interest exclusively. Buyer's agents can't legally release your confidential information to the sellers.

But they can pass along to you any information about the sellers they know that could strengthen your hand in negotiations.

Space doesn't permit a complete look at the full pros and cons of each of these types of agency relationships (that would require another book). My primary purpose is to alert you to the fact that "your" agent may be working for the sellers. Also, many state laws don't require agents to disclose until you're ready to make an offer on a property. By that time you may already have revealed your finances, how well you like the house, or that your landlord has ended your lease and you have to find someplace else to live within the next 60 days.

Follow This Advice

Here's the best advice to follow: Set ground rules for your relationship *before* you begin to work with a real estate agent. Each type of agency has its advantages and disadvantages. As long as you know the ground rules for what you can disclose and what you should keep to yourself, you can work with any type of agent. Mistakes are most likely to occur when you simply assume "your" agent is really your agent.

In addition, consider an agent's character, competence, and knowledge. Who you choose to work with is just as important as the type of agency relationship. Most real estate professionals—people who are committed to a career in real estate—don't view home buying and home selling as an adversarial contest. Buying (or selling) a home is not like filing a lawsuit. In contrast to lawyers whose "ethics" permit them to mislead and deceive, consumer laws (as well as Realtor ethics and personal reputation) oblige real estate agents to treat all buyers and sellers fairly.

No doubt, more and more homebuyers are choosing buyer's agents. It is the wave of the future. But in many areas of the country, dual agency and traditional (seller) agency still account for a large number of agency relationships. So, no matter what type of agency you choose, remember who's working for whom. It's tough to secure a win-win agreement when you don't know if your confidential disclosures will be passed along to the sellers.

MISTAKE # **73**

I tried to buy directly from an owner to save the commission but instead lost $5,000.

LESSON: *Buying without an agent can cost you more than you save. Be careful.*

When Danny Boatman decided to stop renting and buy his own home, he called several real estate agents whose names he had seen on for-sale signs. "They didn't impress me much," says Danny. "One just wanted to talk all the time but never listened. Another one kept showing me houses and neighborhoods he didn't know anything about. I'd ask him questions and he would answer, 'I dunno, but I can find out for you if you want.' This was a hassle I didn't need.

"So I decided to concentrate on for sale by owners [FSBOs]. That way I wouldn't have to deal with agents, and I could get the sellers to give me a lower price, since they would be saving the commission. It seemed like a smart move. Unfortunately, I got suckered. My smart move cost me $5,000. That's a mistake I won't make again."

Danny actually made not one but three mistakes.

Don't Choose Agents Randomly

First, for all practical purposes, Danny selected agents randomly. He might as well as flipped open the yellow pages to the real estate section, pressed his finger to the page, and started telephoning. The chances are that if Danny or anyone else merely pulls an agent's name out of the telephone book or off a for-sale sign, they're not going to come with a first-class professional. Real estate sales follows the same 80–20 rule found in most fields. Eighty percent of the agents do 20 percent of the business, and the top 20 percent of the agents do 80 percent of the business.

To locate a real estate professional, ask relatives or friends for recommendations. Read the newspapers for names of top producers. Call the sales manager of the most highly regarded real estate firms and find out who among their agents has provided the highest quality services to the most buyers. In other words, work with an agent who has a proven track

record. Helping people buy and sell homes requires knowledge, competence, and possibility analysis. You don't want a chauffeur. You need a
pro. Danny Boatman failed to understand this critical difference.

FSBOs Don't Always Sell at Lower Prices

Second, Danny mistakenly assumed that if he bought direct from an
owner he would get a lower price. Since the owners wouldn't have to
pay a commission, they could pass along their savings to him. But why
would they want to? Most sellers don't take on the burden and expense
of selling their own home so they can give buyers a better price. They do
it to pocket more money for themselves.

In fact, as often as not, people selling their own homes overprice
them. They're hoping to find some "bargain-hunting" buyers who will
be hoodwinked into believing they are saving money because there's no
agent involved. In addition, even if the home appears to be priced right,
it may suffer from hidden defects. In today's lawsuit-happy world, professional agents will insist that sellers disclose their home's shortcomings. Owners who sell on their own, in contrast, are noted for "forget-
ting" about the erratic furnace or the fuses that blow every time the
toaster and microwave are turned on at the same time.

Always Place Deposits in Escrow

Third, here's how Danny lost his $5,000. After negotiating the price and
terms of their purchase agreement, the sellers asked Danny for an
earnest money deposit of $5,000. This amount would be credited against
his down payment at closing after Danny had arranged his mortgage financing. Danny knew earnest money deposits were customary, and
since he planned to put a total of $15,000 down, a $5,000 good faith deposit didn't seem unreasonable. So he wrote the sellers a check. That
was his biggest mistake.

As it turned out, Danny could not get his financing approved within
the 30 days allowed by his purchase agreement. To make matters more
difficult, other buyers wanted the house and they were already preapproved by their lender. The sellers gave Danny an extra week to close,
but to no avail. He couldn't close. The sellers went ahead and sold to the
other buyers.

When Danny asked for his deposit back, the sellers told him they would send him a check after the other buyers completed their purchase. Should that new deal fall through, they promised to give Danny another chance to come up with his financing. Danny reluctantly agreed because he really wanted the house. But the new sale did close. The sellers moved to Tacoma. And Danny never again saw his $5,000.

Danny then hired a lawyer who wrote the sellers and demanded them to return his deposit. The sellers' lawyer responded by saying that Danny had forfeited the deposit when they had given him extra time and yet he still couldn't get his financing put together.

Danny disagreed. "We didn't discuss anything about forfeiture," Danny told his lawyer. "Well," the lawyer said, "we can sue them in federal court. But that will cost you a lot more than $5,000, and I can't guarantee you'll win, or that if you win, you can actually collect. There's not really anything I can do. You might as well kiss your $5,000 good-bye."

Guidelines to Follow

No one denies that, on occasion, you can negotiate directly with sellers and save money. (Or maybe the home you like best isn't listed with an agent.) But if that's the route you choose, be careful. Remember this advice:

1. If you buy direct, you'll not only give up the services agents provide to help you find a home but also the services that carry you through negotiations, financing, and closing.

2. Get the home professionally inspected for condition and appraised for value. Take special care if the sellers offer you easy financing.

3. Open up an escrow closing account for your deposit with a title insurer, escrow firm, or realty firm. (In fact, even when buying from a FSBO, you can still employ a buyer's agent to help negotiate a win-win agreement and to provide other services that will keep your transaction progressing smoothly. In these cases, many by-owner sellers are willing to pay a two or three percent sales commission to your agent.)

MISTAKE # **74**

We didn't know we could withdraw our offer.

LESSON: *You may withdraw your offer at any time before the sellers accept it.*

As you prepare your offer to purchase a home, you'll have to decide how long you want to give the sellers to accept it. Commonly used real estate sales contracts include a clause that reads something like this:

This offer prepared and delivered to the Sellers by the Buyers on _____, 19___, at _____ and shall remain open for ___ days, *or until revoked by the Buyers.*

In regard to this clause, some homebuyers overlook or misunderstand the meaning of the last six words. In effect, these words give you the right to withdraw your offer any time before the sellers have accepted it. If you tell the sellers you'll leave your offer open for three days, but then change your mind for any reason whatsoever, simply notify your agent (preferably in writing, but that's not essential). Even if your contract doesn't include these words or something similar, you still may withdraw your offer.

On occasion, agents forget to fully explain your right to withdraw. Some agents don't like to emphasize the point because homebuyers (especially first-time buyers) often get second thoughts about the wisdom of their decision to buy. To squelch these worries, the agent might gloss over your right to pull back. He or she might lead you to believe you're obliged to keep the offer on the table for the specified number of days.

Of course, you shouldn't withdraw just because you start focusing on what might go wrong. Such thoughts are natural. You should get rid of negative emotions by replacing them with thoughts of how much you're going to enjoy the home and home ownership. But if you discover new information (you're getting transferred or you've noticed a shortfall in your bank balance), or you run across another home that better fits your needs, then you might want to exercise your right of withdrawal.

Counteroffers Kill Offers

Also keep in mind that if the sellers change any part of your offer, you're released from obligation. Any counteroffer kills a previous offer. Should you offer $89,500 and the seller counters with a price of $89,501, your bid of $89,500 is dead. You could bring it back to life if you wanted. But if you reject the sellers' $89,501, they can't unilaterally declare (without your agreement), "Okay, then, we'll accept $89,500."

From a negotiating standpoint, keep the sellers guessing about what you plan to do. Let them know you're considering other options. The sellers should realize that if they wait too long to accept your offer or if they counter too high, they could lose you as a prospective buyer. Maintain a cooperative, win-win demeanor. But don't tip your hand.

MISTAKE # **75**

We never met the sellers. We didn't know anything about them.

LESSON: *Get to know as much as you can about the sellers.*

Some real estate agents do everything they can to keep buyers and sellers away from each other. For good reason. Agents have seen sales fall through because of personality clashes. Or they fear that sellers (since agents in the past have nearly always represented sellers) might give away a choice bit of information that will help the buyers.

"Why are you selling?" the buyers ask.

"Oh, Mack's been transferred," the sellers respond. "We have to be in Omaha by the end of next month."

Although the keep-the-buyers-and-sellers-apart sales strategy sometimes is best, as a rule I don't recommend it. Before you make your first offer, you should learn all you can about the sellers. What kind of people are they? Do they seem generous and open? Or are they rigid and argumentative? Do they take a great deal of pride in their home? Are they moving reluctantly, or are they eager to leave? Have they already bought another home? Why are they selling? What are their most important needs: emotional, personal, financial? What are their worries and concerns?

What Do the Sellers Really Want?

The sellers aren't really trying to sell a house. They're actually reaching for more distant goals. Selling their home is a means to those ends. Naturally, then, the sellers won't judge the price and terms of your offer by absolute standards. They will judge it according to how well it helps them move toward what they are ultimately trying to achieve. That's why it's a big mistake not to get to know the sellers. Without understanding their real needs, you may miss a great opportunity to find high value/low value win-win trade-offs that can benefit both of you.

Let's say the sellers had previously accepted two offers that both fell through because the buyers couldn't arrange financing. With these experiences in their background, the sellers may be quite anxious. They don't want to be strung out again. So, if you can assure them you have the resources to buy (bank statements, credit report, lender preapproval letter, job security), they most likely would be willing to give you a lower price.

Broaden Discussions beyond Price

All too frequently, homebuyers and sellers aim most of their negotiating power toward price. The sellers want a higher price. The buyers want a lower price. Stalemate. Don't get caught in this trap. To prevent it—or escape from it—you need to meet the sellers, talk with them, and learn all you can about their perceptions, past home-selling experiences, feelings, and needs. But agent concerns about personality clashes are valid. So, when meeting and talking with the sellers, follow these guidelines:

- Meet the sellers as soon as possible. The sooner you get a fix on who they are and what they're like, the better you can begin to map your negotiation strategy. Also, sellers are generally more open with information when you first look at a home. At that point they're eager to please. They want to excite your interest. If you wait to meet them until after you've made an offer, they'll be guarding their disclosures more closely.

- Get as many concessions as you can before you ever begin negotiations. "You're asking $125,000, is that right? Just so we can fairly compare the price of your home to others we're looking at, have you thought about how much less you would accept?" Or: "You're asking $125,000, right? Can you tell me what personal property (appliances, drapes, rugs, patio furniture, gazebo, etc.) you're willing to include?" Or maybe: "Have you considered how much financing you're willing to carry back in a note?" By "innocently" suggesting concessions in this way, you're not "negotiating" with the sellers. You're not really even asking for concessions. You're merely trying to gather information so you can fairly rank the sellers' home against other houses that are up for sale. Sensing you are exploring other options, many sellers will sweeten the deal before you write your first offer.

- Inquire, don't interrogate. The way you ask your questions is far more important than the questions themselves. Phrase them as innocuously as you can. Don't intimidate, accuse, threaten, or debate. Remember Peter Falk as Columbo, the perpetually "disoriented" detective. Columbo didn't interrogate suspects. He gently probed. Use similar tactics. Encourage the easy flow of information. Don't try to extract it.

- Establish rapport. Try to find common ground. Talk about the last Cubs game or that old favorite, the weather (certainly not politics—perhaps religion or ethnicity, if you share a common faith or cultural heritage). Negotiations are about people, not money. Treat the sellers as people, not merely owners of a house you might want to buy.

- Compliment, don't criticize. As you walk through the sellers' home, sincerely compliment their beautiful grandfather clock. "Does it have an interesting history? How long have you owned it?" Comment on other belongings they seem to take pride in. Have the owners decorated or remodeled their home with taste, flair, or creativity? If so, tell them. What about the yard? Do the sellers have a green thumb? Can you genuinely admire their tomatoes or roses?

At this first meeting, develop a cordial attitude. Establish a *relationship* bank account so you will have something to draw on later if (when) you need it. To sharply criticize the sellers' home won't loosen them up to accept a lower price. But it may very well turn them against you and make later negotiations more difficult. (Of course, also corral your enthusiastic exclamations: "Wow! This is exactly what we want. It's so much nicer than the other houses we've seen.")

- Share information about yourself with the sellers. Let them get to know you. Skip the bravado. But accent personal characteristics that tell the sellers you're decent, credible people who like (not love) their home. Creating trust and building a relationship can't be a one-way street.

MISTAKE # **76**

The worst they can do is say no.

LESSON: The worst they can do is say get lost.

Nothing destroys trust faster than a lowball offer. When you lowball the sellers, you signal that you're going for a win-lose negotiating strategy, with the sellers as the losers.

Joan McGill recalls her lowball experience. "We really wanted this house," says Joan. "But my husband considered himself a hotshot negotiator. So, even though the house was priced just a little over market at $325,000, he convinced me we should start with an offer of $260,000. 'All they can say is no,' he assured me. 'At the worst, they'll probably compromise. We can still get the house at a bargain price of around $290,000 to $300,000.' Well, he clearly missed that one. We got the house all right—at a price of $325,000." After our lowball offer, the sellers simply refused to negotiate with us. They just said, 'The price is $325,000. Take it or leave it.' So we ate crow and took it."

Most sellers are emotionally involved with their homes. A lowball offer insults them. Besides, if the sellers are listed with a real estate agent, they've got a good idea of what their home is worth. And if they doubt the agent's price, 9 times out of 10, the sellers figure higher, not lower. So what chance does a lowball offer have of getting accepted? Slim and none.

Put yourself in the shoes of a seller. Your home is worth $210,000. Out of the blue, someone offers you $150,000. How would you respond? You'd probably think: (1) the buyers don't know what they're doing, so why even talk with them; (2) they think we're so ignorant we don't know the value of our own home, and they're trying to take advantage of us; (3) the buyers believe we're desperate and they want to prey on our misfortune; or (4) the buyers aren't serious buyers. They are just shotgunning lowball offers to see what might turn up. (In fact, this tactic is taught in some of the get-rich-in-real-estate seminars.)

Anyway you look at it, buyers who lowball destroy trust. They destroy the possibility of working out a win-win purchase agreement. Most sellers respond to a lowball offer by flat out rejecting it, counteroffering at the full asking price, or telling the buyers to get lost. "Stop wasting our time!" This is not to say you'll never find ignorant or desperate sellers who will accept a lowball offer. Or, if your priority is to buy at a bargain price—without regard to a specific house—then lowballing may be worth a try. But, as Joan McGill and her husband learned, as a negotiating ploy for a home you want, lowballing is generally a mistake.

MISTAKE # **77**

We thought the sellers had accepted our offer.

LESSON: *Get the sellers' signatures on the contract.*

"We had been going back and forth with offers and counteroffers," says Keith O'Hara. "We kept trying to find that magic combination of price and terms that would click for both of us. Finally, it seemed like we found it. We were working with our agent in her office late Friday afternoon and she came up with a solution that would work for us. Next she called the sellers' agent to ask him to run it by the sellers before we wrote it up in a revised contract. About 20 minutes later the sellers' agent called back. He said we had a deal. The sellers could live with our solution.

"Our agent printed out a new copy of the agreement. We signed it, and she said she would drop by the sellers later that evening to get their signatures. 'Congratulations,' she told us. 'You've just bought a great house. I know you're going to be happy with it.' We were elated.

"But our spirits came crashing down less than 24 hours later. That's when we learned the sellers had accepted another much better offer that an agent from another firm brought them on Saturday morning. Our agent had dropped the ball. She hadn't kept her 7:00 P.M. appointment with the sellers. Because of a personal conflict, she had rescheduled the appointment for 1:00 Saturday afternoon. By that time, the sellers had already accepted the other offer with the provision that we would be given a chance to match it. We couldn't. So we lost the house."

The lesson here is simple. In real estate, never assume you have a deal until you have a signed contract. An oral acceptance isn't binding. Once upon a time you could count on people to honor their word—regardless of whether it had been committed to writing. But to a great extent, those days are gone. To be safe, if you receive an oral commitment to an agreement you want to see fulfilled, get the necessary signatures as fast as possible. Don't give the sellers time to change their minds, change the terms, or find a better offer.

MISTAKE # **78**

The listing handout said "wet bar/sink" included.

LESSON: *Itemize in writing all personal property and fixtures included in the sale.*

Exactly what are you buying when you buy a home? Does the sales price include that $1,500 Tiffany light fixture hanging over the dining room table? Does it include the gazebo in the backyard? Does it include drapes, rugs, carpeting, appliances, or the window air conditioner? Does it include the mailbox? What about the lightbulbs in the ceiling lights and outdoor flood lamps?

"We couldn't believe it," recalls Jay Martin. "We got into town after dark around 8:00. We went right to our newly bought house, eager to spend our first night there, even though the moving van wasn't scheduled to arrive until the next day. We opened the front door, reached for the light switch, and flipped it on. Nothing happened. At first we thought the electric company had turned off the power. But when we felt our way to the kitchen, we could hear the refrigerator running. We opened the door to the fridge expecting to get some light; nothing happened. Like lost souls in the dark, we wandered from room to room, flipping on every light switch we could find. Still no light. Finally, we borrowed a flashlight from a neighbor, and we quickly discovered the problem. The sellers had taken every lightbulb in the house with them—including the bulbs from inside the refrigerator and oven.

What Is a Wet Bar/Sink?

When Forrest and Dyan Albertson bought their home, the Realtor handout that described the features of the house listed a "wet bar/sink." In looking at the home before they bought, the Albertsons admired the bar, its fine quality wood, and its unique design. In fact, they had complimented the owners on the bar.

But when the Albertsons moved into their new home, the bar was gone. The only evidence remaining were the imprints on the floor where the bar had stood. "Where's the bar?" Forrest inquired of his real estate agent.

"Oh," she said, "that was the sellers' personal property. The bar wasn't included in the sale."

"What do you mean, 'not included'?" Forrest shot back. "The house listing handout you gave us said the wet bar/sink was included."

"That didn't refer to the bar," the agent said. "That referred to the wet bar sink. You get the sink, not the bar. That bar was worth over $1,000."

I once bought a house that had a large antique mirror bolted to the bricks above the mantel on the fireplace. When I took possession of the house, the mirror and the bolts were gone. I got the holes where the bolts had been.

Assume Nothing, List Everything

Each of these stories teaches the same lesson: Never assume the sellers plan to leave any "personal" property with the house. Sellers have removed items as trivial as lightbulbs and mailboxes. At times they remove items of high value, such as chandeliers, gazebos, and wet bars. They may even take things that are bolted to floors, walls, or ceilings. There have been court cases where after contracting with buyers, sellers have removed toilets and furnaces. No matter how obvious it is to you that the item belongs with the house, the sellers may entertain different ideas.

In some instances, the sellers show their pettiness. In others, the sellers interpret ambiguity in their own favor. And sometimes sellers take things they know rightfully belong to the buyers. But they may justify their actions: "Those buyers stole the house from us, so it's only right we even the score." Or, with larceny in their hearts and a keen sense of the impractical, the sellers may say to themselves, "What are the buyers gonna do, come to North Dakota to get us?"

There is a body of law (real property, fixtures, personal property) that attempts to define "what stays" and "what goes" in a home-buying transaction. Like all law, though, it's riddled with contradictions, conflicting court opinions, and gray areas—not to mention the difficult and expensive burdens of using lawyers to enforce a claim—even when you're sure the law favors your view. (I believe there's a Yiddish curse that says, "May you have a lawsuit you believe you can win." You might also recall Dickens's *Bleak House*.)

The law may offer recourse but rarely satisfaction. The best way to prevent mistakes of "what goes" and "what stays" is to assume nothing. Write out a complete list of everything included in the home's sales price. Go through the house room by room with the sellers and your real estate agent. Identify, itemize, and list. Leave no chance for doubt, confusion, or ambiguity. Then attach the signed list to both your copy and the sellers' copy of the purchase agreement.

Don't Rely on Oral Promises

Never depend on an oral promise of the sellers. "You're such a nice couple," the sellers say. "Since we have no use for them in our new house, we'll leave you the washer and dryer. They're old, but they'll serve you until you can buy your own."

When making their promise to you, the sellers may not know their daughter also needs a washer and dryer. But where will these appliances end up when the daughter says, "Mom, you know I hate going to the laundromat. If you're giving your washer and dryer away, you should give them to me." At that point, if you haven't written the washer and dryer into your purchase agreement, even the most well-intentioned sellers may be tempted to help their daughter at your expense.

MISTAKE # **79**

We fell in love with the house and just had to have it.

LESSON: *Keep your love to yourself. Put your options on the table.*

In his best-selling book *You Can Get Anything You Want,* Roger Dawson, the world-renowned negotiating expert, tells how a negotiation slipup cost him $30,000 when he was buying his family's home. Roger writes that one day while teaching his daughter to drive in the secluded hills of Southern California, he spied the house of his dreams. "Everything about the house was perfect," he says, "and it was for sale."

Posing as a reluctant, if not altogether indifferent, buyer, Roger relates how he plotted his negotiation strategy—only to see it evaporate when his wife and daughter returned to look at the house without him. "They oohed and aahed over every feature, and by the time they were through with their tour, they had demolished my reluctant buyer plan," says Roger.

It also didn't help matters when his wife told the sellers Roger really thought their house was wonderful. At that point the sellers knew the Dawsons were hooked. With a ticket price of $15, Roger says many people think a tour of Hearst Castle is expensive. But he calculated that one house tour by his wife and daughter cost him $30,000.

Express Like, Not Love

When talking with sellers, you've got to walk a fine line. Yes, you want to show interest, develop a cooperative, problem-solving attitude, and prevent critical remarks that may offend. Yet, you can't go overboard with lavish praise. Nor do you want to tell yourself, "This is the perfect house, we've simply got to have it."

In other words, keep your other options open—both in your own mind and in the minds of the sellers. When the sellers believe you've eliminated other houses from consideration, they'll naturally use that information to bolster their own position. Should you tell yourself "Nothing else will do," you abandon the strongest negotiating power any buyer has—the willpower to walk away from the deal. Sometimes emotions do get the better of us. But remember, once you relinquish your "walk away willpower," you might as well hand the sellers a blank contract and let them fill in the numbers.

MISTAKE # **80**

Our negotiations centered too much on price.

LESSON: To most sellers, price is the main event. It's up to you to win agreement by emphasizing other important points.

"The mistake many home sellers make," says Realtor Bill Sloane, "is that they stop listening if the purchase price offer is too low." Sloane is pointing out a well-known fact. To most sellers, price is the main event.

Everything else is intermission. That's why lowball offers can so easily knock negotiations off the track before they even get going.

If you realize this fact, however, you can often use it to your advantage. By not pushing the sellers too hard on price, you sometimes can get nearly anything else you want. Let me illustrate with one of my own home-buying experiences from some years ago.

A Truly Win-Win Agreement

In this instance, the sellers and I were sitting at their dining room table going through a contract form point by point. The first point was price. Although the sellers had their house priced fairly, I offered $5,000 less. The sellers rejected. I said, "Well, let's put that issue on hold and see if we can agree on some of the other points." In abbreviated form, here's how those other points went:

- The sellers agreed to a lease-purchase plan with closing 15 months after I took possession of the property.
- The sellers agreed to a cash deposit of just $2,500.
- They agreed to give possession within six weeks.
- They agreed to let me store all my household furniture in their den for the month prior to my taking possession of the property. (I had sold my previous home and was giving quick possession to the buyers, so I was going "homeless" for a month.)
- The sellers agreed to include in the sale about $2,000 worth of furniture and appliances.

These people were the easiest sellers I had ever dealt with. But when we eventually returned to price, they still didn't want to budge. Then, finally, after we talked some more, the husband said, "Look, here's what we paid for the property. At what you're offering us, we would take a $3,000 loss. We want to at least get what we paid."

Now, here's where negotiation experts differ. Some would say at this point you've got the sellers committed to everything but price. Hang tough and you can still get the price concession you want. The sellers are so close to a deal, they won't let you walk away. If they did, they would just have to start over again with someone else—if and when that some-one else appears. If they're smart, the sellers won't take that risk.

For reasons explained earlier (and later, see Mistake #83), I don't en-dorse this view. If the sellers have been willing to yield on every point that's important to me, why not let them score a point, too? Besides, once you've gotten nearly all you want, why push so hard you might up-set the entire applecart? So, following a win-win approach, I increased my offer by $3,500 on the promise the sellers would take responsibility for cutting down and removing a dead tree from the backyard. They quickly agreed. We had a deal we were both happy with.

How to Bargain for a Low Price

Now, let's go back to the beginning of the negotiations. What would have happened early on if we had heavily debated price? Even if I had been able to pull the sellers down to my offer, that "success" probably would have destroyed my chances of getting all the other things I *needed* to make the deal work. A hollow victory indeed.

On other occasions, I have reversed this approach somewhat. When through my early inquiries I've learned the sellers have needs stronger than price, I emphasize how I am willing to help them meet those needs (e.g., their preferred possession date, their need to know the transaction is actually going to close). Then, once the sellers understand they are re-ceiving nearly all the terms and conditions they want, I feel I can justify my request for a concession on price.

The important thing to remember is that sellers don't demand their price for purely economic reasons. For many, price is laden with emo-tional content. A low offer doesn't just hurt their pocketbook. It affronts their psyche.

Should you enter negotiations with the idea that you're negotiating price alone, more than likely, one party will "lose" and the other party will "win." On the other hand, when you adopt the view you are negoti-ating (searching for) an *agreement,* you and the sellers can both emerge winners.

MISTAKE # **81**

"Split the difference" sounds like a good compromise to me.

LESSON: *Don't compromise, conciliate.*

In negotiation lore, the story is frequently told of a mother who hears her two children bickering at the dinner table. Each child wants the only remaining slice of cake. Tiring of this debate, the mother takes the cake, slices it in two, and gives half to Craig and half to Shawn. "There," she says, "as you get older you must realize you can't have everything you want. You must learn to compromise. Remember this as an important lesson."

This well-intentioned mother thought she was teaching her kids a valuable lesson, whereas, in fact, she had imprinted them with one of the greatest obstacles to win-win negotiating. By "splitting the difference" before fully exploring her children's wants and a wide range of options, this mother mistakenly framed her kids' debate along a single continuum. Compromise simply meant deciding how much cake to give each child.

Look for Ways to Broaden the Issues

On the other hand, had the mother framed the problem multidimensionally, more than likely she could have figured a better solution. What if one child really preferred the icing? What if the children shared a television set and each preferred different programs? What if the children shared after-dinner cleanup responsibilities? What if the children had money from an allowance? What if Shawn didn't really want the cake, but simply liked to annoy Craig?

Had the mother recognized a wider range of potential wants, trade-offs, and outcomes, she may have produced results more satisfying (or just) for both children. The true art of negotiating doesn't depend on one's readiness to strike a compromise. Instead, it depends on seeing beyond a single issue stretching across an either-or continuum.

Conciliation Sparks Creativity

In Mistake #80, I told how the sellers I was buying a home from agreed to let me use one of the rooms in their home to store my household furniture. Alternatively, I wanted an earlier date of possession and they wanted a later date. What would have happened had we focused our negotiations exclusively on possession date? I would have said, "I have to be out of my present home on February 1. So I need possession on that date."

The sellers may have responded, "But we can't get into our new home until March 1. A February 1 possession date is out of the question. We can't possibly give you possession before February 28.

"Okay," I might say if I'm thinking compromise, "let's split the difference. I'll agree to February 15. I'm willing to meet you halfway."

Although meeting the sellers halfway has the ring of justice, reason, and fair play, in many situations, it doesn't make sense, or it overlooks another more satisfying outcome. In this case, February 15 was actually undesirable for both of us. So that "position" never found its way onto the table. By looking at my real problem—what to do with my furniture for a month without incurring the high costs of multiple moves into and out of storage—we struck upon the solution of storing my household goods in a large room they used but didn't really need. We both were satisfied with this outcome.

Nine times out of 10, thoughtful conciliation beats win-lose compromise. And this was one of them.

Compromise Provokes Extremes

Here's another point that works against compromise as a desirable negotiating strategy. People who negotiate with a compromise mind-set too often want to begin their negotiations at the extreme. Naturally, if you believe the sellers will split the difference, it's to your advantage to offer $95,000 for a $120,000 house. Should the sellers accept your meet-you-halfway tactic, they will sell you the house for $107,500.

But few sellers are that obliging. The tactic of bid low and compromise is too familiar and obvious to work effectively. As negotiating expert Herb Cohen likes to emphasize, "A tactic perceived is no tactic at all." You're more likely to negotiate successfully if you bake a bigger cake. Expand your knowledge of wants, needs, trade-offs, and possibilities. To paraphrase Emerson, foolish compromises are the hobgoblins of little minds.

MISTAKE # **82**

We let our agent negotiate for us.

LESSON: *Use an agent as an intermediary but negotiate for yourself.*

Writing in *Real Estate Today,* a national trade magazine for Realtors, sales agent Sal Gebbia tells of an offer he received on one of his listings. Sal says that after receiving the purchase offer from a *buyer's agent,* this agent told Sal, "This is their [first] offer, but I know my buyers will go up to $150,000."

"Of course," Sal adds, "I told my sellers that information, and we were pleased with the outcome of the transaction."

The lesson here is very plain. Never let your agent do your negotiating for you. Don't give your agent information you do not want the other side to learn. Don't let on to your agent that you're willing to pay a higher price than your first offer. Use your agent as a fact finder and intermediary. But guard your emotions, confidences, and intentions.

Many buyers (especially first-time buyers) mistakenly rely too heavily on their agents to actually come up with the terms of their offer and carry out their negotiations. These buyers will ask their agents, "What price do you think I should offer? What's the most you think I should pay? Will the sellers concede points or agree to carry-back financing?" Then the buyers follow whatever the agent recommends.

Unfortunately, these buyers are abdicating their negotiating responsibilities. If you follow their example and shift too much decision-making power to your agent, you run the following risks.

You May Be Working with a Subagent

Remember, you may be working with the sellers' subagent. As a subagent, "your" Realtor's legal duty is to the seller. Thus, in favoring the sellers' interests, the agent may persuade you to enhance the price or terms of your offer. Or the agent may disclose your confidences to the sellers.

Now, as a practical matter, many "subagents" don't strictly follow the letter of the law. Even though technically they're representing sellers, in their heart and efforts they may feel more loyalty to you. I know many "subagents" who work hard for their buyers—even to the detriment of the sellers.

Nevertheless, since you don't know for sure how "your" agent will use the information you share, carefully limit your disclosures. Likewise, when it comes to offering price and terms, rely on your agent for facts about the sellers, neighborhood statistics, selling prices of comp houses, and general market conditions. Listen to the agent's price recommendations and accept the benefits of his or her experience. But don't delegate your decision making. You may be led into paying more than you need to.

Be Cautious of Buyers' Agents

As explained earlier, a number of brokerage firms and sales agents have been promoting "buyers' agency." Since sellers are represented by their own agents, buyers also need someone to look out for their interests. Marilyn Williams, a Vancouver, Washington, real estate broker, says, "Buyers should think of their agents as attorneys. Would you want to have one attorney representing both parties in a divorce settlement?"

Superficially, the idea sounds reasonable, and there's no doubt the number of buyers' agents is going to grow fast. Yet, even if you choose to employ a buyers' agent, you still need to guard your disclosures and negotiating strategy. First of all, like the agent Sal Gebbia referred to earlier, even buyers' agents may disclose your confidences—either intentionally or unintentionally.

Second, we're all subject to subtle influences. A buyers' agent may talk you into offering a higher price or better terms because it will make his or her job easier. For example, in which case do you think your agent will work hardest for you: when the agent knows you've offered $185,000, but you've said you're willing to go up to $200,000, or when you offer $185,000 and say "If they don't accept this offer, I'd like to go out and look at four or five other houses"?

Watch What You Say

In sum, regardless of whether you're working with a sellers' subagent, a buyers' agent, a dual agent, or a facilitator, watch what you say. Don't tell your agent everything and then turn the negotiations over to her with the simple instructions, "Do the best job you can," or "Why don't you try $135,000 and if that doesn't fly, we can go to $145,000."

In fact, it doesn't matter whether we're talking about lawyers, insurance agents, financial planners, real estate sales agents, or any other type of professional relationship; conflict of interest always lurks in the background. As a general rule, you've got to walk a fine line. Release enough information to achieve the results you want, but not so much you invite your agent to sacrifice your interests to the interests of someone else (including your agent).

MISTAKE # **83**

We pushed to get the absolute best deal we could.

LESSON: *The deal's not over till it's over.*

"We chose to work with a buyers' agent," recalls Barry Tausch. "We felt a buyers' agent would work harder to get us the best deal possible. As it turned out, though, maybe we pushed too hard.

"We knew the sellers were getting a divorce. The wife had moved out of the house and in with her boss. Without income from the wife's paycheck, the husband was facing tough times. He couldn't handle the family expenses on his own. Although they had a lot of equity in the house, the husband was hurting for cash. He really needed a fast sale. By using this information to our advantage, we got the sellers down at least $12,000 or $13,000 below market. Bad deal for them. Good deal for us.

"The only thing we had to agree to was a 30-day close. We didn't think this would be a problem because we already had been prequalified. But it was. There was one foul-up after another.

"In the meantime, the sellers got a backup offer for $7,500 more than our price. To make a long story short, the husband held such resentment against us for 'stealing' his house, he wouldn't cut us any slack. As soon as we missed the close date, he demanded payment. When we couldn't deliver, he pulled out of our contract and sold to the backup buyers."

Leave Something on the Table

Negotiating expert Bob Woolf says, "There isn't any contract I have negotiated where I didn't feel I could have gone for more money or an additional benefit." Why leave money on the table? Because skilled negotiators know, "The deal's not over till it's over." If you push too hard, you create resentment and hostility in the other party. Even if they've signed a contract, they'll start thinking of all the ways they can get out of it. Even worse, if you stumble on your way to closing, they won't help you up. They'll just kick dirt in your face.

Especially in the purchase of a home—where emotions run strong on both sides—you're usually better off to "leave something on the table." In many instances, the purchase agreement is only stage one of your negotiations. Later problems may pop up with respect to property inspections, the appraisal, financing, possession date, closing date, surveys, or any number of other things. Without goodwill and mutual respect, problems on the way to closing can easily cause an agreement to fall through.

CHAPTER 7

The Best Loan at the Lowest Cost

❝It's easier than ever for young people to buy a home," writes Bill Rumbler of the *Chicago Sun-Times.* Lenders and builders are bending over backward to help first-time buyers. They're lowering interest rates, reducing (or eliminating) down payments, and cutting closing costs. "On top of that," reports Rumbler, "many lenders, builders, and credit counselors provide home-buyer counseling."

Roger Showley of the *San Diego Union-Tribune* agrees. "It's a great time to go from renter to homeowner," says Showley. "The government [the National Homeownership Strategy] *wants* to put people in their own homes and is encouraging lenders to target first-time buyers."

Although the great explosion of new loan programs, easier qualifying standards, and counseling services may at times confuse (or even overwhelm) you, take heart. Within all of these choices, you're nearly certain to find a low-cost loan possibility that can move you into home ownership. The key is to educate yourself, plan your finances, and avoid mistakes that can cost you money—or even worse, take you out of the mortgage game. In other words, learn from the home-buyer experiences in this chapter, and you will find the home loan that's best for you.

MISTAKE # **84**

We never heard of special financing for people like us.

LESSON: *If you have the will, you can find a way.*

"We always heard that to buy a house you needed 20 percent down and excellent credit," says Rene Wolpe. "Otherwise we would have bought years ago. Until recently, when we learned of the National Home-ownership Strategy, we never knew people like us could qualify for special financing."

The Wolpes have made the most common and most costly mistake in real estate. They excluded themselves from home ownership because they mistakenly believed they couldn't qualify for financing. But as Kathy Ortiz of the San Diego Home Loan Counseling Center points out, "There are a lot of loan programs, and there is a program for almost everyone."

Ortiz goes on to say that most of the people she helps are like the Wolpes. They just don't realize how many different ways there are to finance a home. "A large majority of our clients come in here really hesitant and lack the confidence that they can qualify. But when they leave, they leave with confidence because they have developed an understanding of the home-buying process and they know their options."

Javier and Maricela Samaniego are living proof of what Kathy Ortiz is referring to. This young couple with a 16-month-old son never believed they could own their own home. They were paying $550 a month for rent and had meager savings. But thanks to Union Bank's Economic Opportunity Mortgage, they were able to buy. "I thought that without this," says Maricela, "we would have had to come up with more money, and since we didn't have much money to work with, it really helped us a lot. . . . We now have so many plans for the house. It really changed everything for us. The money we were paying in rent is now going somewhere."

With the help of Realtors, home builders, mortgage lenders, government agencies, and home counseling centers, hundreds of thousands of

Americans like the Wolpes and the Samaniegos are discovering that "traditional" rules of mortgage financing no longer block most renters from home ownership. Although never etched in stone as many potential homebuyers have believed, in today's push to expand home ownership (especially among minorities and low- to moderate-income individuals and families), lenders are reaching out to all credit worthy (not credit perfect) people who want to become homeowners. Although you will need to check your local area to see what's available, here's a brief sampling of the types of home finance programs you might use. (Also see Chapter 10.)

Community Reinvestment Programs

For years civil rights activists and various consumer groups have accused banks and other mortgage lenders of "redlining." According to critics, bank officers take a red marking pen and draw a circle around minority or low- to middle-income neighborhoods. "These areas are too risky," say the bankers. "We can't finance homes there. Property values may go down."

When bankers do cut off mortgages to an area, they set in motion a self-fulfilling prophecy. If people can't get the money they need to buy and fix up homes in a neighborhood, the neighborhood will decline. Fortunately, lenders now recognize a more positive truth. If they do make loans available, people will invest in their own homes. Neighborhoods will turn around. Values will increase.

In response to neighborhood activists, federal antidiscrimination laws, the National Home Ownership Strategy, and the profit motive, mortgage lenders are "rolling out the red carpet" for borrowers who in past years may have been turned away. "We are in a heavy campaign to spread the word to the community that home ownership is not out of reach for low-income families," says mortgage specialist Fred Thomas III. "This is truly a window of opportunity for folks who previously were shut out of the home-buying system."

Loan Details Differ

The specific details of these community reinvestment home finance plans differ among lenders. Some offer low- or no-down-payment plans.

Others eliminate or reduce closing costs and fees. Most relax qualifying standards and offer counseling to help individuals and families shape up their finances, improve their credit, and become familiar with the process of buying a home. A large number of lenders combine all these benefits into one program.

Ray Sims of GE Capital Mortgage Services says, "We expect to create business where we haven't seen it before. . . . We see this as a potentially large underserved market."

Even though community reinvestment loan programs are geared toward "low- to middle-income" borrowers, the income limits often go up to $40,000, $50,000, or $60,000 a year. Sometimes no limits apply whatsoever. American Savings Bank has advertised; "If you pay $1,000 a month or more for rent, you should consider buying a $200,000 house." So, don't rule yourself out because you think you earn too much money. Most community reinvestment home finance programs reach well into the middle class.

State and Local Governments

"It's a great program," says Rebecca Hoffreiter. "Anybody that needs it should go for it." Rebecca's talking about a home finance plan sponsored in part by the Pennsylvania Housing Finance Agency (PHFA). Under this innovative lease-purchase plan, renters can move into home ownership with as little as $1,000 in up-front cash. Then for a period of one to three years, a part of the homebuyers' monthly payments go into a forced savings account. Once they build up enough money for a five percent down payment, the buyers obtain a mortgage and close on their purchase.

"This is certainly a great program, and we're really excited about it," says Craig Cunningham. Craig is director of marketing for K. Hovnanian, one of the new home builders who agreed to participate in this lease-purchase program. On the other side of the country, Harry Jensen of Jensen Mortgage says, "We're putting people in $120,000 homes who could have only qualified for a $60,000 home. At the beginning, the Realtors I know were incredulous." Harry's praise is aimed at a shared equity mortgage plan sponsored by the San Diego Housing Commission.

Under this plan, the Housing Commission contributes up to $25,000 in down-payment funds. Homebuyers need only come up with three percent of the home's purchase price from their own pocket. As an added advantage, the city Housing Commission's down-payment money doesn't require any monthly repayments. If the homeowners sell within 15 years, they must then repay the down-payment money along with some profit to the Commission. On the other hand, after 15 years the loan is completely forgiven.

Throughout the United States, both state and local governments have created dozens of different types of programs that offer special assistance financing. There are low-interest mortgage bond programs, mortgage credit certificates, low-cost home repair or renovation loans, down-payment assistance plans, and even sweat equity and urban homesteading. Some states have also created their own version of the VA (U.S. Department of Veterans Affairs) mortgages.

Fannie and Freddie Get Creative

The largest suppliers of mortgage money in the country are two congressionally chartered corporations called Fannie Mae and Freddie Mac. Since the kickoff of the National Homeownership Strategy several years ago, both of these lenders have relaxed their underwriting standards and lowered down payments for first-time buyers.

Through loan programs sponsored by Fannie and Freddie, you can borrow as much as 95 to 97 percent of your home's purchase price—up to around $215,000. In fact, at present (for homebuyers with excellent credit), Fannie Mae is giving a trial run to "flex mortgage." With this loan, borrowers put only three percent down. Even better, the three percent need not come from cash savings. You could borrow the down payment from family; obtain a gift, grant, or loan from your employer; or even take a cash advance against your credit card.

Only time will tell whether the flex mortgage proves successful. But Fannie and Freddie are committed to creating new and easier ways for renters to finance homes. As long as borrower default rates (foreclosures) remain low, these giant mortgage lenders will "keep their doors open" to almost any homebuyer who can demonstrate financial responsibility.

Where to Look

Locating the community reinvestment mortgage, first-time buyer loan program, or other special assistance finance plan that's right for you may take some work: Talk to Realtors, loan officers, mortgage brokers, government agencies, and home-buying counselors. Read the business and real estate sections of the major newspapers in your city or state. Just stay alert and persevere. You can find an easy qualifying, low- (or no-) down-payment home finance plan with your name on it.

MISTAKE # **85**

We thought FHA loaned only to low-income people and involved too much red tape.

LESSON: Don't overlook loans insured by the Federal Housing Administration.

"We earn $48,000 a year," says Sam Wright. "We didn't know we could get an FHA loan, since we fall well outside the low-income category. Anyway, whenever you get involved with the government, you've got too much red tape to wade through."

Sam has made a common mistake. Many Americans erroneously believe FHA mortgage loan programs are intended only for low- to middle-income individuals and families. In truth, FHA places no limits on income. It doesn't matter whether you earn $12,000 a year or $120,000; as long as you've got acceptable (not perfect) credit and earn enough to make your mortgage payments, you can qualify. As to red tape, the FHA does have its bureaucratic rules and regulations. But these shouldn't present a problem for borrowers who are working with a DE (direct endorsement) lender. These lenders can complete and approve the loan paperwork directly, without submitting it to the FHA.

Two Drawbacks of FHA

Compared to many other types of home mortgages, FHA loans have only two drawbacks. First, if you plan to buy a higher-priced home,

—— 185 ——

FHA loan limits may be too low. In general, maximum FHA loan limits range between $90,000 and $157,000. The top limits apply to high cost areas such as Boston, San Francisco, San Diego, and New York. The lower loan limits apply to the more moderate housing cost areas such as many of those found in Florida, Arkansas, Alabama, and West Virginia. (However, no matter where you live, you can find some homes suitable for FHA financing. For example, even high-cost San Diego has 24 neighborhoods where homes average less than $170,000. And condominiums and townhouses are priced much less.)

A second drawback of FHA loans is cost. Compared to many mortgages, FHA insurance and fees can add several thousand dollars to your closing expenses. To offset these higher expenses, though, the FHA does let you roll most of the costs into your loan. You don't have to pay much at closing.

Benefits of FHA Home Financing

Overall, in deciding whether to use an FHA loan, weigh its drawbacks against these benefits:

1. *Low down payment:* It's usually five percent or less.
2. *No savings required:* Even the relatively small FHA down payment need not come from your own cash savings. Your parents or other close family members may loan (or give) this money to you.
3. *Easier qualifying:* FHA lenders often will not be as picky as other lenders. The primary purpose of FHA is to expand home ownership. FHA lenders can't broaden home ownership by turning down people who want to buy homes.
4. *More liberal qualifying ratios:* This means FHA loans expand your borrowing power (see Mistake #86).
5. *Counseling:* HUD/FHA offers counseling through hundreds of not-for-profit organizations located throughout the country. These counselors can help you plan your finances to achieve home ownership. And should you suffer a layoff, health problem, or other financial setback after you've bought your home, FHA counselors can reduce your mortgage payments and help you sort through and solve your budget problems.

6. If you finance your home with an FHA loan and mortgage interest rates drop, you can "streamline" an FHA refinance to take advantage of the lower rates. Streamlining means you don't have to again jump over any qualifying hurdles. A streamlined refinance requires no credit check, no income verification, no appraisal, no points. No conventional lender offers this super deal.

7. When you sell your home, your buyers can, with easy qualifying, assume your FHA fixed-rate mortgage at the same rate you're paying. If interest rates fall, they too will be able to streamline a refinance at the new lower rates.

These last two FHA benefits, streamlining and assumability, provide especially good value. As economic hard times have hit some homeowners, they haven't been able to refinance their conventional loans because their income, their home's value, or both have fallen. They've been stuck with old mortgages of 9 to 13 percent even as market rates hovered between 7 and 8 percent. In contrast, through streamlining, FHA borrowers have been able to cut their mortgage payments by hundreds of dollars a month—even when they could not have qualified for new financing.

As further benefit, FHA assumability will give you a competitive edge over other sellers when you put your home up for sale. If interest rates are high, you can pass along your lower rate to buyers. If market interest rates have fallen, you or your buyers can streamline a refinance. Your buyers avoid the hassle and cost of taking out a new loan. In addition, qualifying for an FHA assumption is usually easier than qualifying for a new loan.

All in all, I believe the benefits of FHA greatly outweigh its drawbacks. Although only you can decide what's best for your circumstances, don't make the mistake of overlooking FHA. During the past five years FHA has helped more than 3.5 million Americans become homeowners. This is one government agency that is working hard to put renters into their own homes.

HUD Homes

HUD (U.S. Department of Housing and Urban Development) is the parent of FHA. When FHA borrowers fail to make their mortgage payments, HUD takes back the homes and offers them for sale at bargain prices, on bargain terms, or sometimes both. The exact deals HUD offers depend on the number of homes it has to sell relative to the number of potential homebuyers.

When sales are slow, HUD creates all kinds of buyer incentives. In more robust markets, incentives become less generous and HUD prices its homes closer to their market values. Nevertheless, even in hot markets, patience, perseverance, and maybe a little luck, can get you a good buy on a HUD home.

Note, though, that HUD does not sell directly to buyers. To bid on a HUD home, you must go through a real estate agent who is authorized by HUD. To find these agents, look through the realty firm ads in your local newspaper or consult the yellow pages of your telephone directory. You might also call the HUD office nearest to where you live and request a list of their registered agents.

If you want to stop renting now, a HUD home might prove to be your best opportunity. Put a HUD agent to work for you. There are no guarantees. But passing up this possibility could be a mistake. Nearly anyone (with tolerably good credit) can afford to buy a HUD home.

VA Mortgages

While discussing the home-buying and home-financing possibilities sponsored by the federal government, I should also mention the Department of Veterans Affairs (VA). If you have served in the armed forces (including the National Guard), contact the VA. See if your years of service qualify you for a VA *certificate of eligibility*. With VA eligibility, you can buy a home priced up to around $215,000—with virtually *no cash* required for a down payment or closing costs. Some new home builders even advertise, "VETERANS—$1 MOVES YOU INTO YOUR OWN HOME." If you are an eligible veteran with tolerably good credit, don't overlook this possibility.

Nonveterans Can Also Benefit from VA

Nonveterans can use VA programs in two ways. First, you may "assume" a VA mortgage that has been originated by an eligible veteran. In other words, say a veteran bought and financed a $200,000 home two years ago. Now she finds she has been transferred to a job in another city and needs to sell. The outstanding loan balance is $203,000 (at the time of purchase, some of the closing costs were added to the mortgage). Today's market value of the home is $207,000. Pay the veteran $4,000 (or whatever amount you both agree to) and, with a small assumption fee, you can simply take over the veteran's mortgage. A quick, low-cost, low-down way to buy a home!

Another VA possibility for nonveterans is to buy a VA home. Similar to FHA, VA "takes back" some of the homes it finances when veterans don't make their scheduled mortgage payments. It then turns around and offers these homes on easy terms to anyone (veteran or nonveteran) who meets VA's relatively easy qualifying standards. (For more details on how to buy HUD or VA homes, see my book *Investing in Real Estate*, also published by John Wiley & Sons, Inc.)

MISTAKE # **86**

We wanted a fixed-rate mortgage. ARMs were too risky.

LESSON: *Before you pass up an ARM (adjustable rate mortgage), make sure you understand and explore your options.*

"When we started shopping for a home," recalls Ari Kyle, "I read that you should avoid an ARM whenever you can get a 30-year fixed-rate mortgage for less than 10 percent. Since at the time, 30-year mortgages were fluctuating around 8 percent, we didn't even consider an adjustable rate. With fixed rates that low, why take the risk of an ARM?"

Although Ari asked this question rhetorically, the answer is not as obvious as he thinks. In fact, like Ari, far too many homebuyers pass up ARMs without fully considering why some type of adjustable-rate mortgage might prove to be their best choice. Before you make this mistake, answer these questions:

1. Is there a strong probability you will sell your home within seven years?
2. Do you expect your income to increase during the coming years?
3. Would you like to increase your home purchase price range by $10,000 to $40,000, or even more?
4. Would you like to cut your closing costs by $1,000 to $3,000?
5. Do you expect to keep your home for more than seven years?
6. Do you enjoy a financial cushion in your budget and savings accounts?

If you can answer yes to at least three of these six questions, you should fully explore your ARM options.

Save Money with ARMs

First, the shorter the length of time you plan to own your home, the more you should consider an ARM. That's because nearly all ARMs cap your monthly payments. As a rule, you can nearly always find an adjustable that will cost you less than a fixed-rate loan if you plan to sell within seven years. As a minimum, take a look at 5/25 or 7/23 (sometimes described as a 30/5 or 30/7) adjustables.

These types of ARMs fix your interest rate and monthly payments for the beginning five or seven years of the loan. Then they periodically adjust to keep your rate in line with the market. Even this limited type of adjustable *may* save you between .5 and 1.5 percent in interest rates as compared to a fixed-rate mortgage. For instance, when 30-year fixed-rates were at 7.25 percent, I saw several 5/25 ARM plans with interest rates as low as 5.75 percent.

On a $100,000 loan, your payments for a 7.25 percent 30-year fixed-rate loan would have cost $682 a month. If you selected the 5/25, your payments would drop to $583 a month. Although the precise cost differences between 30-year fixed-rate loans and various types of ARMs change daily, it pays to explore the market. When you plan to sell within seven years, the chances are good you can find an ARM that limits your risk at the same time it reduces your monthly payments. You have the best of both worlds.

On top of this, if you're fairly certain your income is going up throughout the coming years, you should be able to handle increases in your ARM's monthly payments. Take a careful look at your future expenses and factor in salary raises. Is there some breathing room? If there is, don't needlessly worry about an adjustable-rate mortgage (as long as its payment increases are moderately capped, of course).

Qualify for a Larger Mortgage

As an additional benefit, ARMs help you qualify for a larger mortgage. They do this in two ways. First, since ARMs start with lower interest rates, for the same amount of monthly payment, you can borrow more. A payment of, say, $800 a month will pay off a loan of $109,000 at eight percent over 30 years. With an ARM's qualifying interest rate of say, six percent, you could borrow $133,000. Second, even better, if you can afford it, some ARM lenders will qualify you with more liberal qualifying ratios. For example, with a fixed-rate loan, the lender might limit your payments to $800 a month. But with an ARM, the lender might qualify you for a monthly payment of, say, $840. Instead of borrowing $109,000 (with an eight percent fixed-rate loan), the six percent ARM with liberal qualifying would permit you to borrow $140,000.

Lower Points and Fees

To further encourage you to use an ARM, sometimes ARM lenders cut their loan origination fees and closing costs. This benefit, however, may not be the advantage it once was. To meet competitive pressures, some lenders also have been offering low cash-to-close deals on their fixed-rate loans. Nevertheless, don't forget to at least compare adjustable- and fixed-rate mortgages on the basis of cash you need to close.

Longer-Term Cost Savings

Nearly all experts agree that ARMs may save you money if you plan to sell within seven years or less. But you also might save money over the longer term. Here's why.

Say you're faced with a choice between a 30-year fixed-rate loan at 8 percent and a 7/23 that starts at 6.75 percent. You want to borrow

$100,000. With the fixed-rate plan, your payments will cost $733 a month. With the 7/23, you'll pay $648. So, for at least the first seven years, you'll save $85 a month, for a total of $7,140.

Instead of pocketing this monthly savings of $85, though, let's say you add it to your mortgage payment. Even though you're only required to pay $648, you go ahead and pay $733 ($648 + $85 = $733). This tactic causes you to pay down your outstanding mortgage balance much faster. By making these extra payments, your mortgage balance after seven years would have fallen to approximately $83,000. On the other hand, your mortgage balance with the fixed-rate plan at 8 percent would have dropped to just $92,480. Obviously, if you sell at this point, you're way ahead of the game with the ARM.

But what if you don't sell? As long as your new adjustable rate stays below 9.5 percent, your monthly mortgage payments won't amount to any more than $740—about the same as you've been paying. At 10.5 percent, your payments would increase only to $798 a month. Now, what if interest rates are lower when your loan adjusts after seven years? Not only will you have accumulated an additional $9,480 in home equity, but your monthly payments won't increase and may actually go down.

Of course, these figures are illustrative only. Because the *relative* costs of ARMs versus fixed-rate loans change frequently, you'll have to work the numbers with your mortgage loan advisor that are current at the time you buy your home. Still, this basic fact holds true. For some homebuyers, the right ARM can put them thousands of dollars ahead of where they would have been with a fixed-rate mortgage.

The Fixed-Rate Solution

Some mortgage loan officers agree with everything I have just stated, but they still argue that for most homebuyers the fixed-rate mortgage (FRM) can give comparable benefits with less risk. Here's their reasoning:

1. Some fixed-rate loans can be obtained without heavy front-end costs and fees. Therefore, the total first year costs of ARMs versus FRMs may not differ as much as is commonly supposed.

2. Should interest rates fall, you can inexpensively refinance your "no cost" FRM at the lower interest rates. (Of course, this refi-

nance option presumes that both you and your home continue to meet any applicable qualifying and *loan-to-value* requirements.)

3. Instead of using an ARM to qualify for a larger mortgage, locate a special first-time buyer fixed-rate mortgage that offers easier qualifying, a lower-than-market interest rate, or perhaps both. Or get your seller to *buy down* the FRM interest rate for the first two or three years of the loan.

4. With an FRM you need not worry about *payment shock.* (Payment shock results when a quick jump in an ARM's interest rate boosts your mortgage payments by hundreds of dollars a month.)

5. Even if you plan to sell within three to seven years, take the security of a fixed-rate mortgage. Why? Because your plans may change. Or, if interest rates have dramatically increased (say from 7.5 percent to 10 percent), you may not be able to qualify for a loan on another house. In other words, higher interest rates may put your move-up possibilities on hold until interest rates fall (whenever that may be). Then you would be stuck with your high rate ARM.

The Debate Continues

Which is best? An ARM or a fixed-rate mortgage? As you can see from the above discussions and viewpoints, no one can answer that question definitively. It depends on how FRM points, fees, and interest rates compare to those of ARMs at the time you buy. Plus, the answer depends on your personal financial situation as well as your "sound sleep" quotient.

Will an ARM really save you money? Can you afford the risks of an ARM? Can you sleep soundly with the knowledge that your mortgage payments could dramatically increase (even though they probably won't)? Don't prejudge the answers to these questions. Get together with a smart and concerned loan originator who will walk you through a wide variety of loan products and potential outcomes. Look at specific dollar amounts. Don't focus on "small" percent changes in rates. A two or three percent increase (decrease) in your mortgage rate can increase (decrease) your payments by hundreds of dollars a month.

Only then—after you have reviewed the numbers in light of your present and future circumstances—should you choose the best loan for your needs. In other words, to locate the best loan at the lowest cost, don't act on your preconceived ideas. Compare actual dollars, and actual risks.

MISTAKE # **87**

We didn't negotiate for seller financing.

LESSON: Even when you can qualify for financing from a mortgage lender, also consider the possibility of seller financing.

Julio and Tara Scott had only enough cash for a 10 percent down payment. So when they bought their home, their bank charged them a higher interest rate and required them to buy private mortgage insurance (PMI). In addition, because the mortgage insurer applied tight qualifying standards, the Scotts weren't able to buy as much house as they wanted. In other words, they ended up paying more and getting less.

What the Scotts overlooked was a financing method referred to as an 80–10–10 sale. Here's how this technique works: You put 10 percent down; you borrow 80 percent of your home's purchase price from a bank or S&L; and the sellers carry back the other 10 percent as a seller-financed *second mortgage*.

Save on PMI

Since under this plan the bank has made an 80 percent loan instead of a 90 percent loan, it faces less risk. In exchange for this lower risk, the bank will drop its requirements for PMI, give you a better interest rate, and probably relax its qualifying income ratios or other credit standards. You can get more house for less.

Benefits to Sellers

Now, you might ask, "What's in it for the sellers? Why would they accept this kind of deal?"

Most important, the sellers get their house sold. For most sellers, that's their number-one priority. When you write up your offer, you make an 80–10–10 plan a condition of the contract. Second, because it's easier to qualify at the bank for an 80 percent loan, the sellers can feel secure that your purchase will actually close. Many sellers fear they will pull their house off the market for four to eight weeks, then their sale falls through, and they're back at square one. Anything you do to reduce this fear stands out as a plus in the sellers' eyes. (A preapproval letter also helps achieve this goal.)

Third, the interest you agree to pay the sellers will exceed the amount they could earn on their money in a certificate of deposit or savings account. With CDs paying four to six percent, a return of seven to nine percent to the sellers on a second mortgage can look pretty good. Fourth, an 80–10–10 sale will probably take less time to close than a 90–10 sale with private mortgage insurance.

Other Variations

Of course, an 80–10–10 sale represents just one variation of combined seller-bank financing. If you're really short of cash, you could try for an 80–15–5 plan, or even an 80–20–0. In fact, any combination is possible. If your credit has some blemishes, you could decrease the bank's percentage to 60 to 75 percent—say 70–20–10. Just remember: The lower the bank's loan-to-value ratio, the greater your chance for loan approval, the less likely you'll have to buy PMI, and the lower your interest rate.

Eliminate the Bank Altogether

Homebuyers who can't qualify for bank financing know they must turn to some type of seller financing or *nonqualifying mortgage assumption.* But even when you can bank qualify, still consider negotiating a completely seller-financed purchase. Here are four reasons why seller financing is beneficial:

1. You can often get the sellers to accept a lower interest rate than typical mortgage lenders.
2. Sellers don't charge application fees, "garbage" fees, or loan origination fees. You need less cash to close.

—— 195 ——

3. Seller financing involves less paperwork and a quicker closing.
4. You can tailor the exact terms, amounts, and payment schedule to your and the sellers' needs. You don't have to get stuck in the red tape of lender rules and regulations.

More than 40 percent of the homeowners in the United States and Canada own their homes free and clear. These homeowners are prime candidates to carry back all or a substantial part of your financing. But sometimes you have to do more than ask. You have to make seller financing an essential condition of your purchase offer. Then itemize and explain the benefits. If you make your offer reasonable and responsive to the sellers' needs (remember win-win), you'll find that many can be persuaded to accept.

MISTAKE # **88**

Those were the fastest two years of our lives.

LESSON: *Beware of seller financing that falls due in less time than it takes to wear out a pair of shoes.*

"We never worried about it at the time," says Ruth Mehta. "We were sure interest rates would come down and our home would appreciate. We couldn't imagine any trouble refinancing. But interest rates didn't come down. Our home didn't appreciate. And those were the fastest two years of our lives."

When Ruth and her boyfriend, Sid, bought their home, they used a 70–20–10 financing plan. They borrowed 70 percent of their home's price from the bank; the sellers financed 20 percent; and Ruth and Sid put 10 percent down. This technique made it easier for the couple to qualify for bank financing, and it saved them money. Not only did the bank give them a lower interest rate, the sellers even agreed to accept an interest rate less than the bank was charging. But here's the catch: Ruth and Sid agreed to pay off the sellers' loan within two years. And they couldn't do it.

Ruth and Sid had fallen into a common trap. Sometimes sellers who carry back financing will grant their buyers very favorable terms for a year or two. After this relatively short term, the seller financing falls due. The buyers then have to either come up with the money themselves or arrange new financing.

Risks of Short-Term Financing

Although in and of itself, there's nothing inherently wrong with short-term financing, it does present risks that too many homebuyers ignore. Ruth says, "We were so eager to stop throwing rent money down a rat hole, we were willing to accept almost any terms the seller wanted. Back then, two years seemed like a long time. With the prospects of home ownership so close, we shut our mind to the risks. As far as we were concerned, there weren't any. We told each other interest rates had to come down. We told each other our home would probably go up in value by at least 10 to 15 percent. Talking between ourselves was like talking in an echo chamber. Neither of us listened critically. We just repeated what the other one said."

Sid and Ruth's sleepless nights and anxious days demonstrate the risks of short-term financing. Over a period of one to three years, no one can accurately predict interest rates or home appreciation rates. Although it's often easy to tell yourself you'll be able to refinance, experience too often has proven otherwise.

Minimize Those Risks

In fact, as many Southern Californians and New Englanders learned a while back, short-term home values can fall even when interest rates have hit their lowest levels since automobile tailfins were popular. Many of these homeowners couldn't refinance their short-term seller carry-backs. Although a new loan would have meant lower payments, their home values would no longer support the amount of mortgage they needed.

To prevent getting caught in refinance limbo, do the following:

1. Insist on a loan term of at least five to seven years. Don't risk short-term future shock for the immediate joy of home ownership.

2. If you do agree to a shorter-term loan, include an escape clause that extends your due date if home values are depressed or if interest rates have risen.

3. As an additional safeguard, develop a plan to create value. Shorter-term finance plans work best when you buy a home at a bargain price. Then redecorate, remodel, or renovate to boost its loan value (or future selling price).

Special Note on Lease-Options

One of the most popular short-term seller finance plans is the lease-option. Most lease-option agreements call for buyers to execute their option to buy within one to two years. Usually, buyers use this time to save money for a down payment, strengthen their credit record, or pay off some of their other bills. For tens of thousands of former renters, the lease-option has been their admission ticket to home ownership.

If you do choose a lease-option home finance plan, however, remember you face the risk that interest rates will go up before you are able to buy. Just as with short-term mortgages, try to protect your position. Write a clause into your agreement that gives you more time to close if interest rates head north. You especially want to follow this advice if you're paying substantially more for your option and lease payments than you would be paying in straight rent for another similar home. Don't leave yourself wide open to the danger that you won't qualify for the financing (refinancing) you need.

MISTAKE # **89**

I paid $2,500 down to lease-option a townhouse but then found out later that my bank wouldn't give me a mortgage on it.

LESSON: *Not all properties or "down payments" meet lender rules and regulations.*

Like many tenants, Eric Coffey was tired of wasting money on rent. But financially, he wasn't quite ready to buy. Eric wanted time to pay off his car loan, cut down his credit card debt, and build up more savings for a down payment and cash reserves. So he decided to look for a seller who would give him a lease-option.

"After just three weeks of searching," recalled Eric, "I felt lucky because I found just what I wanted. It was a large end-unit townhouse with two bedrooms, two-and-a-half baths, fireplace, and a lower-level study. At $129,500 it was priced right, and the seller agreed to an 18-month lease-option. Our terms looked like this: I paid $2,500 to move in; my monthly rent payment was $1,200; and out of that $1,200, I received a *rent credit* of $500 a month toward the purchase price.

"I was quite pleased with this arrangement," Eric continued. "Everything went well for the first 16 months. Altogether, I had accumulated $18,000 toward my down payment and cash reserves. I had the option payment of $2,500, rent credits of $9,000, and additional savings of $6,500. That was more than enough for a 10 percent down payment and closing costs. I had even paid down my bills like I planned."

Be Wary of Complexes or Buildings with Large Numbers of Renters

"But my bank still turned down my loan application," said Eric. "The loan officer said too many homeowners in the complex were renting out their townhouses instead of living there themselves. To further complicate matters, the bank would not count my rent credits as part of my down payment. I'd been doing business with this bank for eight years. I had never made a late payment on my car loan or bounced a check. Yet the lender wouldn't make me the mortgage. I began to panic that I was going to lose the townhouse and all the money I'd put into it.

"In the end, we did get things worked out. The bank made a 70 percent loan, the seller carried back 20 percent, and I contributed my 10 percent. But it was really touch-and-go for a while."

When Eric entered into his lease-option agreement, he had overlooked the fact that many lenders won't give mortgages for condo, townhouse, or co-op complexes with high numbers of renters. Once a building or complex drops to less than 60 or 70 percent owner occupancy, lenders believe values in the complex may start to decline. When a project "tips" too much toward rentals, upkeep and maintenance often deteriorate.

"Funny Money" Down Payments

Eric also faced a second problem. Some lenders are suspect of "funny money" down payments. They prefer cash down from your bank account. If instead you want to use your car, a stamp collection, or rent credits as part of your down payment, the lender may feel you and the sellers are manipulating the numbers. In the past, many lease-option sellers have simply overpriced the homes they were selling. In exchange, they give buyers a large rent credit so it appears like they're building equity—at least on paper. But in fact the rent credit is just whittling down the price to where it should have been to begin with.

Say you agree to pay $110,000 for a condo (or house) that's actually valued at $100,000 (review Chapter 3). Over two years you build up $11,000 in rent credits that you want to count as a down payment. From the lender's viewpoint, those rent credits are "funny money." Even after counting them against your purchase price, you'll still owe just about what the home is really worth. So the lender says no deal. You've got to come up with a lot more real cash.

The solution to both these problems is, first, to avoid condo, co-op, or townhouse developments that are close to tipping toward renters. (This is good advice regardless of whether you're using a lease-option.) Second, make sure your option terms can pass a lender's sniff test. If your agreement doesn't smell right, the lender probably won't go for it. The lender will try to make sure your rent levels, rent credits, and purchase price make sense in terms of the market. A lender doesn't want to make a 80 or 90 percent loan-to-value ratio loan that actually turns out to be a 95 or 100 percent loan.

MISTAKE # **90**

We paid too much for our mortgage.

LESSON: *Learn the tricks of the trade.*

Until several years back, some real estate agents routinely received kickbacks from mortgage lenders. Although RESPA (the Real Estate

Settlement and Procedures Act) supposedly outlawed this practice, it was common in many cities throughout the United States for lenders to pay agents under-the-table referral fees. In fact, unethical agents even *demanded* lenders pay them kickbacks for bringing in loan customers.

Beth and Ted Cippolla were one couple who fell victim to such an agent. "We trusted him," says Beth. "He told us we didn't need to waste time calling a dozen lenders because he had a special arrangement with a mortgage company who would give his buyers the best mortgage terms possible. Sure, he had a special arrangement all right. But the arrangement wasn't to get us the best deal. It was to get Harold [their agent] a free trip to Hawaii. It cost us an extra $900 in closing costs and one-quarter percent on our mortgage interest rate."

HUD Gets Tough on Kickbacks

In an effort to stamp out abuses like the Cippollas suffered, HUD has cracked down on illegal kickbacks and referral fees. In several well-publicized court cases, HUD has gone after offenders with civil fines and criminal prosecutions. In addition, HUD has strengthened its rules and regulations. "Under current law," says HUD division director David Williamson, "if agents aren't providing a bona fide financial service, they aren't entitled to referral fees, extra compensation, or anything else of value."

However, what HUD has taken away with its left hand, it has given back double with its right hand. Under HUD's new rules, agents may not accept under-the-table referral fees; but they can act as loan originators. In other words, real estate brokerage firms have been given the green light to compete directly with lenders, mortgage brokers, and mortgage bankers. In fact, some of the larger realty firms have even bought or set up their own mortgage companies. When a realty firm actually provides mortgage services (not just referrals), it can legally charge buyers (borrowers) for these services.

The effects of these changes will not be clear for several years. HUD and the National Association of Realtors maintain consumers will gain. They say as long as real estate agents fully disclose all fees, homebuyers will enjoy a greater choice of mortgages.

Mortgage Bankers Oppose "One-Stop" Realty Firms

The Mortgage Bankers Association, though, sees realty firms invading their turf and doesn't like it. The mortgage bankers say "one-stop" shopping will reduce competition. Real estate agents will steer home-buyers— especially first-time homebuyers—to lenders who are affili-ated with the realty firms. And there's no guarantee those lenders will offer borrowers the best terms or interest rates. Stephen Brobeck, with the Consumer Federation of America, agrees with the mortgage bankers. This group has gone on record to oppose HUD and the Real-tors.

In response, Realtors have countered that they would be foolish to steer their buyers to uncompetitive loan products or mortgage lenders. It wouldn't take long for word to get out, and then that realty firm would lose not only its mortgage business, it would lose real estate sales. "Con-sumers have never been shy to squeal when they are not satisfied," says Realtor spokeswoman Sally Sciacca.

At present, no one can say whether "one-stop shopping" will actually benefit homebuyers. So, become a savvy borrower. Don't accept your real estate agent's loan products or referrals without first checking the rates, terms, and qualifying standards of other lenders. HUD's rules can work well only if you don't forget to think for yourself. Count on your real estate agent to advise and suggest. But remember, it's up to you to make an informed choice.

Loan Originators Can Increase Your Costs

In today's highly competitive mortgage market, most mortgage origina-tors work on commission. They want to find you a loan. Otherwise, they don't get paid. That's the good news.

The bad news is that loan originators can earn higher commissions by placing you into higher-cost loan products. In other words, to a cer-tain degree, the interest rate, points, and fees that you pay are subject to negotiation. If your loan officer says, "The best I can do is a rate of 8.25 percent and two points," don't take that as his or her final quote. Just like a car salesperson (or any other type of salesperson), the loan officer may be testing you.

If you accept, great. If you balk, the loan officer can say, "Oh, wait a minute, I've just thought of something else. Maybe I can get the lender to shave a point off those origination fees. They owe me a favor."

Protect Yourself

To protect yourself against paying too much, ask to see the loan officer's rate sheet. The rate sheet shows the "wholesale" cost of the loans. The bigger the spread between the wholesale rate and the interest rate and fees you pay, the larger the loan officer's commission. In fact, ask the loan officer straight out, "What's the amount of your commission on this loan?" If it's $4,000, you know that more than likely you've been placed into a high-cost loan. If the commission is $400, there is far less chance you're being taken for a ride. ("Typical" commissions run about 1 to 1.5 percent of the amount you borrow.)

Of course, neither the wholesale-retail spread nor the amount of the loan officer's commission—taken together or separately—provides the entire picture as to whether you are getting the best possible loan given your needs and financial qualifications. But it is one important piece of the puzzle. So, don't simply accept your loan originator's recommendations and quotes at face value. Do some investigating. Then negotiate, negotiate, and negotiate.

Credit Blemishes

In the language of mortgage lenders, homebuyers typically are classified into the credit categories of A, B, C, and D. The lower your grade, the more you must pay for your mortgage. But just like in school, the "grade" you receive depends on who's doing the grading. Whereas, even with credit blemishes, one mortgage lender might give you an "A," another might downgrade you to "B" or "C" status—and, correspondingly, try to persuade you to pay a higher interest rate and fees. (At the same time, of course, the loan rep earns a higher sales commission.)

If you get "downgraded" because of credit blemishes, don't meekly accept that category. Ask why. Is the loan rep bamboozling you so he or she can make more money? Or do you really deserve the downgrade? Also, try to learn how long it will take—or what you can do—to reach

"A" status. Maybe you should defer buying for a while until you can qualify at lower rates.

· Also, talk with other mortgage companies. If your blemishes consist of nothing more than a few late payments, you can probably find an "A" grade mortgage. Even when you've suffered more serious setbacks, sometimes it's possible to provide an "excuse" that will move you into an "A" category (see Mistake #93).

Just keep in mind that loan originators can earn higher commissions when they persuade borrowers to accept higher fees and interest rates. If your credit is severely blemished, you may face little choice. You may have to pay more for your loan than "A" borrowers (but still subject to negotiation). Nevertheless, don't passively accept the downgrade. Learn the specific reasons and then seek second, third, fourth, or even fifth opinions. One mortgage company recently told me that 50 percent of "B" and "C" borrowers could have been qualified for an "A" grade.

Discriminatory Pricing versus Negotiating Skills

In Mistake #16, we talked about two types of discrimination: (1) stereo-typical ("We don't make loans to _____. They're bad risks."), and (2) discrimination through "neutral" rules or practices that adversely impact some identifiable groups of borrowers (e.g., African Americans, Hispanics, immigrants, women, singles, single-parent families).

As company policy, lenders have nearly eliminated stereotypical "turndowns." However, studies do indicate that some borrowers pay more for their mortgages than other borrowers—even when their credit records and incomes are fairly similar. And as it turns out, the borrowers who pay more are the borrowers most likely to fall into some legally protected category. Does this suggest that lenders are engaged in illegal discriminatory pricing? Not necessarily.

What it does suggest, though, is that these borrowers are far less likely to negotiate their interest rates and loan fees. When the loan rep says, "Gee, this is the best I can do," these borrowers accept the loan on the terms offered. They don't realize that they should respond with their own negotiating gambit, "Really, that's the best you can do? Well, Providence Mortgage quoted us a much better deal. Sorry, we're just wasting our time here."

The lesson is plain: Many loan originators will charge you higher interest and fees—if you let them. If you fear the lending process, are inexperienced in negotiations, or are otherwise uneducated about mortgage loan practices, you are fair game—regardless of your race, sex, ethnicity, nationality, sex, or family status.

To protect yourself, assert yourself (politely, of course). For when some loan reps sense a vulnerable and powerless prey, they go for the kill.

30-Year Loans versus 15-Year Loans

Mortgage lenders joke among themselves about the many telephone calls they receive where the caller asks, "What's your best rate?" Nine times out of 10, the caller really means, "What's your best rate on a 30-year, fixed-rate mortgage?" Yet, the 30-year, fixed-rate mortgage is nearly always the "most expensive" loan over the short run—and it's far more expensive than the 15-year, fixed-rate loan—over both the short run and the long run. Consider the comparisons on a $200,000 loan shown in Table 7.1. The original monthly payments on a 30-year loan cost less than the payments on a 15-year loan. But that's where the advantage ends. After five years you will still owe $190,122 for the 30-year loan (compared to a $156,188 balance on the 15-year loan). And after your first 10 years of ownership, you'll owe $79,862 more on your 30-year loan as compared to the 15-year loan ($175,385 − $95,523 = $79,862). And after 15 years your 15-year mortgage will be paid off, but

Table 7.1	**Comparison of 30-year and 15-year Fixed-Rate Outstanding Mortgage Loan Balances**		
	30 Year Fixed-Rate @ 8%	*15-Year Fixed-Rate @ 7.5%*	*Difference*
Monthly Payment	$ 1,467	$ 1,854	$ −387
Balance @ 5 yrs	$190,122	$156,188	$ 33,934
Balance @ 10 yrs	175,385	95,523	79,862
Balance @ 15 yrs	153,507	00	153,507
Balance @ 20 yrs	120,911	00	120,911
Balance @ 30 yrs	00	00	00
Total Interest Paid	$328,120	$133,720	$194,400

you'll still owe $153,507 on your 30-year loan. In total, the 30-year loan not only will cost you a much slower payoff but also $194,400 in additional interest expense.

So, why do so many borrowers choose the higher-cost 30-year loan? Of course, the answer is the lower monthly payment for the first 15 years. Not only does the original lower payment help borrowers qualify for a larger mortgage, many borrowers say they don't want to pay down their loan quickly. They would rather invest their "extra" money in stocks. Or they say, just for safety, we want the 30-year loan's lower payments, but we plan to go ahead and make larger payments so we can get rid of this debt faster.

Only you can judge whether and to what degree the above reasons may influence your choice of loans. But before you decide, compare the 15-year versus 30-year numbers very closely. Experience proves that for many (if not most) homebuyers, the 30-year choice proves far more costly. (Also see Mistake #93.)

Prepayment Penalties

Some borrowers choose the higher-cost 30-year mortgage with the idea of refinancing into a 15-year loan later when rates drop or when their income goes up. Be careful, though, if you are adopting this strategy. Some lenders now are putting prepayment penalties into their mortgages. This means that if you try to pay off your loan early (say within the first three to five years), the lender may stick you with a $2,000 to $4,000 penalty (maybe more).

In some cases, loans with prepayment penalties aren't necessarily bad since, technically, these loans can be originated at slightly lower interest rates. In other words, you might be offered a 30-year fixed-rate loan (no penalty) at 8.25 percent, but with a prepayment penalty, the rate drops to 7.75 percent.

Unfortunately, some loan reps don't fully explain these choices, nor do they automatically give you the interest rate break that loans with prepayment penalties warrant. So, once again, a word to the wise: Ask your loan rep to fully advise you concerning the features and costs of the mortgages that you are considering. If your loan includes a prepayment penalty, make sure you get a discounted interest rate.

Table 7.2 **Illustration of Different Payback Calculations**

$100,000 Mortgage @ 30 years

Interest rate	Points/Amount	Monthly payment	Months to break even
1. 8.0	0/0	$733	00
2. 7.75	1/$1,000	716	58 months
3. 7.5	1.5/$1,500	699	44 months
4. 7.25	2.0/$2,000	682	39 months
5. 6.75	3.0/$3,000	648	35 months

Points versus Interest Rates

Nearly all lenders offer a broad variety of trade-offs with respect to points (fees paid at the time the mortgage money is loaned) and interest rates. For example, let's say you're looking at the choices shown in Table 7.2.

The question is, "Which of these choices is the lowest cost?" The answer: It all depends on how long you keep your mortgage. Clearly, if you keep your loan over three years (36 months), the 6.75 percent/3 point loan will save you the most money. Although you must pay an additional $3,000 at closing to get this lower rate, this loan will save you $85 a month over the 8.0 percent/0 points loan. In other words, in comparison to the 8.0 percent mortgage, you'll earn back your $3,000 in points in just over 35 months ($3,000 ÷ $85 = 35.29).

The above figures are for purposes of illustration only (the actual trade-offs you see will differ from these). Yet, this type of calculation is a good method (though not precisely accurate) to select the lowest loan *based upon your circumstances.*

A trustworthy and competent loan rep will go over interest rate/points trade-offs with you to figure out which look best for you. A greedy loan rep will steer you into interest rate/point combination that yields the largest sales commission. Don't make the mistake of asking your loan rep, "Which one is best?" Instead, ask him or her to work through the numbers with you. Then, after a full explanation, you decide.

Closing Costs and Fees

At the time you apply for a loan, your lender will provide a "good faith" estimate of the closing costs and fees that will be charged at settlement.

In addition to points (discussed above), closing costs may include charges for an appraisal, credit report, prorated taxes, mortgage application, flood insurance, title insurance, mortgage insurance, homeowners insurance, garbage fees, and numerous other expenses that in total can run into the thousands of dollars.

The question is, how can you reduce the amount of these costs that you have to pay? First, before you apply for a loan, get some idea of the closing costs that buyers "typically" pay. Then, in your home purchase negotiations, shift some of these costs to the sellers (or at least keep this tactic in mind). Second, in some markets and for some loan products, lenders differ greatly in the costs they levy against buyers. So, when shopping lenders, compare costs and fees as well as points and interest rates. And third, if the closing costs seem high (or even if they don't), ask that the lender reduce or eliminate them. It is perfectly reasonable for you to question and negotiate a lender's costs and fees.

Watch Out for Bait and Switch

Notice above, I placed "good faith" in quotation marks. That's because some lenders will quote you one amount for costs, fees, points, and interest rate. Then, after they get you into the loan approval process, they will "discover" a credit blemish or some other "defect" in your application. "Sorry," such a lender might say, "we're going to have to charge you more because . . ." At that point, don't give in without a fight. You may be a target for the old "bait and switch" sales tactic. In fact, if you do suspect this type of unethical (perhaps illegal) behavior by the lender, tell them to honor their commitment or you will file a complaint with the various regulators. Also, you could switch lenders and demand that the offending lender forward your file to the new lender. That way, your new approval process won't start over from square one.

Bad Faith Lock-Ins

Some unethical lenders also play tricks with lock-ins. At the time you apply for a loan, the lender may (for a fee) lock you into an interest rate of 8.25 percent for say, 45 days. Then, if market interest rates head up, the lender may "discover" problems in your application that delay settlement beyond the 45 days. "Sorry," the lender says, "rates have increased, and we have to bump you up to 8.75 percent."

If you believe that the lender has purposely dragged its feet to push you into a higher rate, don't accept it. Complain. Demand. Threaten to go to the regulators. More than likely you'll get the original rate restored.

False Float-Downs

Some lenders will lock in your maximum mortgage interest rate, yet will also give you a float-down if rates fall between the time you apply and the date your loan closes. "Good news," your loan originator tells you, "rates have fallen and we can now close your loan at 7.75 percent instead of 8.0 percent. You're going to save $26.30 a month."

Well, yes, that's good news. But it may not truly reflect the full drop in rates that has occurred. If market rates are really at 7.5 percent, by fooling you into accepting 7.75 percent, your loan originator is going to pocket a nice-sized "overage" commission. So, even with float-downs, take care. Make sure you're receiving the full float-down that you are entitled to.

"Hot" Products/"Hot" Lenders

In highly competitive mortgage markets, mortgage costs such as points, rates, and closing expenses may not vary much among lenders. However, on occasion, some mortgage lenders decide to "buy market share" or push a "hot" loan product in an effort to strike a desired balance within the lender's total portfolio of mortgage products. In these cases, if you're in the right place at the right time, you could score a real bargain loan.

So, when shopping for a loan, keep your mind open to various alternatives. I know of borrowers who have picked up super-priced ARMs even though they had mentally committed to a fixed-rate product. The opposite is also true. In other words, it's just like going to a restaurant with your appetite set on sirloin steak. Then you learn the lobster-prime rib combo is on special at $9.95. In that situation, why pay $12.50 for sirloin?

APRs and ARMs

When you compare the costs of mortgage loans, you will undoubtedly see the term APR (annual percentage rate). To comply with government truth-in-lending laws, nearly all mortgage interest-rate advertising includes this figure. The APR is always higher than the stated interest rate because it reflects your total cost of borrowing (interest, fees, points, prepaids, and certain other expenses). Presumably, by comparing APRs among various loan products and lenders, you will be able to select the lowest-cost loan.

Unfortunately, life is not so simple. In the first place, APRs that apply to ARMs make no sense. Under the law, they are calculated as if the ARM interest rate will not change during the life of the loan (except for the scheduled boost up from the teaser rate to the initial contract rate). Yet, the very idea of an *adjustable* rate mortgage means that the interest rate will change. So, APRs for adjustable-rate mortgages give us mathematically precise, yet totally inaccurate figures. True APRs for ARMs cannot be calculated in advance.

To put it bluntly, in its effort to force lenders to tell the truth about the costs of their mortgage loans, the government misleads borrowers. When comparing ARMs, you cannot rely on the stated APRs. You may find a COFI (Cost of funds index) ARM with an APR of 7.86 percent and a one-year treasury ARM at an APR of 7.21 percent. But since no one knows how these respective ARM indexes will change over time, no one can accurately predict which one represents the lowest-cost loan.

Fixed-Rate APRs

Although it might appear that the APR would apply accurately to fixed-rate mortgages, that is true only in the unlikely event you pay off the loan balance precisely according to schedule over the full life of the loan. If you pay ahead (or behind) of schedule, your actual APR will increase. Similarly, if you sell your house or refinance your mortgage, your actual APR will exceed the APR figure the government requires lenders to calculate.

In mandating APR disclosures, the government was addressing a real need: helping consumers compare the total costs of mortgage loans. In practice, though, you must look beyond the APR. To obtain the best loan at the lowest cost, you must compare loan products according to your personal financial situation, your tolerance for risk, and the expected period over which you think you will hold your loan.

This takes us back to the payback calculations shown in Table 7.1. If you're contemplating a "loan for life," it's *generally* better to pay higher points in trade-off for a lower interest rate. In situations where you might move or refinance "tomorrow," it *generally* makes sense to accept a higher interest rate in exchange for lower upfront points, costs, and fees. In either case, you will still want to calculate a "years to break even" figure. Then evaluate them in reference to your circumstances and preferences.

Summing Up: Loan Costs and Possibilities

Getting the best loan at the lowest cost can't be left to chance. Nor can you simply "dial for dollars" and ask lenders, "What's your best rate?" Instead, learn the many ways that unscrupulous (or inexperienced) loan reps can lead you into paying more than you should. Give due consideration to your many loan possibilities. Understand the necessity of assertive and informed negotiation. And, most important, work with a trustworthy loan rep who demonstrates savvy, knowledge, competence, patience, and concern. A top loan rep operates with the philosophy, "You'll never come in second by putting the customers first."

Just as a top real estate agent does far more than "show houses," a top loan rep does far more than "give rate quotes and process applications."Put a top loan rep on your side, and you'll get the loan that's right for you.

MISTAKE # **91**

Our lender canceled our loan approval because I went into labor early and had to take temporary leave from work.

LESSON: *Don't change your loan status before you close your mortgage. Your lender may revoke your approval.*

Kristi Colburn and her husband, Pat, did all the right things to buy their home. They saved diligently. They ran up no large debts. They kept their credit record spotless. They both worked steadily since graduating from college seven years earlier. And before they started their home search, they received preapproval (not merely a prequalification) of their loan application. (A prequalification tells you how much house you can probably afford according to the lender's standards. With a pre-approval, the lender actually commits to making you a loan.)

"Everything was going great," says Kristi. "We found a terrific three-bedroom, two-and-one-half bath in Brighton less than 15 minutes from work for both of us. Our offer was accepted and we went into escrow. After years of waiting and months of searching, we were just two weeks away from becoming homeowners. Our loan officer told us from now until closing would be smooth sailing. Just paperwork formalities—nothing to be concerned about.

"Instead of smooth sailing, though, during the next two weeks, our sailing ship lost its wind and we hit choppy seas," recalls Kristi. "Eight months along in my pregnancy, I started to feel severe labor pains. It became too difficult for me to work, so I went on disability leave. Ten days later I delivered our daughter Jessy—as healthy and strong as a baby can be.

Gain a Daughter, But Don't Stop Work

"But at the same time we gained a daughter, we lost our loan. The day after I got home from the hospital, the loan officer called and said I needed to go back to my job immediately or the lender would refuse to close the loan. The mortgage approval was conditioned upon both our incomes, he said. Of course, we knew that and I did intend to return to work—but not for two or three months. The loan officer replied that wasn't good enough. He said I had to go back now.

"In trying to find a satisfactory solution, over the next six weeks we went through sheer agony. Our apartment lease expired and we had to move in with Pat's parents. My mom agreed to cosign our note. My employer assured the lender my job was waiting for me any time I was ready to end my maternity leave. We increased our down payment to 20 percent. The lender switched us from the fixed-rate loan we wanted to an ARM.

"Each time we would make one of these concessions or accept a new lender demand, the loan officer would reschedule our closing date. Then he would call and cancel until we agreed to something else. It was ridiculous.

"But you won't believe what happened next," Kristi added. "After meeting all the lender's additional requirements, and suffering through three cancellations and reschedulings, the loan officer informed us the loan committee had once again changed its decision. If we wanted the loan, I would still have to go back to work immediately, receive a paycheck, and then show the lender my paystub.

"At that point, we were totally frustrated and exhausted. There was nothing we could do. We needed a home and weren't about to start looking for another apartment to rent. So I had no choice. I went back to work, got my paystub, and, finally, escrow closed."

Your first reaction to Kristi's ordeal might be that the lender discriminated against Kristi because of her pregnancy and the birth of her daughter. But no matter how absurdly the lender handled Kristi and Pat Colburn's loan processing, it acted within its rights. Whenever a mortgage applicant changes his or her *loan status* prior to closing, the lender can revoke its loan approval. Since, technically, Kristi's job income had stopped, the lender wasn't required to count it. Without the income, the Colburns no longer qualified. Not fair or reasonable. But it is the law.

Many Factors Affect Loan Status

In Kristi's case, her loss of income (even if temporary) triggered the change in the Colburns' loan status. However, all the factors a lender considers in its loan decision will actually contribute to your loan status:

- Income
- Bills, debts, and expenses
- Length of employment
- Job security
- Credit record
- Available cash
- Net worth

- Type of loan, interest rate, amount of your scheduled payments including property taxes, homeowners' insurance, and mortgage insurance (if any)

Upon learning that their mortgage had been approved, Phil and Sue Grubbs went out and charged $3,000 of new furniture for their home. When the lender learned of these additional bills through a last-minute credit reverification, the Grubbs lost their mortgage approval. Their additional bills knocked them out of qualifying. Jack Reeves was preapproved for his home loan and then accepted a better job at higher pay. Thinking this was good news, Jack told his loan officer. The loan officer revoked Jack's preapproved commitment. The lender thought new jobs were too insecure. "Come back after a year," the loan officer told Jack.

When it comes to approving and closing loans, lenders show a split personality. Sometimes they will lean over backward to bend the rules to get a borrower qualified. On other occasions they act as if they've locked their common sense in one of their money vaults. So a word to the wise: After you've applied for a loan, don't do anything that can adversely change your loan status. If you do, your lender may give you the same kind of hassle (or rejection) that hit the Colburns, Grubbs, and Reeves.

MISTAKE # **92**

My loan fell through because of poor credit. But it wasn't *my* credit that was bad.

LESSON: *Get your credit record and finances in shape before you begin to shop for your home.*

Gwen Davis knew she had excellent credit and had never made a late payment in her life. So she didn't bother reviewing her credit report before she began shopping for a home. As Gwen now realizes, that shortcut proved to be a mistake. It cost her the home she wanted.

"I couldn't believe it," says Gwen. "I was in shock. The loan officer told me the credit report showed I was two months behind on my car loan and that my Visa card had been canceled for nonpayment. 'I don't even have a car loan,' I told him. 'Look on my mortgage application. Or I can show you the title to my car.'

"The loan officer sympathized with me but said his hands were tied. If the credit report erred, it would be up to me to straighten it out. Until I could show him a clean record, my application would not even be considered.

"My next step," Gwen continued, "was to try to get to the bottom of this. So I went to the credit bureau and got a copy of my credit report. Sure enough, the black marks were there for all the world to see. But as I knew, they didn't belong in my file. What had happened was the credit bureau had mingled my record with the record of Gail Davis—my ex-husband's new wife.

Beware: Credit Bureacracy at Work

"At this point, my education concerning the credit bureaucracy was just beginning. I soon learned that to discover a problem is one thing. To fix it is something else. To get those black marks off my record required endless phone calls, a dozen letters, and threats from my attorney. To make matters worse, Gail didn't lift a finger to help. She wasn't eager to see delinquent accounts reappear in her file. All told, it took four months to clear my name. By then, the sellers had already sold their home to other buyers. I really wanted that house, too."

You can prevent Gwen's mistake by contacting your local credit bureau or one of the national credit repositories (Experian, TransUnion, Equifax). Ask them to provide you a copy of your credit report. (They may charge a small fee.) Then examine the report carefully. If you discover bad credit that doesn't belong to you, tell the credit bureau. Immediately do what's necessary to get it removed. As Gwen Davis found out, that process can sometimes take months.

Make Your Best First Impression

On the other hand, if you find some late payments or other blemishes that are yours, realize that these may stop many lenders from granting you a mortgage. At a minimum, make sure all your installment accounts are current. Should you owe outstanding past-due debts, judgments, or tax liens, you will need to pay them. Very few mortgage lenders will lend money to someone who has not paid legally valid obligations. This practice even extends to disputed claims. The lender won't take your word. By whatever means you can, you will have to clear them from your record. You will have to negotiate, litigate, or otherwise satisfy the claims.

The best way to guard against a turndown is to review your credit record, get your finances in the best shape you can, and search for the right loan originator and loan product for your situation. Getting approval for home financing is like a matching contest. Figure your strengths and weaknesses. Then before you formally apply, try to identify the lender(s) whose qualifying criteria best fits your borrower profile. In other words, prepare to make your best first impression.

MISTAKE # **93**

Our lender turned down our loan application.

LESSON: *Prepare, prepare, prepare.*

"Our lender turned down our loan application. What can we do?" Every year I hear this lament from hundreds of potential homebuyers. Nationwide, the total number of turndowns runs into the hundreds of thousands. Sadly, though, most of these rejections need not have occurred. In the great majority of cases, the people who were turned down hadn't done their homework.

Preparation Counts

Far too many potential homebuyers simply think they either "qualify" or "don't qualify" for financing, as if this were some type of genetic determinism. They go to a lender, fill out the application forms, then hope for the best. (Of course, a top loan rep would never permit this foolish practice, but most people who are turned down have not sought the advice and counsel of a skilled loan originator. More than likely, they have dealt with a "paper processor.")

Before you apply for a mortgage, evaluate four areas of importance: (1) capacity, (2) collateral, (3) credit, and (4) compensating factors.

Capacity

Nearly every mortgage lender judges whether you bring in enough income to cover your monthly bills, living expenses, and housing costs-to-be (mortgage payments, homeowners insurance, property taxes, homeowner association fees). *In general,* lenders say your total housing costs shouldn't run any more than 28 percent of your income; and your housing costs plus other monthly payments shouldn't exceed 36 percent of your monthly income. These percentages are called qualifying ratios.

However, do not mistakenly believe that those figures are set in stone. That's why you need a top loan rep. He or she will go over all of your numbers *prior* to your application. Then he or she will help you "arrange" your numbers in such a way that loan approval (for the loan program selected) is substantially assured. For example:

1. *Qualifying ratios:* Although 28/36 qualifying ratios are "traditional," many loan programs and lenders approve loans with ratios as high as 44/44. FHA and VA frequently approve borrowers with ratios of 33/43—or even higher. First-time buyer programs, too, typically permit high ratios.

2. *Installment debt:* Quite likely, you make monthly payments on various credit-card accounts, car loans, student loans, and maybe alimony or child support. Lenders and loan programs count these debts differently. In addition, you may be able to pay off or consolidate some accounts. These efforts will improve your qualifying ratios.

3. *Income:* Even the amount of income you bring in may not prove as simple to count as you think. What if you're self-employed, a commissioned sales rep, or expecting a big raise? What about part-time work, overtime, or a second job? What if you receive alimony or child support? Can you bring in the income of a co-borrower? Do you expect to houseshare or bring in rental income from tenants? How should your spouse's income be figured?

— 217 —

Although it is reasonably easy to fill in the numbers on a form to see if you "qualify," it takes skill, knowledge and experience to "arrange" your numbers in their best light. Then, once you've been made to look as good as you can, a top loan rep searches for the mortgage program (and lender) that will best fit your borrower profile.

Collateral

Sometimes, lenders who want to reject an otherwise creditworthy borrower will use a "lowball" appraisal. To guard against this problem, (1) verify the features and selling prices of a large number of comparable sales; and (2) provide the lender's appraiser with the comp sales data that you (or your real estate agent) has discovered.

In addition, lenders prefer large down payments (i.e., low loan-to-value ratios) as opposed to low down payments (i.e., high loan-to-value ratios). So, should your loan approval look "iffy," try to raise more cash for your down payment. If you're planning to increase the home's value through improvements, tell that to the lender.

In the total scheme of things, lenders reject relatively few loans for reasons of inadequate collateral. But even so, it doesn't hurt to do what you can to convince the lender that your home offers solid value.

Credit

In moving into the electronic age, lenders have developed a new twist on evaluating your creditworthiness. It's called credit scoring (sometimes referred to as a FICO [Fair-Isaacs Company] score). To calculate this score, the lender puts a broad variety of borrower profile characteristics into a computer program. Then the computer prints out a number typically ranging between 500 and 800 (although higher and lower scores may be possible).

When scores come back above 680, loans are almost automatically approved. For scores in the range of 620 to 680, the lender takes a closer look. And for scores below 620, the borrower will be asked to provide more information, explanations, and justifications in support of the loan request.

Right now, it's too early to tell what FICO will mean for mortgage borrowers. Lenders say that rapid approval of the "slam dunks" will permit them more time to work with "marginal" or "credit-impaired" borrowers. Critics say that lenders will become so obsessed with the "right" numbers that homebuyers who don't fit the FICO profile will find themselves shut out of the mortgage market.

Compensating Factors

I suspect that if some lenders do simply look for high FICO scores, others will target borrowers with lower scores. In that case, just as now, compensating factors will still play a big role in the mortgage approval process.

What is a compensating factor? It is any evidence that you can provide to support your willingness and ability to make your mortgage payments on time. Here are some examples:

- Low family living expenses
- Energy efficient house
- Low or no costs of commuting
- High net worth (for your age and income)
- Regular pattern of savings
- Low use of credit
- Upward career path
- Rent payments equal to or exceeding your mortgage payments-to-be
- Sterling credit history
- Large cash reserves (or liquid assets)

In addition to positive compensating factors, you can also provide compensatory evidence to offset negatives such as credit problems, bankruptcy, foreclosure, or judgments. Lenders will forgive isolated instances of trouble—if you can convince them that the circumstances were beyond your control or resulted from some adversity of life. Disability, unemployment, divorce, spendthrift ex-spouse, real estate market collapse (e.g., as happened in the past in Texas, Southern California, and New England), or high and out-of-the-ordinary medical expenses are creditable types of explanations.

Beware of Stacking Risk Factors

Although today's lenders look beyond the "traditional" qualifying rules of the past, they still proceed cautiously if a borrower stacks up too many risk factors (e.g., low down payment, credit blemishes, short time on job, high ratios, large family with one breadwinner, high installment debt, large number of open credit accounts, payment shock, etc.). So, if your present financial circumstances "push the limit" in more than a few areas, get together with a home-buyer counselor or loan rep. Then make changes for the positive wherever possible. Mortgage lenders want to make loans. But they also want to get their money back according to schedule and without hassle.

Summing Up: Qualifying Depends on You

Follow the lessons displayed in this chapter and work with a trustworthy and skilled loan originator. You will obtain mortgage approval. As with most other achievements in life, a successful loan application requires preparation. Learn the "rules." Then learn how to make the "rules" work for you. Arrange your finances. Explore the many loan possibilities. Provide strong documentation of compensating factors and explanations. You'll get the loan you need. (For more on "possibility" analysis, see my book, *Yes! You Can Own the Home You Want,* also published by John Wiley & Sons, Inc.)

CHAPTER 8

Become a Satisfied Homeowner

You're about to enter the wealth-building and personally satisfying experience of home ownership. But hold back a moment longer. Before you commit, let's run through a final check of several more issues. Are you confident this is the right home for you? Or are you being unduly influenced by others? Do your advisors really understand your priorities and possibilities? Or are they pushing you toward decisions based upon their own interests and biases?

Review the property's condition and the inspection report. Have you reasonably protected yourself against after-closing surprises and unanticipated expenses? Have the real estate agents and mortgage loan rep secured all agreements, documents, and verifications that are necessary to effect a smooth closing?

In this chapter we look at some of the common mistakes that homebuyers make as they move into the final stages of home buying and the early stages of home ownership. Attend to these details that others often overlook and you can count on a home-buying experience that will reward you for years to come.

MISTAKE # **94**

Our friends told us we were getting a great deal.

LESSON: *Critically evaluate the advice of friends, relatives, real estate agents, and attorneys.*

After finding the home he wanted to own, Bruce Carver enlisted several of his friends to take a look at the house he had selected. "This house is great," they told him. "You're really getting a good buy." Of course these words of encouragement were exactly what Bruce wanted to hear. Bruce wasn't actually seeking an honest opinion. More than anything, he wanted support for a decision he had already made.

Bruce had fallen in love with the home's rear deck and canyon views. He didn't want to hear about the small size of the home's bedrooms, its lack of closet and storage space, or the home's needed repairs, which included an aging and leaky roof. Sensing Bruce's enthusiasm for the house, his friends avoided giving him the advice he really needed. Nevertheless, Bruce used the opinions they did offer to calm anxieties that lurked in the back of his mind about the home's problems.

Bruce bought the house, but high costs of repairs and cramped living conditions soon dampened his enchantment with his deck and canyon views. Bruce admitted that he believed he had made a mistake. Along with being captivated by the home's desirable features, Bruce had misinterpreted and misused the advice he had sought.

Naturally, like Bruce, when you buy a home you'll turn to advice from friends, relatives, your real estate agent, and maybe a lawyer. But before you interpret and rely on this advice, answer these questions:

Advice or Approval?

Do you really want critical counsel? Or do you want someone who simply agrees with you? There's an old saying among consultants and research analysts that most clients want to use advice like a drunk uses a lamppost—for support, not for illumination. If support is what you really want, your friends will probably oblige. But if that's the case, make sure you recognize such advice for what it is.

Knowledge or Ignorance?

Do the people you're asking for advice really have the information, experience, and expertise necessary to tell you what you need to know? Unless your friends or relatives have recently been shopping for a home in the same neighborhood where you've been looking, they probably can't tell you whether you're getting a good buy. If your lawyer sister hasn't seen a real estate contract since her Real Property I course in law school, chances are she's not someone who should review your home purchase agreement.

You may be working with one of the best real estate agents in the state. But if your home tour takes you into neighborhoods or communities where your agent can't find her way without constantly studying a map, it's probably time to bring in another agent who's more familiar with the area. Whether friend, relative, lawyer, or sales agent, just because someone is willing to offer an opinion doesn't mean he or she actually knows enough to give you the advice you need.

Your Preferences or Theirs?

Do your advisors really understand your needs and goals? Or are they applying their own preferences or standards? Here's an area where nearly everyone could do better. Often when we ask for advice, we don't really explain our needs, goals, or the most important things we're trying to achieve. Sometimes we don't even know ourselves. On the other hand, when we offer counsel, it's just as likely we will shade our advice toward our own biases, preferences, and standards. We won't (or can't) see the other person's perspective.

If you ask your brother to tell you what he thinks of that darling three-bedroom ranch in Windsor Heights, he could answer, "What? That dump? I wouldn't even think about living in that house or neighborhood." Now, has your brother answered according to your needs? Or does he have some personal bias against ranch-style homes or Windsor Heights? What if your agent tells you Troy Woods is not a good area? Should you accept that advice at face value? Or should you question why

the agent holds that view? Maybe the agent doesn't like Troy Woods because he doesn't think much of its schools. But if you don't have kids or
you're planning to send your kids to a private school, the reasons for
your agent's objections might even work to your advantage. Maybe with
less attractive schools, homes in Troy Woods provide more house for the
money. Rather than being helpful, your agent's (or brother's) advice
could actually work against your most important needs.

If people fail to understand what you want, or if they can't put aside
their own biases, don't pay much attention to their advice.

Conflict of Interests?

Do your advisors' interests conflict with your own? Whenever you're interpreting or relying on the advice of other people, keep in mind that their
interests may conflict with yours. Some unethical real estate agents may
try to talk you into a house (or financing) that doesn't meet your needs just
so they can gain a commission. Your parents may talk against an outlying
neighborhood because they'd rather see you live closer to them. Your
friends could advise you not to buy a home because they're jealous; or
maybe they think that if you move you will drift apart as friends.

Everyone has their own reasons for the advice they offer. They may
want to help you make a better decision. But they may have their own
interests to promote, too. So, when someone says, "This is what you
ought to do," take a moment to reflect on this advice. Before accepting
it at face value, think through the actual concern, knowledge, facts, care,
experience, and motives that lie behind the advice.

MISTAKE # **95**

The lawyer created more problems than he solved.

LESSON: *Keep the lawyer(s) under control.*

"Although I wasn't in the market to buy a house," says Ramon Williams,
"that's exactly what I did. One day I happened to drive by a for-sale-by-

owner open house. Just out of curiosity, I decided to go in and take a look. Sure enough, by the end of the afternoon the owners and I had reached an agreement. But rather than proceed on our own—or bring in a real estate agent—we thought it best to consult a lawyer. Unfortunately, the lawyer we went to created more problems than he solved.

Lawyer Wins, Clients Lose

"First off, instead of simply formalizing our agreement, the lawyer sided with the seller. It turned out they had both played football (in different years) at the same Dallas high school. For at least the first hour of our two-hour office conference, the seller and the lawyer talked Texas football.

"After that, the lawyer offered his unsolicited opinion that the seller was not getting a good price for his home, and then tried to rewrite other terms where we had already reached an agreement. By the time the conference ended, the cordial relations the seller and I had originally developed were quickly moving toward hostility. The seller wanted to revise, I wanted to carry through our original intent.

"The point was that we had a written and signed agreement. We didn't go to the lawyer for advice about what either of us should have done. We just wanted him to make sure the language we used in our agreement actually meant what we had wanted it to mean.

"Eventually, our basic agreement held with just a couple of more concessions on my part. Then the seller and I left the meeting by instructing the lawyer to redraft our final agreement in legalese. The contract came back okay, but our surprise came when we got the bill of $1,050. Seven hours of billing at $150 an hour, including the hour wasted on talk of Texas football. At least at this point the seller and I agreed. The bill was outrageous."

Ramon Williams's bad experience with the lawyer who handled his home-buying transaction is not unusual. As evidenced by the proliferation of lawyer jokes, record numbers of complaints to bar associations, and increasing attorney malpractice cases, consumer satisfaction with lawyers has reached an all-time low. In fact, former Chief Justice of the United States Warren Burger has even charged that half of the lawyers practicing before the U.S. Supreme Court are incompetent.

Lawyer Abuses

If you do choose to bring a lawyer into your home-buying transaction, guard against three widespread problems: overbilling, an underqualified lawyer, and gratuitous advice.

When discussing fees with a lawyer, look beyond the hourly rate. Get a firm estimate of the total bill. In my dealings with lawyers, I've found that some bill eight hours for the same work another lawyer could perform in two. I once hired a lawyer to answer a question. He billed for 12 hours of research and still couldn't adequately answer the question. When I consulted another attorney, I got a sensible answer in less than 30 minutes—no research required.

Also make sure your lawyer routinely handles the type of problems you're presenting. Divorce lawyers may know next to nothing about real estate contracts, escrow, and title insurance. Verify the lawyer's *successful* experience in home-buying transactions.

Beware of gratuitous advice. Many lawyers love to talk and give their opinions regardless of whether they know what they are talking about. I was once in a mortgage closing where in response to a buyer's question the attorney began to explain the mortgage interest figures on the settlement sheet. But rather than admit he didn't know how to calculate mortgage interest, the lawyer tried to bluff his way through. On other occasions, I've listened to lawyers give (unsolicited and incorrect) advice about sales prices, investment returns, zoning ordinances, neighborhood desirability, and a myriad of other things.

Several years back, a real estate lawyer hired me to perform a market analysis for some land he had bought recently on which he planned to build a small shopping center. To his dismay the lawyer soon learned that the steep grade of the site would have made a shopping center development prohibitively expensive. In this case, the lawyer had "advised" himself about commercial site selection; that advice cost him over $200,000.

Lawyers should understand the area of the law where you need help. But they also should know what they do not know. Further, they should not give advice that extends beyond their own experience and expertise. Just as important, don't make the mistake of asking lawyers for opinions in areas outside their competence and experience. Even lawyers with the best intentions have trouble resisting that temptation.

Finally, realize that nationwide, far more trouble-free home-buying transactions take place without lawyers than with them. In fact, in Maryland so many homebuyers were successfully buying homes without lawyer involvement that the lawyers lobbied for a law that would *force* buyers to hire lawyers.

MISTAKE # **96**

We shouldn't have taken escrow allowances for repairs.

LESSON: *When you buy a home that needs extensive repairs, get a substantial price discount.*

When you're looking at a home that needs work, you can get the sellers to credit you with an escrow allowance; bargain for a price discount; or maybe go for a combination escrow allowance and price discount. However, do not accept an escrow allowance or price discount that exactly matches the estimated costs of repairs. You want substantially more. The chance for underestimates is just too great.

Repairs Often Exceed Estimates

"We knew the house needed work when we bought it," says Kay Schall. "So we got an estimate for repairs before we placed a contract on the home. In total, everything came to around $13,000. To pay for these repairs, we wrote a clause into our offer where the sellers would credit us $13,000 at closing. Unfortunately, this escrow allowance didn't come close to covering the repairs we've had to make. So far we've spent $26,136, with the end still not in sight. We now know what it means to own a 'money pit.'"

Kay and her husband made a common mistake. When they accepted an escrow allowance for the estimated cost of repairs, they assumed that the repairs could actually be completed for the amount of the estimate. For small repairs, the risk of underestimating may not be too great. But for more extensive work, no contractor can really tell for sure how much the repairs will cost. Here are some of the unexpected problems the Schalls ran up against:

- Previous owners of the house had remodeled it without building permits or city inspections. As a result, before permits could be issued for the new work, the old work had to be inspected. That meant opening up walls so the inspector could see whether the earlier construction had been performed according to code. It hadn't. Therefore, the old remodeling had to be redone.

- The fireplace in the living room, too, had to be completely rebuilt because it had wood instead of metal framing. A second fireplace in the dining room had to be sealed up permanently because of problems with the chimney.

- A wood patio deck had to be torn out because it was built without proper termite barriers between it and the ground.

- A tiled exterior entrance to the home had to be jackhammered to oblivion and then rebuilt with poured concrete with steps of a new height and width to comply with the building code.

- Not only did the whole roof need to be reshingled, much of the wood had to be replaced, and in an area above the old remodeling, the roof had to be raised a foot.

The Capuanos

When Katie and Joe Capuano bought their rundown clapboard home in Stony Brook, Long Island, they figured the age of the house at 60 years and believed they could restore it with a modest amount of work—much of which Joe could do himself. But once the Capuanos got into the restoration project, it became clear that far more work would be necessary than they had anticipated. "Once I started pulling things out, I realized the house was at least 100 years old," says Joe.

By the time they've completed their "modest" restoration, Joe and Katie will have spent more than $55,000 to gut the interior of their house, replace a crumbling foundation and wall beams, add on an extension, and install new siding. "When it's done," says Katie, "it will be everything we could have wanted."

The Capuanos seem to be taking their unexpected expenses with a bit more aplomb than the Schalls. But the experiences of the Schalls and the Capuanos both teach the same lesson: Unless you want to accept the risk of repairs and restoration costs that exceed your estimates, don't accept a dollar-for-dollar escrow allowance or price discount. Instead, build into your figures a large reserve for error—or require the sellers to make the necessary repairs and improvements before you close your purchase.

MISTAKE # **97**

We accepted an escrow allowance of $6,000 for termite damage. Our repairs cost $18,347.

LESSON: *All termite inspections are not created equally.*

Before you become a homeowner, most mortgage lenders will require you or the sellers to provide a termite clearance for the house. Generally, a licensed termite inspector comes out, looks around the house with a flashlight, and, at critical points, pokes into the wood with a knife or screwdriver. If no evidence of termites is found, the inspector issues a clearance certificate and sends it to the escrow agent. But if the inspector finds evidence of infestations, he will estimate the cost of treatment and repairs.

Typically, when treatment and repairs are necessary, the sellers either pay for the work or give you an escrow allowance. Which is better? Here you face the same kind of situation as with other kinds of repairs. If the sellers remedy the problem, your risk is reduced. On the other hand, if you accept an escrow credit and can get the work done for a lesser amount, you can come out ahead. The question is, do you want to take a chance?

Ian and Magenta Cordall took a chance and lost. They accepted a $6,000 escrow allowance for termite damage and ended up paying $18,347 for treatment and repairs. "We had no idea," says Ian, "that the inspector's estimates weren't guaranteed. By the time our work was finished, the contractor had to tear out the den and completely rebuild it."

This type of unpleasant surprise occurs because all termite inspections aren't created equal, and even the best ones can miss serious damage.

Termite Inspectors Only Sample

Primarily, a termite inspection is a sampling process. The inspector pokes here and there hoping to spot any problems that might exist. But there's always the possibility the inspector won't hit the right spot, or the damage may be hidden and relatively inaccessible. Either way, actual damage could exceed reported damage. (It's even possible for an infested house to receive a clean bill of health.)

How do you protect yourself?

1. Tag along with the inspector as he tours the house. Did he get under the house and poke around in the crawl space? How about the attic? The foundation? Did he especially check areas where wood (treated or untreated) comes in contact with the ground? How thoroughly has the inspector actually "sampled" the home for termites?

2. Ask the inspector questions. Try to learn the areas of the house that are most vulnerable to infestation. Find out whether other homes in the neighborhood have had a termite problem. See if he discovers any signs that the house has been treated previously. If so, how extensive was the previous damage? Were there any recurrences?

3. If the inspection and treatment results in a warranty, what does it cover? Will it pay for all necessary repairs? Or does it only require the company to re-treat the home with another dose of pesticides?

4. If the company locates infestation and estimates repairs, who bears the risk for underestimates? Is the company merely issuing a good-faith estimate? In that case—unless the firm has been negligent in its inspection—you must pay the repairs if additional damage is found after work begins. Some exterminators, though, guarantee their estimates. When they miss problems, they bear the costs to correct them.

Avoid simply accepting a termite inspection, clearance report, or damage estimate at face value. With some, you can sleep easy knowing you've covered (or limited) your exposure to loss. With others, you just have to hope those pesky little critters have satisfied their appetites somewhere else. Because if they haven't, you'll be the one who's picking up their dinner check.

MISTAKE # **98**

We thought the roof warranty was good for 20 years.

LESSON: Determine exactly what types and amounts of repairs your warranties cover.

"When we bought our house," says Kip Phillips, "the sellers showed us their receipts for a new roof they'd put on four years ago. Plus, they pulled out this engraved certificate that stated in bold print: 20-Year Warranty. With the receipts and the warranty, we didn't think we would have to worry about paying for roof repairs for a long time to come.

"But just 18 months later, the roof started leaking. We learned the shingles were cracking and the entire roof would have to be replaced at a cost of $3,400. At that point, we were really glad we had that 20-year warranty, which the owner had transferred to us.

"So, the next thing we did was to contact the shingle manufacturer's local distributor. 'No problem,' he told us, 'we'll send someone out right away to process your claim.' Faithful to his word, several days later a company representative came out to the house. After inspecting the roof, he agreed the shingles needed to be replaced. He then proceeded to write us a check for $600.

Read the Fine Print

" 'Six hundred dollars!' we said. 'Replacing that roof is going to cost $3,400. How do you expect us to accept a meager $600?'

" 'Because that's the amount the warranty provides,' he said.

" 'What do you mean?' I asked. 'We've got a 20-year warranty.'

" 'True,' he said, but then he pointed to the fine print.

"That's when I knew he might as well have said 'Gotcha.' The fine print stated the company was not liable for the costs of taking off the old roof, installing the new roof, or paying for adhesives, wood repair, or any other labor or materials. The warranty covered only the prorated cost of the shingles over a 20-year expected life. In other words, our 20-year roof warranty amounted to nothing more than reimbursement for 70 percent (14/20) of the price of the shingles. To complete the job, we were still going to be out-of-pocket $2,800."

From this experience, Kip Phillips learned an important (and expensive) lesson: Don't count on warranties to reimburse you for repairs or replacements unless you've first verified exactly what types of repairs and amounts of protection the warranty offers. Real estate broker Carl Steinmetz says his realty firm stopped dealing in home warranties because "we just had too many cases in which the buyers were discontented with the policy. They always thought it should have covered something, but then it didn't."

Of course, not everyone agrees with Carl. California Department of Insurance spokesman John Fogg reports his agency gets fewer complaints about home warranty policies than any other type of insurance. And the real estate brokerage firm Joan M. Sobeck, Inc., thinks so highly of warranties that some of its agents buy the policies as a service to their sellers and buyers. Another broker says, "First-time buyers often don't know much about fixing up a home. . . . [As a result] those folks are really drawn to the protection of a warranty."

How to Analyze a Warranty

So, what's the bottom line on home warranties? Read the fine print and look for answers to these questions:

- Does the warranty cover labor, materials, and parts? Or is it limited to certain named items (e.g., roof shingles, furnace combustion chamber, air conditioner compressor)?

- Will you receive full reimbursement? Or will payments be prorated?

- Regardless of coverage, will you be required to pay for service calls? Some warranties charge homeowners anywhere from $50 to $200 each time a repairman is called out to the house.

- If you're buying an existing home with a warranty, ask what items are excluded from coverage (e.g., roof, foundation, air conditioner, pool equipment, well pump, sprinkler system, plumbing, wiring).

- How long will the warranty last? Most overall warranties with existing homes end after one year. New home warranties may cover major structural items for 10 years but limit coverage on appliances, furnace, and air conditioner to just one year. (Of course, in some instances the manufacturers of these items separately warrant their quality and performance. You'll need to check these separate warranties to determine how you're protected.)

- Does the warranty cover preexisting conditions? If when you buy your home the pipes are rusty or the furnace is clunking and clanging, the warranty may exempt these items from coverage. Many (but not all) warranties only guard against unexpected breakdowns or malfunctions—not sure things. So don't count on a warranty to substitute for a thorough inspection of your home by a professional inspector.

- What is the warranty company's track record for honoring claims? Does it run you through a maze of paperwork and proofs? Or does it enjoy a reputation for fair settlements?

• Is the warranty company in good financial shape? In the past some homebuyers have lost out on collecting for their claims because the warranty company disappeared or went bankrupt. If you're buying a new home, check to see who stands behind the warranty. Some builders warrant their own work. Others provide protection through independent warranty companies.

Although you certainly want your builder to stand behind his or her work, in most cases it's better to receive your new home warranty from a financially strong insurer. Too many builders run into tough financial trouble when housing markets head toward the low point of their up-and-down cycle.

Also, don't be fooled when builders tell you they've been in business for 25 years. To gauge financial stability, the real question is how long has their present company been in business. Some builders open a company, run it into bankruptcy, and then start another one. Over a period of 20 or 30 years, builders like these may open and close six or eight different firms. Each time they bankrupt a company, they leave their previous homebuyers without a way to collect the claims they may have for defects in their homes.

During the past 10 years, warranty programs have grown enormously. And in general, homebuyers, sellers, and builders have all benefited from this trend. But as with all types of insurance, don't assume that a warranty will cover your losses. To prevent mistakes, read the fine print.

MISTAKE # **99**

Our homeowners' insurance didn't cover our losses.

LESSON: *Don't take your homeowners' insurance for granted. Closely check your coverages.*

When fire swept through the Oakland-Berkeley, California, hills, Ron and Betty Bugaj lost their $500,000 home and all their personal belongings. The Bugajes were not alone. In one of the worst residential firestorms in U.S. history, more than 3,300 other homeowners suffered total losses. As tragic as the fire was, though, for many of these families their troubles were just beginning. "The damage we really suffered," said Betty, "was in our negotiations with the insurance company."

Like more than 1,000 other firestorm victims, the Bugajes learned after the fire that their homeowners' insurance policy would pay far less than they expected. To get the amounts they thought they were entitled to, the Bugajes wrangled back and forth with their insurance company for over 10 months. Adding to their hassle was the $75,000 in lawyer bills and consulting fees their negotiations with the insurance company cost them.

In the end, the Bugajes and most of the other firestorm victims did settle with their insurers—but only after the California Department of Insurance, various consumer advocacy groups, and widespread unfavorable publicity pressured the insurance companies to give in. Although to some extent several insurers had tried to lowball their policyholders, most of the settlement problems resulted because homeowners had not purchased the insurance coverage they actually needed (or thought they had).

Review Your Specific Coverages

The important lesson of the Oakland-Berkeley hills firestorm was not that most insurance companies are bad guys. Rather, it's that far too many homeowners don't actually understand their insurance coverages. They just buy a homeowners' policy and assume (incorrectly) they have the protection they need. This is a big mistake you should avoid.

To make sure your policy adequately protects your home and belongings, ask your insurance agent or check your policy to find the answers to these questions:

What Perils Are Covered?

In insurance language, a peril is a cause of loss. No insurance policy covers every type of loss. Some policies exclude hurricanes, floods, mudslides, sink holes, earthquakes, and riots. Sometimes freezing pipes and roof collapse due to a buildup of snow and ice are not covered. Apart from war and civil rebellion, though, you can usually buy an endorsement or rider to cover perils that basic policies don't insure.

What Property Is Covered?

With tens of millions of Americans now working in their homes, it's important to realize some of your business property or business inventories may not be covered under your homeowners' policy. Nor are your pets, golf cart, or snowmobile. Similarly, if you own any expensive antiques, jewelry, furs, artwork, or a collection of stamps, coins, or baseball cards, you'll want to find out whether they're covered, and, if so, for how much. More than likely, you'll have to pay extra to secure adequate protection. If you're a writer, store an extra copy of the manuscript you're working on with friends or in a safe deposit box. (Dozens of writers in the Oakland-Berkeley fire lost computer disks and partially completed books and articles.) Your homeowners' policy won't pay for the value of your past work, or even the market value of a finished manuscript.

Also, if you live in a co-op, condo, or townhouse, make sure you clearly determine the property covered by the homeowners' association coverages, and the property coverages that remain your responsibility. For example, if a water pipe bursts within a wall and causes water and plumbing damages, who pays for what? Check your association rules and regulations.

How Much Will the Company Pay?

This issue causes the most problems between homeowners and their insurance companies. Unfortunately, there's lots of room here for confusion and ambiguity.

First, let's consider your house. Generally, you can choose either replacement cost coverage or actual cash value coverage. With a replacement cost policy, your insurer agrees to pay you enough to repair or replace your house at today's prices. Under actual cash value coverage, the company subtracts a figure for depreciation from the costs of replacement. Naturally, it's better to have replacement cost coverage. Otherwise, the older your house and the greater its wear and tear, the less you can collect.

However, regardless of which type of coverage you select, here are some questions where misunderstandings frequently occur (as they did in the Oakland-Berkeley fire):

- How much will you be able to collect if you choose not to rebuild?

- What happens if government regulations prevent repairs or rebuilding? (For example, some homes now located in coastal areas, floodplains, wetlands, or hillsides could not be rebuilt because of new safety or environmental regulations.)

- What if new government regulations (safety codes, environmental laws, building regulations) significantly increase the costs to reconstruct (replace) your existing home? In the Oakland fire, many destroyed homes were 30 to 70 years old. Thus, they couldn't be rebuilt as they previously had been built. Extra regulations added as much as $50,000 or more to their rebuilding costs. Yet, homeowners' policies often exclude these types of costs because they're not really "replacement" costs. This fact came as a big surprise to many homeowners when they learned that to rebuild they were going to have to come up with substantial amounts of cash from their own pockets. (A *guaranteed* replacement cost policy is one way to meet this problem.)

- How much will your policy pay for your home's unique architectural or historical value? (Usually nothing unless you've requested special coverages.)

- If your insurer drags its feet while settling your claim, are you entitled to interest payments on the proceeds when the company finally does pay?

- How much are your policy limits? Regardless of how much it costs to replace your home, the company typically won't pay any more than your policy limits. So, make sure you periodically increase the limits of your policy to keep up with rising costs of construction.

- If you choose an actual cash value policy, how will your insurance company calculate depreciation?

—— 237 ——

Discuss all these questions with your insurance agent before you suffer a loss. After a loss occurs is the wrong time to try to sort out shortfalls in your coverage.

Also give due attention to your household furniture and personal belongings. To collect as much as possible for the contents of your home, you should choose guaranteed replacement cost coverage. But keep a list and photographic (or video) inventory of your personal property. Under the terms of your policy, you'll be required to prove your loss. Photos or videos stored in a safe place (away from your home, of course) can serve as good proof of what you owned. Besides, without a detailed inventory of your possessions, chances are you'll forget or overlook a lot of things that you're entitled to collect for.

What Liability Protection?

In addition to protecting your home and its contents, your homeowners' policy will protect your against liability for personal injuries. Typically, this provides "slip and fall" coverage where someone is injured on your property. It may also cover you for accidents such as running into someone while on your bicycle or hitting someone with a golf ball with your mean slice.

If you live in a condominium, co-op, townhouse, or subdivision development where you're a member of a homeowners' association, check to see what type of liability coverage the association carries. In some states, you can be held personally liable (along with other homeowners) when someone is negligently injured on the common areas of the property (swimming pool, bike trails, tennis courts, clubhouse, hallways).

According to attorney Benny Kass, a specialist in condominium and homeowners' association law, too many community associations "are pitifully underinsured and represent a significant risk to association members."

How Much Are the Premiums?

Apart from fully understanding your insurance coverages, before you offer to buy a home, determine how much adequate insurance protection will cost you. During the past 10 years, property insurance companies and homeowners have suffered billions of dollars in losses (Hurricane

Andrew, the Oakland-Berkeley firestorm, the Los Angeles riots, the Midwest floods, the Los Angeles-Malibu fires). As a result, some companies have raised their premiums and made insurance much more difficult to obtain in some areas with high loss potential.

In Florida after Hurricane Andrew, for example, many major insurance companies canceled tens of thousands of homeowner policies, and several insurers tried to withdraw completely from writing policies in hurricane areas. In California, many insurers have eliminated or severely limited the coverages they offer for earthquake losses. At present, no one can predict how all these troubles will work themselves out. But for these and other reasons, it does mean that you will need to check your coverages and your premiums very closely. You can't assume that you'll be able to get the coverages you need at a price you can afford.

MISTAKE # **100**

After we bought our house, the property taxes jumped by $1,200 and we got hit with a $600 special assessment for new sidewalks.

LESSON: *Prior to buying, find out how much you must pay for property taxes.*

When Stan and Beth Hill bought their home, the information sheet their Realtor gave them listed property taxes for the most recent year at $1,700. Shortly after the Hills bought, however, their taxes shot up to $2,900. In addition, the city notified Stan and Beth that it was installing new sidewalks throughout their neighborhood. Their share of these costs would total $600, to be added to the Hills' tax bill for the coming year.

Past Taxes Don't Equal Future Taxes

In looking to the past rather than the future, Stan and Beth made a common mistake. They assumed their property taxes would cost about the same as the sellers had been paying. But in many cities and counties throughout the United States, you can't make that assumption.

Under the laws in most states, county assessors periodically estimate a home's value for the purpose of levying property taxes. The period for reassessment, though, might be annual, quadrennial, whenever the assessor's office gets around to it, or sometimes when a property is sold and a new deed (and sales price) is recorded in the county records. In addition, in many areas homeowners are entitled to various exemptions (homestead, mortgage, senior citizen). So even when two homes are assessed at the same value and the valuations are current, the property taxes can vary greatly.

In Stan and Beth's case, their property tax surprise arose for two reasons. First, the home had not been reassessed for four years, and during that period values in the neighborhood had increased about 35 percent. Second, seven years earlier the sellers had built on a new 800-square-foot master bedroom suite that enhanced the home's value but had not been noticed by the tax assessor.

As a result, on the books at the courthouse, the home carried an assessed value of only $106,300. But when the Hills' purchase price of $179,000 came through the records office, it triggered an immediate reassessment of the home's current market value. The property taxes on the Hills' home went up by over 60 percent.

Learn How Property Taxes Are Calculated

To prevent this type of surprise, learn the ins and outs of the property tax system in your area. If the home you're planning to buy is underassessed, or if the sellers qualify for more exemptions than you are entitled to, you might see a steep rise in your property tax bill.

On the other hand, by learning the ins and outs of property taxes, you might also discover an overassessment. In recent years some homes in the Northeast, California, Florida, Oklahoma, Texas, Arizona, and several other states have sold for less than their peak prices of earlier years. So their current market values may have fallen below their assessed value. When that's the case, you can expect to see your property taxes fall.

Here are some of the property tax questions you should discuss with your real estate agent or the tax assessors office:

- What is the current market value of the home you're buying?

- What is the current assessed value of the home? (In some tax juris-dictions, the assessed value is stated as a percentage of the home's market value. Therefore, you should look at both the tax assessor's appraised value and the assessed value before you conclude a home is underassessed.)

- After you buy, can you expect the *assessed* value of the home to in-crease, decrease, or remain about the same?

- Are you entitled to any exemptions that can reduce your property tax bill?

- What is the local millage rate? (One mill equals a thousandth of a dollar. A millage rate of say, 17, would mean a property tax of $17 for every $1,000 of assessed value.)

- Will any improvements you plan to make to the home increase its assessed value? (Some types of improvements will add signifi-cantly to your assessed value—if the tax assessor learns about them. Built-ins, room additions, a swimming pool, or wall-to-wall carpeting, for example, typically increase a home's assessed value. A new roof, furnace, or hot water heater may not. Every tax asses-sor's office has its own way of operating. You'll have to check for the specifics as they may apply to the home you buy.)

- What amount of taxes can you expect to pay? (To calculate this fig-ure, you need to multiply the millage rate expressed as a decimal by the home's expected assessed value. Seventeen mills, for exam-ple, converts to .017. With an assessed value of $100,000, your property taxes would run $1,700 a year.)

Special Assessments

Besides property taxes, from time to time local governments may levy special assessments. These charges usually pay for new sidewalks, sewers, sewage disposal plants, street widenings, parks, or other types of "infrastructure." In most cases special assessments will range between $300 and $1,000. But on occasion they can go as high as $2,000 or $3,000, or even more.

Since special assessments can upset a budget, find out whether any asessements are planned for your neighborhood. Also, learn of proposed "infrastructure" changes before you buy. Better parks may add to your home's value. But widening the street through your neighborhood or in front of your home could bring more traffic and take away from the value of your home.

MISTAKE # **101**

We didn't know title insurance companies offered discount policies.

LESSON: *Before you set up escrow, ask whether the sellers have a title policy that can be transferred to you and your lender. It could save you money.*

One of the most important steps in your home-buying process will be the title search. Before you and your lender release funds to the sellers, a title company (or lawyer) will verify that they actually own the property and that any outstanding liens or claims against the home will be taken care of prior to closing.

Years ago most title searches were performed by lawyers, who would then offer an opinion as to whether title to the home was marketable ("free and clear"). Although still common in some areas of the country, most lenders and homebuyers today no longer use lawyers to assure title. Instead, they wisely buy a title insurance policy.

Obtain Title Insurance

When a lawyer makes a mistake or otherwise misses a defect in the home's title, the only way you can make him or her pay for your losses is to hire another lawyer to sue the first one. That's an expensive, time-consuming, and uncertain proposition. With title insurance, the insurance company agrees to pay the legal expenses necessary to defend the title to your home against other claims. If unsuccessful in its defense, the company will pay for covered losses.

Of course, like all insurers, title companies write their policies with various exceptions and limitations. For example, if your next-door neighbor's garage sits a foot onto your side of the property line at the time you bought your home, the insurer may exclude that known problem from its coverage. Also, basic title policies cover only the lender. Adding your name to the policy may cost slightly more.

In general, title insurance has proved to be a wise purchase for most homebuyers. It dramatically reduces the possibility that you'll be drawn into a long, drawn-out legal battle when some ex-husband of a long-ago owner shows up and claims that his ex-wife forged his name to the deed when she sold the house as part of their divorce settlement. For most homebuyers, it is a mistake not to buy title insurance.

Secure an Owner's Endorsement

Once a decision to buy is made, though, other mistakes are also common. The first is that many homebuyers don't realize title companies offer two types of coverages: lender's policies and owner's policies. As mentioned earlier, to protect your equity in the property, you (or the sellers) may need to pay an additional premium. Plus, inquire whether you can obtain increasing amounts of protection as your home appreciates in value. Title policies last for as long as you own your home, but most policies limit the amount of coverage to your home's original purchase price.

Also, many homebuyers do not know they should find out whether the sellers of the home have a title policy that can be updated and transferred to them. If your sellers do have title coverage, by sticking with the same company you might save several hundred dollars. If you can't save money that way, you should compare insurance premiums among title companies. In some states these premiums are set by law, so you won't find any differences among companies. But many states encourage competition, and shopping around can pay off.

Stay on Schedule

Title problems on the way to closing have become common. With the huge volume of home mortgages being traded among lenders in the secondary market like baseball cards, the paper trail for existing liens and previous mortgage satisfactions sometimes can prove cumbersome to follow. Therefore, title checks should proceed as soon as escrow is set up.

On occasion, loan officers or loan processors busy themselves with credit reports, document verifications, and appraisal and leave the title search and property survey to the last minute. When problems then crop up, closing has to be delayed, which disrupts moving plans for both buyers and sellers. Although most title defects and boundary disputes eventually get straightened out, doing so can take several weeks to several months. In general, good planning and timely processing of the paperwork can free you and the sellers from this type of troublesome situation. (Although real estate agents aren't responsible for escrow, top agents do monitor progress to keep the closing on schedule.)

MISTAKE # **102**

Our closing was like showdown at the Great Western Corral.

LESSON: *The best closing is a no-surprises closing.*

Most mortgage closings go smoothly. On occasion, though, failure to prepare or last-minute changes can create turmoil. "We felt it was a bad sign," says Wendy Kantor, "when the real estate agent telephoned us two days before closing and told us the sellers had decided to take the refrigerator and window air conditioners with them. However, these items were already included in our purchase price. So the agent said the sellers would give us a credit for their value and we could work out the details at closing.

"But at closing, the sellers only wanted to give us $500. That figure wasn't acceptable to us. We thought $1,000, maybe even $1,250 was closer to the mark. Besides that, we found a $600 mistake in the closing statement and another $1,300 in garbage fees that we hadn't expected. By the time that closing finally settled, it was like showdown at the Great Western Corral."

Get Everything Settled before Closing

I can empathize with Wendy because I once went through a mortgage closing disaster much like hers—only I was the seller. In my case, several days before closing my agent telephoned and said the buyers had come up short on cash and asked whether I would be willing to carry back $2,000 in seller financing. I said no. Since I was moving out of town, I didn't want to worry about collecting $2,000 from a distance of 1,200 miles. If the buyers didn't pay, I could end up spending more than $2,000 in lawyer's bills just to collect.

However, once we got into closing, the buyers proceeded as if I was going to help them with their financing. As I later learned, my agent had set us up. He figured that once we were sitting in closing—both of us with loaded moving vans—we would be forced to work out some kind of compromise. And that's what we did.

But from that experience, I learned the same lesson Wendy Kantor learned: Make sure all the details of the transaction are known and agreed upon by all parties prior to closing. In fact, to avoid these kinds of last-minute showdowns, many mortgage loans and home-buying transactions are closed through escrow without buyers, sellers, agents, lender, and attorneys all meeting together around a conference table. I've been involved in both types of closings and definitely favor the escrow approach.

Check the Figures and Arithmetic

Nevertheless, even with in absentia escrow closings, you still must carefully check the figures on your closing statement to make sure they're totaled correctly and that the lender hasn't thrown in some "garbage fees" that were not properly disclosed to you in the lender's good-faith Real Estate Settlement and Procedures Act (RESPA) disclosure statement. Plus, stay alert for last-minute tactics to renegotiate amounts in the sellers' favor. Unethical sellers (and buyers) or their lawyers use this technique to force concessions they otherwise couldn't get. Again, full preparation and agreement prior to closing can help prevent this gambit.

MISTAKE # **103**

We couldn't believe the way the sellers left the house for us.

LESSON: *Arrange a final walk-through and inspection of the house just prior to settlement—ideally, after the sellers have moved out.*

"We couldn't believe the mess," recalls Derek Chapman. "We walked into the house the day after settlement and discovered the sellers had left piled-up boxes of trash throughout the house; the inside of the oven looked like a grease pit; the carpeting and floors were all tracked up with mud (evidently from their movers); and the dining room chandelier was missing. We also learned the den did not have hardwood floors as we thought.

"When we first looked at the house," Derek continued, "the sellers had a large area rug in the den so all we saw was the hardwood floors around the edge of the room. Naturally, we assumed the floor under the rug was also finished hardwood. But it wasn't. That part of the floor was unfinished pine. I guess we should have pulled back the rug just to make sure. But it really wasn't anything I had even seen before—or would have imagined."

Verify You're Getting What You're Paying For

Derek Chapman's experience teaches several lessons. First, don't assume. When you're inspecting a house, get nosy. Pull back rugs, open the cabinets, drawers, and the oven door. Look behind pictures or other wall hangings. Maybe even look under the furniture. It's better to discover flaws, stains, cracks, or unfinished floors before you make your offer rather than after.

Second, if at all possible, schedule settlement after the sellers have moved out. Then, prior to closing, do a final walk-through and inspection. Learn whether the sellers have left the home in satisfactory condition and confirm that they have not taken any personal property, appliances, or fixtures that were supposed to stay with the house. Inspecting a vacant house also gives you another chance to discover any defects that were previously hidden by the sellers' selective placement of furniture, area rugs, or wall hangings.

It's far easier to work out problems before the sellers have received their money than after they've deposited their settlement check. This is especially true when the sellers are moving out of town. Once the sellers are gone with their money, as a practical matter, you don't have much leverage. You might be able to sue, but that will nearly always cost you more in time, money, and misery, than you could ever hope to collect.

No Walk-Through? Here's What to Do

If you can't do a final walk-through before the settlement and after the sellers' move date, put a clause in your purchase offer whereby 10 percent (or so) of the sellers' sales proceeds are escrowed until you've had time to check out the house.

As another tactic, put a compulsory arbitration clause in your purchase agreement. With this kind of clause, you and the sellers use an arbitrator instead of a lawsuit to settle disputes. As you might expect, lawyers often advise against compulsory arbitration because it cuts down on their billings. From most buyers' perspective, though, saving on lawyer's bills and court costs stands as an advantage, not a disadvantage. Through arbitration, you also can settle your disputes much quicker than with a lawsuit. Arbitration may not be right for everyone, but it's definitely a method of resolving disagreements that you should consider.

Of course, your goal is to avoid lawsuits, arbitration, and disagreements with the sellers. And a final walk-through of the house still forms your best precaution.

New Homes: Get What You Think You're Paying For

When it comes to new homes, "don't make the mistake of assuming without asking," cautions William Young, who serves as director of consumer affairs for the National Association of Home Builders. Young's advice is aimed at buyers of new homes who expect their homes will include all the same amenities and custom features they've seen in their builder's models. But, as homeowner Paul Jakulski discovered, that's seldom the case.

Paul was conducting a preclosing walk-through of his newly built $185,000 split-level ranch home when he discovered that, unlike the model homes he was shown, his home lacked skylights, which were very important to him. "Without the skylights," Paul complained to the builder, "the house is way too dark."

The builder sympathized with Paul but pointed out that in their contract, skylights were optional and not included in the basic price. Since Paul hadn't specified he wanted them, the builder didn't put them in. To do so now that the home was virtually complete would cost twice as much as if they had been installed during the construction process.

Paul's mistake happens all too frequently. So if you plan to buy a new home that's not yet completed, check two things. First, don't assume those gold-plated bathroom fixtures or the marble fireplaces in the den and master bedroom are standard features. Read your purchase contract closely. Look for those cost-increasing words such as "optional" or "upgrades." With some houses, the upgrades and options are what transform the frog into Prince Charming.

Second, keep tabs on the construction process throughout the time your home is being built. Don't wait until final walk-through to discover the features you wanted aren't the features you're getting. Even when you've accurately listed your options and upgrades, builders and contractors can make mistakes.

In addition, if you decide on changes during construction (as you undoubtedly will), make them as early as you can and put them in writing. The earlier you specify changes, the less it will cost you. And memories are too fragile and building sites too hectic to rely on ad hoc talks with your builder, a sales representative, or a contractor. Whether buying a new home or an existing home definite understandings lead to a no-surprises home-buying experience.

MISTAKE # **104**

The sellers wouldn't move out of the house.

LESSON: *Put a penalty clause in your contract that will force the sellers to either move or pay.*

"A funny thing happened when first-time buyers Janie Brown and Paul Kelley showed up with a bottle of champagne at their new home in La Mesa. The sellers refused to move out." So reports Marsha Kay Seff in the *San Diego Tribune.* But according to Seff, Janie and Paul kept their spirits up, put the champagne back in the refrigerator, and after two weeks of legal process, proceeded to evict the sellers.

Surprising as it may seem, sellers (or tenants) who refuse to move after buyers have closed on a house are not all that uncommon. Take the case of Chauntann Reid. Pooling money contributed by several of her brothers and sisters, Chauntann decided to buy a bargain-priced home at a sheriff's foreclosure sale. After learning the ins and outs of how foreclosure auctions work, Chauntann submitted a successful bid for a two-story brick row house with garage. This lucky new homeowner, though, soon found out that buying a foreclosed home can be easier than moving into it.

Not only did the prior owner of the home challenge the validity of the foreclosure sale, she filed bankruptcy. Both these legal actions stalled any eviction proceedings that Chauntann could have used to take possession of the home.

Five months have now passed since she became a homeowner, but Chauntann and her three children are still living with her sister. With mounting legal fees, property tax bills, and sewer charges that Chauntann must pay to protect her ownership interest in the house, she can't afford to move out and rent her own apartment.

Be Wary of Tenant-Occupied Houses

Getting a tenant out of a house you've bought can present even more difficulties than removing reluctant sellers. As a matter of law, a tenant's lease takes priority over the possession rights of a new owner. If the tenant's rental agreement with the previous owners still has six months to run, then the tenants have the right to stay in the home for six more months (as long as they pay the rent, of course).

Even when the tenants can't turn to the security of a lease, they may seek the protection of various pro-tenant ordinances. Some cities require property owners to give tenants 60 or 90 days' notice, sometimes longer, before they can be forced to move. Similarly, if a tenant is pregnant or files bankruptcy, the law may offer special protection against eviction.

To guard against sellers who won't vacate, put a clause in your purchase contract that obligates the sellers to pay $100 a day (or whatever) for each day they stay beyond the date they're supposed to move out. That type of penalty generally encourages sellers to quickly find someplace else to live.

If you buy a foreclosed home with the "owners" still living there, be aware of the risks. You may be in for a long and expensive legal battle to evict them.

Likewise, should you plan to buy a home that's occupied by tenants, find out the terms of their rental agreement. (It may not make any difference whether the agreement is oral or written.) Then verify the tenants' intentions and planned moving date. Also, check with a lawyer or the local landlord-tenant regulatory agency to see if the tenants are protected against eviction by any laws or regulations. Whatever you do, don't assume that because you're the owner of the house you have rights of possession. Strange as it may seem, that's not the way the law necessarily operates.

New Home Completion Deadlines

If you buy a new home, you're not likely to face any problems with reluctant tenants. But new homebuyers sometimes experience another kind of problem that keeps them from moving into their home as scheduled. Construction of the home may not be completed. Delays in completing a home can result because of bad weather, shortages of building supplies, labor strikes, excessive change orders, or foot dragging by the builder, contractor, or subcontractor.

Although you should work cooperatively with your builder, you nevertheless might want to include a completion delay penalty in your purchase contract. I know of new homebuyers who have had to wait anywhere from two to six months beyond the completion date they were promised. With a delay that long, you should expect a penalty payment if the builder or his contractors are responsible.

More than likely, though, you'll have to negotiate tough to get it. As a rule, builders don't like penalty clauses. But if you're committing to move on a set date, your builder should commit to having a home ready for you to move into. If, within a reasonable grace period, your builder can't meet that commitment, the builder should pay the price of your inconvenience and alternative housing arrangements.

CHAPTER 9

The Biggest Mistakes of All

MISTAKE # **105**

We didn't buy. We were afraid of making a mistake.

LESSON: *Educate yourself. But don't let fear block your goal of home ownership.*

Kyle and Shannon Marks have been shopping for a home for more than two years. Instead of buying, though, they continue to rent. Everytime they get close to an offer, their worries overwhelm their ambition. "You can never be too cautious," says Shannon. "Our home will probably be the biggest investment we ever make. We certainly don't want to make a mistake."

Throughout this book I've emphasized the need to anticipate and prevent mistakes in home buying. As you now know, home buying has become more complex, and there are lots of ways to go wrong. Nevertheless, one of the biggest mistakes of all is to forever put off becoming a homeowner because you fear a mistake. Educate yourself. Shop the market. Get reliable advice from people more knowledgeable than yourself. Then make your commitment.

"You can sit on the fence forever. Eventually, though, the parade goes by," advises corporate relocation executive Keith Bisogno. Or, in the words of country singer Billy Ray Cyrus, "dreams move on if you wait too long."

What Fears Are Blocking You?

"We could afford the house, but the concerns are, what about the future?" says John Schultz. "What if the roof caves in? Oops, you're repairing the roof. Do you have the money to support that?" he adds.

Luis Arroyo feared paying too much. "At first I was wondering if the property was actually worth what I was paying," says Luis. "I kept asking the Realtor, 'Are you sure I'm not overpaying?'"

Terry Faber is worried about whether to buy a single-family house or a condo. She's not sure whether now is the time to buy, or whether a lender will approve her loan. "Although I've got a good job and savings," says Terry, "who knows what could happen tomorrow? Besides, some of those neighborhoods give me doubts."

Do any of these fears apply to you? Do you find yourself wanting to own then backing away? Well, you're not alone. "There are people," says Realtor Susan Swift, "who will run you around looking at 150 different homes and keep telling you, and themselves, they are looking for the perfect thing. But they are afraid in general."

The Risks of Renting

It is odd that so many renters worry about the risks of home ownership. Yet, they do not realize that continuing to rent presents even greater risks. For example: What if interest rates go up? That could cost you tens of thousands of dollars. What if home prices go up? That could cost you tens of thousands of dollars. What if rents go up? That could cost you thousands of dollars. And if you continue to rent, what about the tens (or even hundreds) of thousands of dollars you will lose in home equity?

The real amounts of these losses pale in comparison to the costs of repairing a roof, paying above market value, or choosing the "wrong" home or neighborhood.

"Imperfect" Home Ownership Beats "Perfect" Renting

Yes, exercise caution and good judgment. Yes, fully investigate your potential choices. But to get ahead you've got to move from the rational and cautious to a "leap of faith." In fact, an excessive fear of mistakes is itself irrational. As decision expert Theodore Rubin points out, no decision is perfect. A successful decision results not from the decision itself. It results from your commitment to make the decision work for you.

"If I compare my house to an imaginary dream house," writes Dr. Rubin, "my house comes off poorly and I destroy any chance of enjoying it. On the other hand, if I compare my house to houses that actually exist, it may come off well in terms of any real specifications a home requires to be comfortable. This is a true luxury, one I can appreciate in reality."

Fear of Commitment

Quite often, people who fear buying a home really fear making a decision and then committing to that decision. They say they're holding out for a home that has no flaws, no shortcomings, no drawbacks. But they know such a home doesn't exist.

If you find yourself falling into that trap, put yourself back on the right path by answering these questions:

1. Have you really thought through and ranked your priorities? Have you discovered your most important feelings and values? Are you permitting the opinions and views of others to conflict with or overshadow your own priorities? You can't "have it all," nor can you satisfy everybody. Keep focused on what's most important to you.

2. Are you comparing houses and neighborhoods with an open mind? Have you fully explored your options and possibilities? Have you educated yourself about alternative home finance plans, neighborhoods, types of homes, and price ranges?

   To exercise good judgment, view what the market offers. Put your creativity to work. Don't let wishful thinking push aside market realities. But also don't accept fewer choices than you actually have. Education and creative thinking can go a long way toward reducing your fear, anxiety, frustration, or disappointment.

3. Do you see possibilities and options as problems or opportunities? Too often, fear creates negative thinking. Within a context of neg-

ative thinking, it's easy to let yourself get bogged down by anxiety and hopelessness. You may think, "We'll never be able to find what we're looking for." Or maybe you'll tell yourself, "We can't find anything we like that we can afford."

Fear and negative thinking often go together and block your ability to create choices, options, or possibilities that could work for you. You may resign yourself to renting—or you could jump into a decision "just to get it over with."

On the other hand, when you frame your options in positive terms, you develop self-confidence. As you develop a here's-what-we-can-do attitude, you turn fear into eagerness and excitement. Where fear can generate avoidance and hold you back, a positive outlook can help you see opportunity and commit to action. You will not only make a good decision, through commitment you will make that decision work.

MISTAKE # **106**
___

We thought it over. We're going to continue renting.

LESSON: Continuing to rent will prove to be the greatest mistake of all.

Over the years, hundreds of newspaper and magazine articles have cautioned against buying a home. "These are uncertain times," the articles say. "Buying a home is no longer the sure thing it once was. A renter who invests wisely may well come out ahead of those who buy."

Poppycock. Apart from the fact naysaying "experts" have been wrong in their warnings against buying for more than 50 years (see Chapter 2), a review of four powerful reasons shows why home ownership beats renting:

1. Laws favor home ownership.
2. Home ownership produces the safest and surest opportunity to build personal wealth.

3. Over the course of a lifetime, Americans who own will spend far less money on housing than those who rent.
4. Home ownership yields transcendental benefits that can far outstrip the financial returns.

Laws Favor Homeownership

In Chapter 1 we talked about how the tax laws favor home ownership because you can deduct mortgage interest payments from your taxable income. This deduction—which is not available to renters—may save you thousands of dollars a year in income taxes. In addition, once you begin to build home equity, you will never again pay the high nondeductible interest expenses charged on credit cards, auto loans, and other consumer debt.

Why? Because as a homeowner you can obtain a low interest rate home equity loan (tax deductible, no less) to cover your essential borrowing needs (new car, kids' college education, starting a new business). Plus, as you sell one home to trade up to another, only profits in excess of $500,000 ($250,000 for singles) will be taxed. You certainly can't buy and sell stocks with this tax benefit.

Now, what happens if at some later time you hit a financial tragedy (bankruptcy, creditor judgment, lawsuit damages)? Again, home ownership will help protect you from total loss. In every state, homeowners get to exempt part or all of their home equity from loss to creditors, judgments, or bankruptcy. (Even the I.R.S. rarely goes after home equity to collect unpaid income taxes.)

This benefit is called a homestead exemption. In a few states this exemption is as low as $5,000 to $10,000. In others it typically ranges between $25,000 and $100,000. And in a few states such as Florida and Texas, 100 percent of your home equity is protected—even if it amounts to $1 million or more.

Build Personal Wealth

With inflation rates (at least for now) sitting well below the big increases in the Consumer Price Index we experienced in the late 1970s and early

1980s, the notion has taken hold that home ownership will no longer produce good financial returns. Supposedly, you're better off investing in the stock market. Of course, in terms of rate of return, the fallacy behind that idea can be exposed easily (see Mistake #20). However, even more important than rate of return stands the opportunity home ownership offers to build personal wealth.

In fact, a recent report released by Harvard University's Joint Center for Housing Studies has found that, after allowing for differences in age and income, on average, Americans who owned their own homes enjoyed net worths 20 to 40 times greater than those who rented. Without a doubt, home equity makes up the single largest source of Americans' personal wealth.

A relatively few people may strike it rich in the stock market. But for millions of others, trading stocks means high risk and high losses. On the other hand, building wealth through increasing home equity has consistently proven to be the safest and surest route to a personal net worth of six figures or more. When you combine a decreasing mortgage balance with even modest rates of home appreciation, your wealth multiplies.

Take a close look at the three examples in Table 9.1. These figures reveal how your wealth will grow over time with a beginning down payment of just $10,000 on a home priced at $100,000 and selected appreciation rates of three, five, and seven percent.

As Table 9.1 shows, even with only a three percent average annual rate of appreciation, your beginning home equity of $10,000 will grow to more than $128,301 within 20 years. And by retirement age you would have accumulated home equity of $326,200. Plus, remember, these gains in equity and personal wealth will have built up free of local, state, or federal income taxes (unlike stock market investments).

Don't get me wrong. I'm not trying to persuade you against investing in the stock market, bond funds, mutual funds, or even commercial real estate, precious art, or antiques. On the contrary, I agree with financial advisors who encourage individuals and families to diversify their investments. Most people should not put all their eggs into one basket. However, diversification can come later. As a starting point, first become a homeowner.

Table 9.1   **Building Wealth with Home Equity**[1]

Growing Home Equity at 3% Annual Home Appreciation			
	Years of Ownership		
	10	*20*	*30*	*40*
Appreciated home value	$134,300	$180,600	$242,700	$326,200
Outstanding mortgage balance	77,670	52,299	00	00
Home equity	56,620	128,301	242,700	326,200

Growing Home Equity at 5% Annual Home Appreciation			
	Years of Ownership		
	10	*20*	*30*	*40*
Appreciated home value	$162,870	$265,330	$432,190	$704,000
Outstanding mortgage balance	77,679	52,299	00	00
Home equity	85,191	213,031	432,190	704,000

Growing Home Equity at 7% Annual Home Appreciation			
	Years of Ownership		
	10	*20*	*30*	*40*
Appreciated home value	$196,720	$386,970	$761,230	$1,497,400
Outstanding mortgage balance	77,679	52,299	00	00
Home equity	119,041	334,671	761,230	1,497,400

[1] Assumes a $100,000 home purchase price bought with a $10,000 down payment and an original mortgage of $90,000 at 7.25 interest over 30 years.

Homeowners Spend Less for Housing than Renters

Aside from accumulating wealth through home equity, homeowners build more wealth than renters for another reason. Homeowners typically spend less for housing than renters. Although the exact cost advantages will differ among towns and cities throughout the United States, over time rents will continue to increase as mortgage payments remain the same (or increase only to a capped amount). Then, after your mortgage is paid off, your payments fall to zero.

This cost advantage of owning means that as homeowners grow older, they have more money left from their paychecks after paying for

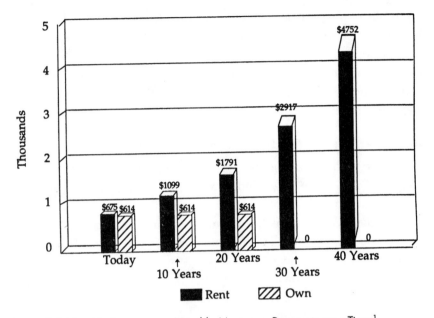

Figure 9.1 Monthly Rents versus Monthly Mortgage Payments over Time [1]

[1] Mortgage payments are based on a 30-year, fixed-rate mortgage at 7.25 percent in the amount of $90,000. Rents begin at $675 per month and increase 5 percent per year.

housing. So, they'll have more money to invest. Look at how rents and mortgage payments compare over time (Figure 9.1).

Based on the monthly mortgage payments and rent levels shown in Figure 9.1, you can see that within 10 years renters will pay substantially more each month for housing than homeowners. After 20 or 30 years, renters (if they can afford them) will be paying thousands more *per month* than homeowners. If homeowners invested an average of only $1,000 a month of these cost savings, say over years 10 through 40, they will accumulate (assuming an annual return of five percent) approximately $675,000. That wealth is in addition to the equity they will have built up in their homes.

There's simply no question that the housing cost savings that homeowners enjoy as they grow older gives them a powerful advantage over renters in their ability to generate personal wealth and create a diversified investment portfolio. But don't just accept the figures here or even the results of the previously mentioned Harvard study at face value. Test this conclusion for yourself. Compare the wealth position of renters and homeowners you know who have reached their 40s, 50s, or 60s. You'll find that the net worths of your older friends and relatives who own their own homes greatly exceed the wealth of those who have remained long-term renters.

Home Ownership Yields Transcendental Benefits

"Hey, we own this. This home is ours," says Melanie Watts. "We never thought of our home as a money machine—although our equity has steadily built up and our payments are lower now than when we bought 12 years ago. We became homeowners because we wanted the good feelings you get when you own instead of rent. I can't describe it, but it's real.

"After owning our own home, I don't think we could ever feel comfortable again as tenants. In fact, we soon plan to buy rental houses and let our tenants put their money into our retirement fund.

"What I'm saying," Melanie continues, "is that the financial returns of ownership are great. But the most important benefit of owning is ownership itself. There's nothing like knowing a small part of this big old world belongs to you.

"Ownership gives me feelings of security and comfort. When I rented I never felt in control of my life. Now I do. To us, home ownership and ownership of property is a transcendental experience. I'm not into Zen or anything like that. But anyone who rents is missing one of the best feelings they can have. Although we intend to become landlords and will need tenants, I still believe most people who rent are making a big mistake."

History shows Melanie is right. Putting off home ownership remains the most common and most costly mistake of all.

CHAPTER 10

50 Ways to Buy When You Are Short of Cash

Millions of Americans believe they can't afford to own. Some say they lack cash for a down payment. Others claim their cash flow comes up short every month. So, they continue to rent because "renting costs less." Yet, far more often than not, these beliefs run contrary to the facts.

Dr. Robert Schuller, minister, inspirationalist, and best-selling author, encourages us to realize that most people live their lives as underachievers. Their persistent excuse rings loud everywhere. "Gee," they say, "here's what I would really like to do—if I only had the money." But, as Dr. Schuller emphasizes, "Nobody has a money problem. First of all, it is always an idea problem." When the "here's what I would like to do" refers to home buying, Dr. Schuller's remarks surely hit home. In today's world of home buying, "not enough money" can no longer serve to justify procrastination. Lack of self-discipline, yes. Lack of knowledge, yes. Lack of motivation, yes. But not lack of money. So, if you think "cash short" blocks you from home buying, think again. At least one of the following 50 ideas is sure to work for you.

1. **FHA 203(b).** Cash-short buyers rely on this fixed-rate program more than any other home finance plan. This plan requires a down payment of between three and seven percent, but you need not use your own cash. You may use borrowed funds or gift money. In addition, qualifying standards (credit and income)

rarely eliminate anyone who can show steady income and good-faith effort in paying bills.

2. **FHA ARM (251).** The same down payment rules apply here as with FHA 203(b). But because the ARM's qualifying interest rate typically starts out less than a fixed-rate loan, you can more easily fit within the qualifying ratio guidelines. Or, alternatively, the ARM permits you to qualify for a larger amount of mortgage than FHA 203(b). As another benefit, FHA ARMs limit your annual rate increases to one percent (no negative amortization), and your lifetime cap is set at five percent.

3. **FHA GPM.** With this finance plan, you qualify for a larger mortgage than with FHA 203(b). But your payments increase gradually according to a preset schedule. In other words, the GPM (graduated payment mortgage) provides you with low monthly payments, vis á vis 203(b), in the early years of your mortgage. Then, later on, your mortgage payments increase.

4. **FHA/VA 203(v).** This FHA program is offered only to veterans. The down payment is less than 203(b), but other qualifying standards remain the same.

5. **FHA 203(k).** This plan works very well for homebuyers who want to renovate, rehab, or otherwise create value for their home. The 203(k) plan permits you to combine a home's purchase price and "fix-up" costs all in one mortgage. It has the same basic down payment and qualifying standards as the FHA 203(b). However, 203(k) also offers several possibilities for zero down purchases by first-time buyers.

6. **FHA qualifying assumptions.** To buy with little (or maybe nothing) down *and* a below-market interest rate, look for sellers with FHA mortgages originated when mortgage rates were in the range of 6.0 to 7.5 percent. Pay the sellers the amount of their equity (or whatever amount you both agree to) and then take over the seller's mortgage payments. Qualifying for this type of assumption is relatively easy and simple.

7. **FHA non-qualifying assumptions.** Millions of these loans were originated during the 1980s. Although most of them have now been repaid or refinanced, some sellers have retained them. The non-qualifying assumption can get credit-impaired buyers into a home without going through any mortgage approval process. Also, the amount of the down payment is subject to no rules. It's whatever amount the buyers and sellers agree to.

8. **HUD homes.** The U.S. Department of Housing and Urban Development (HUD) is the parent of FHA. When FHA borrowers fail to make their mortgage payments, HUD often becomes the owner of these houses. Depending on market conditions, you may be able to buy a HUD home for as little as $300 to $1,000 down. Ask a HUD registered real estate agent for details. Also, regularly read the classified and display real estate ads in your local paper. HUD and HUD agents advertise regularly.

9. **Other HUD/FHA programs.** Over the years the above HUD/FHA programs have proved most popular among homebuyers. But HUD/FHA also makes various other special home finance programs available—sometimes on a temporary or experimental basis. So, check with HUD/FHA for a complete listing of currently available programs. One example is FHA 203(h) which has made little- (or no-) down-payment home mortgages available to people living in areas hit by disaster (flood, earthquake, hurricane, tornado).

10. **VA mortgages.** If you are an eligible veteran, you have absolutely no "cash short" excuse for renting. Easy qualifying and no-cash-to-close are hallmarks of this great benefit for persons who have served in the U.S. military or National Guard.

11. **VA qualifying assumptions.** VA loans may be assumed by non-veterans. So, find a VA seller who has built little equity in his or her home—especially someone who has bought say within the past three or four years—and you can get into home ownership with little or nothing down.

12. **VA non-qualifying assumptions.** Some older VA loans may be assumed without going through any mortgage approval process. The amount of down payment is set through buyer-seller negotiations.

13. **VA homes.** Nonveteran homebuyers may purchase VA foreclosures on very easy terms of financing offered by VA. Contact your nearest VA office for a list of properties available in your area.

14. **State VA programs.** In addition to the federal government's VA mortgage program, some states offer their own version of VA financing. These programs may offer low down payments, below-market interest rates, and low closing costs and fees.

15. **Mortgage bond programs.** Nearly every state offers first-time buyers low-down-payment, below-market interest rate home mortgages. Contact your state and local housing finance agencies for the details of programs offered in your area. Unfortunately, housing finance agencies must limit the total amount of "bond money" that's available. So, keep yourself informed as to pending release dates for mortgage money. Quite often, the available funds go fast.

16. **Portfolio lenders.** Some mortgage lenders (banks, savings institutions, credit unions) hold the mortgages they issue in their own portfolios (rather than sell them to Fannie Mae or Freddie Mac). From time to time, these lenders offer very flexible terms of financing. For example, Washington Mutual in Seattle recently offered a one-percent-down mortgage loan program. Portfolio lenders also may show more flexibility with respect to qualifying guidelines.

17. **Fannie Mae 5% Down.** This loan has relatively tighter credit and income standards, but it's widely available through participating lenders all over the country.

18. **Freddie Mac 5% Down.** This is similar to Fannie Mae's 5% Down program.

19. **Fannie Mae 97.** A three-percent-down program with easier qualifying ratios. Typically limited to people with household incomes no more than 100 (sometimes 120) percent of an area's median household income. Home-buying in targeted neighborhoods may waive the income limits.

20. **Freddie Mac Discover the Gold.** Similar to Fannie Mae 97. Both of these programs reflect part of Fannie's and Freddie's efforts to "break down barriers" and expand home ownership to all Americans and immigrants who can responsibly manage their finances.

21. **New home builders.** As an incentive to buyers, many builders of condominiums, townhouses, and single-family homes offer low-down and/or below-market interest rates. Read the builder ads in your local paper and contact new developments directly. "Wow, we could really afford this. This is so much better than renting." That was the response of Melanie Hiller and Phillip Weizeorick when they visited (and bought) at the new Autumn Lakes subdivision in Aurora, Illinois.

22. **USDA Zero Down.** The United States Department of Agriculture offers nothing-down loans to homebuyers purchasing in small towns and cities—even when those "small towns or cities" are located in large urban areas such as Los Angeles County and San Bernadino County, California. These loans restrict participation to households with income equal to or less than 115 percent of an area's median household income. As with FHA, the qualifying standards are relatively easy for any first-time buyer whose credit history indicates a reasonable willingness to meet obligations. "This is the best thing that's happened to me; I was never able to save a penny," says recent homebuyer John Tunis.

23. **Habitat homes.** Even families with substantially below-average incomes can become homeowners. Habitat for Humanity International (a not-for-profit housing group) builds, sells, and finances homes for thousands of Americans every year—Americans who never dreamed home ownership was possible for

them. Habitat homes offer below-market interest rates. Home-buyers put down $500 to $1,000, and they contribute 300 to 500 hours of work helping to build the house alongside Habitat volunteers and construction professionals.

24. Neighborhood Housing Services. This national not-for-profit organization operates local offices nationwide. In San Diego, for example, the NHS Home Ownership Opportunities Program allows buyers to purchase with nothing down in the City Heights neighborhood. The applicable mortgage interest rate ranges between two and five percent (depending on family income level). A family of four with an annual income of less than $48,600 could participate in this program. Check out NHS programs in your area.

25. The Acorn Connection. Acorn is another national not-for-profit group with local offices that assists people into home ownership. Acorn counsels buyers, helps them clean up their credit, if necessary, and then links them up with mortgage lenders who not only will forgive bad credit but will finance the buyers with little or nothing down and at below-market interest rates.

26. CRA programs. Under the Community Reinvestment Act (CRA), banks must reach out to serve all types of people in all types of neighborhoods. In past years, though, many banks did not take this responsibility seriously. Nor did the law provide serious penalties for noncompliance. More recently, though, penalties have increased, and banks (as part of the National Home Ownership Strategy) have created many different "easier qualifying" low-down-payment mortgage plans—especially for homebuyers who wish to purchase in certain areas targeted for revitalization.

Nothing improves a neighborhood more than homeowners displacing renters—or, even better, renters displacing landlords by buying the homes they previously were occupying as tenants. Call your local banks. Ask them what types of CRA mortgage programs they're offering.

27. **Mortgage Credit Certificates (MCCs).** Although MCC is not a home finance plan, it does improve affordability. With an MCC you are allowed a 20 percent tax credit for the mortgage interest you pay each year. If you pay $12,000 in interest, you will slice your federal income tax bill by $2,400 (.2 × $12,000). This tax credit is in addition to the standard mortgage interest tax deduction. To learn more about MCCs, call your local or state housing finance office.

28. **Fannie Mae rehab loans.** At present this experimental program is aimed at investors (for-profit and not-for-profit) who will buy and renovate a house and then sell it on a mortgage loan assumption (low- or no-down) to first-time buyers. Fannie Mae has modeled the investor acquisition-rehab-buyer assumption features of this program after the FHA 203(k) plan. However, Fannie Mae's maximum loan goes all the way up to $215,000.

29. **Fannie Mae cash-free loans.** Under this "flex-plan" experimental mortgage, homebuyers with excellent credit are permitted to raise their down payment of three percent by borrowing against their credit cards, from family members, or from their employer. In fact, the primary restrictions on this loan concern real estate agents and the sellers. Neither of these sources can lend you the down payment.

30. **Not-for-profit grant money.** Some not-for-profit housing groups make grants to low- to moderate-income homebuyers, which the homebuyers can use as part (or all) of their down payment.

31. **Government grant money.** Similarly, numerous state, county, and local government agencies also may have limited amounts of grant money available to homebuyers. Typically, these grants are tied in with a total home finance plan that combines grant money, liberal qualifying, and maybe even below-market interest rates. Call your county and city housing finance agencies.

32. **First-time buyer programs.** Although many of the above programs are targeted to first-time buyers, some mortgage lenders simply call their programs "special financing for first-time buyers." So, as you "dial for dollars," ask about any first-time buyer programs. Note, too, the term "first-time buyer" often applies to anyone who hasn't owned a home within the past three years. The term may also include people who have been recently divorced or widowed—even though they may have previously owned with a spouse within the past three years.

33. **Land contracts.** This type of seller financing is popular in many parts of the country. Down payment, terms, and interest rate are set by negotiation between buyers and sellers. They are not subject to any underwriting "rules" or government regulations. This type of financing is sometimes referred to as contract-for-deed or installment sale. Sellers and buyers like this financing because it involves no red tape.

   However, the "no red tape" advantage also presents a disadvantage to buyers. Because sellers make land contract purchases so easy, many buyers fail to adequately investigate the condition of the property, the quality of the owner's title, or a fair purchase price (market value). So, before you jump to take advantage of that $500 down, no closing costs, eight percent interest loan, verify property condition, title quality, and value.

   In far too many instances, buyers have faithfully made payments to sellers for periods of 10 to 20 years, only to learn that the sellers could not deliver good title to the property. Similarly, you don't want to buy an overpriced property full of defects.

34. **Lease-options.** Hundreds of thousands of renters have eased into home ownership through the use of lease-options. I agree with Robert Bruss, the respected nationally syndicated real estate investor and attorney, that lease-options offer a great way to buy for anyone who can afford to rent. But, like all home-buying techniques, lease-options do present some drawbacks. Also, I would encourage you to read Robert Bruss's report on lease-options (see "Recommended Reading").

35. Lease-purchases. With a lease-*option,* you are not obligated to complete your purchase at the end of your lease period. However, a lease-*purchase* does commit you to following through. Therefore, some sellers who refuse to accept the uncertainty of a lease-option may find the greater security of a lease-purchase more to their liking. Of course, the terms of both types of agreements depend entirely upon the agreement negotiated by you and the sellers.

36. Sweat equity. With sweat equity, you provide the labor and materials necessary to increase a property's value—often in lieu of a cash down payment. I have seen sweat equity successfully used in combination with lease-options, lease-purchase agreements, land contracts, and new home developments.

For example, say you buy a home that's worth $120,000 on a nothing-down land contract. You promise the seller that you will improve the property through sweat equity. After a year of your work and improvements, the home is worth $140,000. You now owe $119,000. Essentially, your efforts have created a $20,000 "down payment"—or about 15 percent of the home's market value. A lender who loans you $119,000 to pay off the seller would be secure with an 85 percent loan-to-value ratio. Apart from the amounts you spent for materials, you've acquired your home with zero cash down.

37. Self-contracting. A typical builder's gross profit margin ranges between 10 and 20 percent. Eliminate the builder (the general contractor) by serving as your own contractor. Your self-contracting efforts substitute for all or part of your cash down payment. Do you need experience to self-contract? Not necessarily. I have a friend who, without any prior knowledge of construction, self-contracted a beautiful 3,500-square-foot house that's now worth around $250,000.

38. Owner-builder. If self-contracting doesn't seem exciting enough for you, become an owner-builder. Some owner-builders "earn" 40 to 50 percent of their completed home's market value.

In many cities and rural areas, owner-builder schools convert off-the-street amateurs into builders ready to meet the challenge of constructing a new house. If at all interested, check your library or bookstore for owner-builder titles. A number of helpful guides are available.

39. **Real estate owned (REOs).** At times, every mortgage lender becomes the unwilling owner of properties that it has taken back through foreclosure. Lenders vary greatly in how they market these homes and in their offered terms of financing. But as often as not, a thorough search of lenders in your area will turn up some REOs that are available with a bargain price, easy terms, or possibly both (although that combination is more difficult to find).

40. **Manufactured homes.** In days gone by, the ancestors of manufactured homes were called house trailers or prefabs. Today's manufactured homes bear little resemblance to their cheaply constructed forebears. In fact, many are difficult to tell from site-built houses. Even better, manufactured home dealers offer homes with good value and can arrange almost 100 percent financing for their homebuyers. If you already own (or can purchase) a lot, you stand a very good chance of being able to finance the entire price of your manufactured home. (Sweat equity down payments, too, are sometimes possible.)

41. **Family loans.** No one can say for sure, but perhaps as many as 20 to 40 percent of all first-time buyers borrow at least part of their down payment from parents or other family members. Who do you know who can help? Don't be afraid to ask. Most parents want to see their kids become homeowners and are more than willing to lend assistance.

42. **Employer assistance.** Have you checked with your employer to learn whether it offers any home-buying help to its workers? Some employers provide grants, second mortgages, or buydowns. Some have arranged with lenders to obtain below-market interest rates for their employees. Call your credit union.

Although not all credit unions fund mortgages, those that do frequently give great service, lower interest rates, and lower closing costs. Unlike many lenders, most credit unions will not burden you with excessive points and garbage fees.

43. **Shared equity.** Some homebuyers bring in nonresident partners to help them buy a home. Your partner could be a family member, friend, or professional investor. Generally, the partner provides the down payment and becomes a coborrower on the mortgage to strengthen your ability to qualify. You make the monthly payments and keep the property in good repair (perhaps even create value through sweat equity improvements). Upon sale of the home, you and your partner split the profits. The exact terms of your partnership agreement, of course, are shaped through win-win negotiating.

44. **Co-ownership.** In a sense, co-ownership is a form of equity sharing. (Or, vice-versa, you could say that equity sharing is a form of co-ownership.) The primary difference is that under a co-ownership arrangement, you and your equity partner share occupancy of the home. This form of ownership is growing fast among single-parent households. Not only does home sharing add to affordability, the joint efforts of partners also ease the tasks of managing the household and caring for the children.

45. **Buy a duplex.** If you're cash short each month, look for a duplex, triplex, fourplex, or perhaps a home with an accessory apartment. Or find a home that you could comfortably share with housemates. The rental income you collect each month from tenants or housemates will (1) eliminate your budget shortfall, (2) drop your monthly cost of owning far below the costs of renting (especially after tax deductions), (3) increase your mortgage affordability, and (4) increase your price range. Plus, when you own a higher-priced income property, you will build wealth faster.

46. **Buy-downs.** When lenders originate a mortgage, they charge points and interest. A one point loan means a higher interest

rate. A four- or five-point loan will give you a lower interest rate. So, if your monthly budget's tight, get your seller to "buy down" your interest rate by paying the lender's "discount" points. In other words, pay points up front and your lender will discount your interest rate and, correspondingly, your monthly payments.

Why would your sellers pay points? First, to help get their house sold. Second, as a trade-off for a higher price. Of course, lenders are alert to this technique and typically limit the number of points that sellers are allowed to pay. (Remember, to obtain a maximum loan-to-value ratio, the price of a home can't exceed the lender's appraised market value.) Nevertheless, buy-downs (especially temporary buy-downs) can dramatically improve your mortgage affordability and reduce your monthly payments.

47. **Pledged collateral.** Have you, your parents, or other close family members built up a substantial sum in a stock portfolio, retirement plan, life insurance policy, or other type of investment? If so, you can buy a home with nothing down. Simply pledge the valuable asset or funds as security (in addition to the house you're buying). Make your monthly mortgage payments as scheduled, and your mortgage lender won't touch the pledged collateral. Then, at the point you've accumulated a 20 percent equity in your home, your lender will release its lien against the asset.

As another benefit, when you pledge collateral in lieu of a down payment, you won't be required to buy mortgage insurance (PMI). Depending on the amount of your mortgage, this could save you more than $500 a year. Remember, too, your home equity can accumulate through mortgage principal payments, home appreciation, and value-enhancing improvements. With growing equity from each of these sources, you might be able to obtain a lien release for the pledged asset within just a few years.

48. **Seller financing.** A land contract (no. 33, above) represents one type of seller financing. Alternatively, some sellers will finance the sale of their homes with a first mortgage (or trust

deed). Or they may be willing to take back a second mortgage with a combination of lender financing, owner financing, and down payment (e.g., 75–15–10, 80–10–10 or 65–30–5). Seller financing (OWC) is always an option to explore.

As Robert Bruss frequently points out in his syndicated newspaper columns, "You never know whether an owner will accept seller financing until you actually present your offer." Quite often, sellers who have orally said "not interested," will change their minds once they see your signed written offer sitting in front of them.

49. **Creative financing.** This term does not refer to any specific financing technique. Instead, it refers to identifying needs, abilities, and possibilities. Then, from the great variety of techniques available, mix, match, select, and combine a home finance plan that works. Through these efforts, nearly anyone who thinks creatively will be able to become a homeowner.

50. **Revise your budget.** Clearly, most people who lack the cash to afford a home have not placed the goal of home ownership at the top of their list of priorities. Other types of spending and borrowing always seem to shove home ownership into the *someday* category. Partly, it's because other spending is easier. Nearly anyone can buy and finance a new car in less than a few hours. Shopping for a home, arranging financing, completing inspections, and providing documents can require months of effort.

Plus, as often as not, renters don't accept the fact they could achieve home ownership if they cut their spending, increased their savings, and educated themselves about their home-buying possibilities. But you need not fall for these mistakes.

With the above list of financing techniques, you can generate many home-buying ideas that will get you into a home. All that stands between you and home ownership is preparation. Align your budget with the goal of home ownership and, while others continue to pile up rent receipts, you will build wealth and personal satisfaction.

Resources

Homebuyers Checklist

1. Which home-buying priorities are most important?
   A. Comfortable place to live
   B. Bargain price
   C. Bargain terms
   D. Instant equity/create value
   E. Strong appreciation potential
   F. Impress parents, friends, acquaintances
   G. Low maintenance and upkeep
   H. Affordability

2. What are your spending priorities?
   A. Home ownership
   B. Cars (payments and operating expenses)
   C. Furniture
   D. Basic living expenses (food, clothing, insurance, rent, utilities, etc.)
   E. Recreation and leisure
   F. Children
   G. Savings
   H. Vices (smoking, drinking, gambling, drugs)

3. Question the appraisal.
   A. Property address
   B. Neighborhood boundaries
   C. Neighborhood description
   D. Site size
   E. Site quality
   F. Site amenities
   G. Property description
   H. House size/features
   I. House quality
   J. House amenities
   K. Site value
   L. Construction (reproduction) costs
   M. Condition/depreciation
   N. View/inspect comparables
   O. Reasonableness of adjustments
   P. Sales or financing concessions
   Q. Date of "comp" sales
   R. Date of appraisal
   S. Reasonableness of value estimate

4. Consider the home's investment potential.

A. Monthly rents versus mortgage payments

B. Relative price trends among neighborhoods

C. Revitalization potential

D. Area job growth/population growth/demographics

E. Relative affordability among neighborhoods

F. Potential supply of new construction

G. Potential supply of renovations and conversions

H. Trends in construction costs

I. Outlook for inflation/mortgage interest rates

5. Analyze the neighborhood.

A. Accessibility
1. Convenience to jobs, shopping, schools, recreation, etc.
2. Means of access (roads, bus, subway, taxi, commuter trains, ferries, bicycle paths, etc.)
3. Commuting times during peak traffic hours

B. Environment
1. Aesthetics/views
2. Quiet/noise/smells
3. Fiscal: taxes/government services
4. Legal: zoning, building regulations, environmental restrictions
5. Neighborhood demographics
6. Neighborhood lifestyles

7. Anticipated changes
8. School district/quality
9. Microclimate
10. Pride of ownership/appearance
11. Crime rates/types of crime
12. Natural hazards (hurricane, earthquake, flood, fire, mudslides, sinkholes, tornadoes)

6. Analyze the property.

A. Deed restrictions

B. Homeowner association amenities, services, rules, fees, solvency, etc.

C. Building materials

D. Condition

E. Floor plan/livability

F. Energy efficiency

G. Extras and amenities

H. Square footage

I. Fix-up potential

J. Views: protected or unprotected

K. Natural light

L. Site placement: exposure to sun, wind, neighbors, street, Feng Shui, etc.

M. Egress/ingress (from street, from garage or parking)

N. Parking spaces/garage

O. Systems: electrical, HVAC, plumbing, etc.

P. Environmental hazards: lead paint, asbestos, radon,

CFCs, transmission wires, oil tanks, etc.

Q. Soundproofing

R. Maintenance and upkeep: time, trouble, expense

S. Pest control: termites, rodents, roaches, snakes, wasps, bees, deer, possums, etc.

T. Value relative to other homes and neighborhoods

7. Negotiate win-win.

A. Negotiating styles
    1. Adversarial
    2. Passive accommodator
    3. Win-win

B. Issues to be negotiated
    1. Price
    2. Escrow allowances
    3. Seller-paid closing costs
    4. Seller financing
    5. Terms of seller financing
    6. Possession date
    7. Personal property (wet bar, storage shed, drapes, blinds, window a.c. units, furniture, etc.)
    8. Closing date
    9. Contingencies (financing, inspections, third-party approvals, etc.)
    10. Quality of title
    11. Earnest money deposit
    12. Seller disclosures
    13. Pre-closing walk-through
    14. Assumable financing (seller's existing mortgage)

15. Prepaids/prorations
16. Home warranties/appliance warranties

8. Arrange your financing.

A. Types of financing possibilities (see Chapter 10)

B. Underwriting criteria
    1. Qualifying ratios (housing cost, total debt)
    2. Credit history
    3. Income: amounts, sources, stability, growth
    4. Amount of down payment
    5. Amount of cash or liquid reserves
    6. Value of home (collateral)
    7. "FICO" score
    8. Compensating factors/risk factors

C. Loan costs
    1. Application fee
    2. Origination fee
    3. Points/interest rate
    4. Appraisal
    5. Credit reports
    6. Garbage fees
    7. Mortgage insurance
    8. Prepayment penalties
    9. Loan index (ARMs)
    10. Loan margin (ARMs)
    11. Loan caps (ARMs)
    12. Loan ceiling (ARMs)
    13. Negative amortization (ARM, GPM)
    14. Title insurance (lender's policy, owner's policy)

15. Loan rep commission (indirect)
16. Kickbacks or referral fees (indirect)

D. Loan sources
1. Credit unions
2. Mortgage brokers
3. Mortgage bankers
4. Banks
5. Savings institutions
6. Sellers
7. Family, friends
8. Life-insurance cash value
9. Retirement account
10. Sellers
11. Real estate agent/firm
12. Not-for-profit housing groups
13. Housing finance agencies (state and local)
14. New home builders
15. FHA/VA/FmHA (usually through cooperating lenders)

9. Move smoothly through closing.

A. Title insurance/title examination

B. Inspections
1. Physical
2. Pests
3. Environmental
4. Seller disclosures

C. Warranty terms and conditions

D. Site survey

E. Documents for lender

F. RESPA disclosures/check final figures

G. Homeowners insurance

H. Flood insurance

I. Other special coverages or endorsements (earthquake, jewelry, home business, antiques, etc.)

J. Completed purchase contract signed by *all* parties

K. Appraisal

L. Homeowners association resale package

M. Condo/co-op board approval of buyers

N. Cash-to-close requirements

O. Final walk-through of property

P. Get all house keys, copies of warranties, operating instructions for appliances, etc.

10. Enjoy home ownership.

A. Schedule celebration party

B. Perform value-creating improvements/maintenance

C. Build wealth through mortgage payback, appreciation, and improvements

D. Cancel PMI when loan-to-value ratio drops to 80 percent

E. Check mortgage rates every month for profitable opportunities to refinance

F. Enjoy your home; have friends, neighbors, and family over frequently

Sample Appraisal Form

UNIFORM RESIDENTIAL APPRAISAL REPORT File No. _____ SAMPLE

Property Description

Property Address	City State Zip Code
Legal Description	County
Assessor's Parcel No.	Tax Year R.E. Taxes$ Special Assessments $
Borrower	Current Owner Occupant ☐ Owner ☐ Tenant ☐ Vacant ☐
Property rights appraised ☐ Fee Simple ☐ Leasehold Project Type ☐ PUD ☐ Condominium (HUD/VA only) HOA$ ____ /Mo.
Neighborhood/Project Name Map Reference Census Tract
Sale Price $ Date of Sale Description and $ amount of loan charges/concessions to be paid by seller
Lender/Client Address
Appraiser Address

Location	☐ Urban ☐ Suburban ☐ Rural	Predominant	Single family housing	Present land use %	Land use change
Built Up	☐ Over 75% ☐ 25-75% ☐ Under 25%	occupancy	PRICE $(000) AGE (yrs)	One family	☐ Not likely ☐ Likely
Growth Rate	☐ Rapid ☐ Stable ☐ Slow	☐ Owner	Low	2-4 family	☐ In process
Property Values	☐ Increasing ☐ Stable ☐ Declining	☐ Tenant	High	Multi-family	To:
Demand/supply	☐ Shortage ☐ In balance ☐ Over Supply	☐ Vacant (0-5%)	Predominant	Commercial	
Marketing Time	☐ Under 3 mos. ☐ 3-6 mos. ☐ Over 6 mos.	☐ Vacant (over 5%)			

Note: Race and the racial composition of the neighborhood are not appraisal factors.

Neighborhood boundaries and characteristics: _____

Factors that affect the marketability of the properties in the neighborhood (proximity to employment and amenities, employment stability, appeal to market, etc.):

Market Conditions in the subject neighborhood (including support for the above conclusions related to the trend of property values, demand/supply, and marketing time — — such as data on competitive properties for sale in the neighborhood, description of the prevalence of sales and financing concessions, etc.):

Project Information for PUDs (if applicable) - - Is the developer/builder in control of the Home Owners' Association (HOA)? ☐ Yes ☐ No
Approximate total number of units in the subject project _____. Approximate total number of units for sale in the subject project _____
Describe common elements and recreational facilities:

Dimensions	Topography
Site Area Corner Lot ☐ Yes ☐ No	Size
Specific zoning classification and description	Shape
Zoning compliance ☐ Legal ☐ Legal nonconforming (Grandfathered use) ☐ Illegal ☐ No zoning	Drainage
Highest & best use as improved: ☐ Present use ☐ Other use (explain)	View

Utilities	Public	Other	Off-site Improvements	Type	Public	Private	
Electricity	☐		Street		☐	☐	Landscaping
Gas	☐		Curb/gutter		☐	☐	Driveway Surface
Water	☐		Sidewalk		☐	☐	Apparent Easements
Sanitary sewer	☐		Street lights		☐	☐	FEMA Special Flood Hazard Area ☐ Yes ☐ No
Storm sewer	☐		Alley		☐	☐	FEMA Zone Map Date
							FEMA Map No.

Comments (apparent adverse easements, encroachments, special assessments, slide areas, illegal or legal nonconforming zoning use, etc.):

GENERAL DESCRIPTION	EXTERIOR DESCRIPTION	FOUNDATION	BASEMENT	INSULATION
No. of Units	Foundation	Slab	Area Sq. Ft.	Roof ☐
No. of Stories	Exterior Walls	Crawl Space	% Finished	Ceiling ☐
Type (Det./Att.)	Roof Surface	Basement	Ceiling	Walls ☐
Design (Style)	Gutters & Dwnspts.	Sump Pump	Walls	Floor ☐
Existing/Proposed	Window Type	Dampness	Floor	None ☐
Age (Yrs.)	Storm/Screens	Settlement	Outside Entry	Unknown ☐
Effective Age (Yrs.)	Manufactured House	Infestation		

ROOMS	Foyer	Living	Dining	Kitchen	Den	Family Rm.	Rec. Rm.	Bedrooms	# Baths	Laundry	Other	Area Sq. Ft.
Basement												
Level 1												
Level 2												

Finished area above grade contains: Rooms; Bedroom(s); Bath(s) Square Feet of Gross Living Area

INTERIOR	Materials/Condition	HEATING	KITCHEN EQUIP.	ATTIC	AMENITIES	CAR STORAGE:
Floors		Type	Refrigerator ☐	None ☐	Fireplace(s) #	None ☐
Walls		Fuel	Range/Oven ☐	Stairs ☐	Patio	Garage # of cars
Trim/Finish		Condition	Disposal ☐	Drop Stair ☐	Deck	Attached
Bath Floor		COOLING	Dishwasher ☐	Scuttle ☐	Porch	Detached
Bath Wainscot		Central	Fan/Hood ☐	Floor ☐	Fence	Built-In
Doors		Other	Microwave ☐	Heated ☐	Pool	Carport
		Condition	Washer/Dryer ☐	Finished ☐		Driveway

Additional features (special energy efficient items, etc.): _____

Condition of the improvements, depreciation (physical, functional, and external), repairs needed, quality of construction, remodeling/additions, etc.:

Adverse environmental conditions (such as, but not limited to, hazardous wastes, toxic substances, etc.) present in the improvements, on the site, or in the immediate vicinity of the subject property: _____

Freddie Mac Form 70 6-93 Laser Printing by WCA, Inc., 101 Lancelot Ct., Simpsonville, SC 29681 803-967-3922 Fannie Mae Form 1004 6-93
PAGE 1 OF 2

UNIFORM RESIDENTIAL APPRAISAL REPORT   File No.   SAMPLE

Valuation Section

COST APPROACH	
ESTIMATED SITE VALUE . . . . = $ _____	Comments on Cost Approach (such as, source of cost estimate, site value, square foot calculation and, for HUD, VA and FmHA, the estimated remaining economic life of the property):
ESTIMATED REPRODUCTION COST-NEW-OF IMPROVEMENTS:	
Dwelling _____ Sq.Ft. @ $ _____ = $ _____	
_____ Sq.Ft. @ $ _____ = _____	
_____ = _____	
Garage/Carport _____ Sq.Ft. @ $ _____ = _____	
Total Estimated Cost New . . . . = $ _____	
Less Physical	Functional	External	
Depreciation _____ = $ _____	
Depreciated Value of Improvements . . . . = $ _____	
"As-Is" Value of Site Improvements . . . . = $ _____	
INDICATED VALUE BY COST APPROACH . . . . = $ _____	

ITEM	SUBJECT	COMPARABLE NO. 1	COMPARABLE NO. 2	COMPARABLE NO. 3
Address				
Proximity to Subject				
Sales Price				
Price/Gross Liv. Area				
Data and/or				
Verification Sources				

VALUE ADJUSTMENTS	DESCRIPTION	DESCRIPTION	+(-)$ Adjustment	DESCRIPTION	+(-)$ Adjustment	DESCRIPTION	+(-)$ Adjustment
Sales or Financing Concessions							
Date of Sale/Time							
Location							
Leasehold/Fee							
Site							
View							
Design and Appeal							
Quality of Construction							
Age							
Condition							
Above Grade	Total Bdrms Baths	Total Bdrms Baths		Total Bdrms Baths		Total Bdrms Baths	
Room Count							
Gross Living Area	Sq. Ft.	Sq. Ft.		Sq. Ft.		Sq. Ft.	
Basement & Finished Rooms Below Grade							
Functional Utility							
Heating/Cooling							
Energy Efficient Items							
Garage/Carport							
Porch, Patio, Deck,							
Fireplace(s), etc.							
Fence, Pool, etc.							
Net Adj. (total)		☐ + ☐ – $		☐ + ☐ – $		☐ + ☐ – $	
Adjusted Sales Price of Comparable		$		$		$	

Comments on Sales Comparison (including the subject property's compatibility to the neighborhood, etc.): _____

ITEM	SUBJECT	COMPARABLE NO. 1	COMPARABLE NO. 2	COMPARABLE NO. 3
Date, Price, and Data Source for prior sales within year of appraisal				

Analysis of any current agreement of sale, option, or listing of the subject property and analysis of any prior sales of subject and comparables within one year of the date of appraisal:

INDICATED VALUE BY SALES COMPARISON APPROACH . . . . $ _____

INDICATED VALUE BY INCOME APPROACH (If Applicable) Estimated Market Rent $ _____   /Mo. x Gross Rent Multiplier _____ = $ _____

This appraisal is made ☐ "as is" ☐ subject to repairs, alterations, inspections, or conditions listed below ☐ subject to completion per plans and specifications.

Conditions of Appraisal: _____

Final Reconciliation: _____

RECONCILIATION

The purpose of this appraisal is to estimate the market value of the real property that is the subject of this report, based on the above conditions and the certification, contingent and limiting conditions, and market value definition that are stated in the attached Freddie Mac Form 439/Fannie Mae Form 1004B (Revised _____).

I (WE) ESTIMATE THE MARKET VALUE, AS DEFINED, OF THE REAL PROPERTY THAT IS THE SUBJECT OF THIS REPORT, AS OF _____

(WHICH IS THE DATE OF INSPECTION AND THE EFFECTIVE DATE OF THIS REPORT) TO BE $ _____

APPRAISER	SUPERVISORY APPRAISER (ONLY IF REQUIRED):	Inspect Property
Signature	Signature	☐ Did ☐ Did Not
Name	Name	
Date Report Signed	Date Report Signed	
State Certification # State	State Certification # State	
Or State License # State	Or State License # State	

Freddie Mac Form 70 8-93   Laser Printing by WCA, Inc., 101 Lancelot Ct., Simpsonville, SC 29681 803-967-3922   Fannie Mae Form 1004 8-93
PAGE 2 OF 2

CERTIFICATION AND LIMITING CONDITIONS File# SAMPLE

Owner/Borrower	Property Address
Lender/Client	

DEFINITION OF MARKET VALUE: The most probable price which a property should bring in a competitive and open market under all conditions requisite to a fair sale, the buyer and seller, each acting prudently, knowledgeably and assuming the price is not affected by undue stimulus. Implicit in this definition is the consummation of a sale as of a specified date and the passing of title from seller to buyer under conditions whereby: (1) buyer and seller are typically motivated; (2) both parties are well informed or well advised, and each acting in what he considers his own best interest (3) a reasonable time is allowed for exposure in the open market; (4) payment is made in terms of cash in U. S. dollars or in terms of financial arrangements comparable thereto; and (5) the price represents the normal consideration for the property sold unaffected by special or creative financing or sales concessions* granted by anyone associated with the sale.

*Adjustment to the comparables must be made for special or creative financing or sale concessions. No adjustments are necessary for those costs which are normally paid by sellers as a result of tradition or law in a market area; these costs are readily identifiable since the seller pays these costs in virtually all sales transactions. Special or creative financing adjustments can be made to the comparable property by comparisons to financing terms offered by a third party institutional lender that is not already involved in the property or transaction. Any adjustment should not be calculated on a mechanical dollar for dollar cost of the financing or concession but the dollar amount of any adjustment should approximate the market's reaction to the financing or concessions based on the appraiser's judgment.

STATEMENT OF LIMITING CONDITIONS AND APPRAISER'S CERTIFICATION

CONTINGENT AND LIMITING CONDITIONS: The appraiser's certification that appears in the appraisal report is subject to the following conditions:

1. The appraiser will not be responsible for matters of a legal nature that affect either the property being appraised or the title to it. The appraiser assumes that the title is good and marketable and, therefore, will not render any opinions about the title. The property is appraised on the basis of it being under responsible ownership.

2. The appraiser has provided a sketch in the appraisal report to show approximate dimensions of the improvements and the sketch is included only to assist the reader of the report in visualizing the property and understanding the appraiser's determination of its size.

3. The appraiser has examined the available flood maps that are provided by the Federal Emergency Management Agency (or other data sources) and has noted in the appraisal report whether the subject site is located in an identified Special Flood Hazard Area. Because the appraiser is not a surveyor, he or she makes no guarantees, express or implied, regarding this determination

4. The appraiser will not give testimony or appear in court because he or she made an appraisal of the property in question, unless specific arrangements to do so have been made beforehand.

5. The appraiser has estimated the value of the land in the cost approach at its highest and best use and the improvements at their contributory value. These separate valuations of the land and improvements must not be used in conjunction with any other appraisal and are invalid if they are so used.

6. The appraiser has noted in the appraisal report any adverse conditions (such as, needed repairs, depreciation, the presence of hazardous wastes, toxic substances, etc.) observed during the inspection of the subject property or that he or she became aware of during the normal research involved in performing the appraisal. Unless otherwise stated in the appraisal report, the appraiser has no knowledge of any hidden or unapparent conditions of the property or adverse environmental conditions (including the presence of hazardous wastes, toxic substances, etc.) that would make the property more or less valuable, and has assumed that there are no such conditions and makes no guarantees or warranties, express or implied, regarding the condition of the property. The appraiser will not be responsible for any such conditions that do exist or for any engineering or testing that might be required to discover whether such conditions exist. Because the appraiser is not an expert in the field of environmental hazards, the appraisal report must not be considered as environmental assessment of the property.

7. The appraiser obtained the information, estimates, and opinions that were expressed in the appraisal report from sources that he or she considers to be reliable and believes them to be true and correct. The appraiser does not assume responsibility for the accuracy of such items that were furnished by other parties.

8. The appraiser will not disclose the contents of the appraisal report except as provided for in the Uniform Standards of Professional Appraisal Practice.

9. The appraiser has based his or her appraisal report and valuation conclusion for an appraisal that is subject to satisfactory completion, repairs, or alterations on the assumption that completion of the improvements will be performed in a workmanlike manner.

10. The appraiser must provide his or her prior written consent before the lender/client specified in the appraisal report can distribute the appraisal report (including conclusions about the property value, the appraiser's identity and professional designations, and references to any professional appraisal organizations or the firm with which the appraiser is associated) to anyone other than the borrower; the mortgagee or its successors and assigns; the mortgage insurer; consultants; professional appraisal organizations; any state or federally approved financial institution; or any department, agency, or instrumentality of the United States or any state or the District of Columbia; except that the lender/client may distribute the property description section of the report only to data collection or reporting service(s) without having to obtain the appraiser's prior written consent. The appraiser's written consent and approval must also be obtained before the appraisal can be conveyed by anyone to the public through advertising, public relations, news, sales, or other media.

Freddie Mac Form 439 6-93   Page 1 of 2   Fannie Mae Form 1004B 6-93
Laser printing by WCA, Inc., 101 Lancelot Ct., Simpsonville, SC 29681 803-967-3922

— 280 —

Mortgage Payment Tables

Table R.1 below shows how much money you have to pay back each month for every $1,000 you might borrow, at a variety of corresponding interest rates. If the market interest rate for a 30-year fixed-rate mortgage is 9.5 percent, you would have to pay $8.41 per month for each $1,000 of your original mortgage amount. If interest rates are at eight percent, your payment per $1,000 of borrowings would run $7.34 per month. If rates are at 6.5 percent, you would need to pay back $6.32 per $1,000 per month.

Here are three examples:

1. A 30-year loan of $145,000 at 9.5 percent interest requires a monthly payment of around $1,219 ($8.41 × 145 = $1,219).
2. A 30-year loan of $225,000 at 6.5% interest would require a monthly payment of around $1,422 ($6.32 × 225 = $1,422).
3. A 30-year loan of $87,000 at 8.0% interest would require a monthly payment of around $639. ($7.34 × 87 = $639).

Using the above method, you can calculate the monthly payment for any mortgage amount and interest rate. To make the same calculations of monthly payments for 15-year fixed-rate mortgages, use Table R.2.

Table R.1 Monthly Payment Required per $1,000 of Original Mortgage Balance[1]

Interest (%)	Monthly Payment	Interest (%)	Monthly Payment
2.5	$3.95	7.5	$ 6.99
3.0	4.21	8.0	7.34
3.5	4.49	8.5	7.69
4.0	4.77	8.0	8.05
4.5	5.07	9.5	8.41
5.0	5.37	10.0	8.77
5.5	5.67	10.5	9.15
6.0	5.99	11.0	9.52
6.5	6.32	11.5	9.90
7.0	6.65	12.0	10.29

[1] Term = 30 years.

Table R.2	**Monthly Payment Required per $1,000 of Original Mortgage Balance**[1]		
Interest (5)	*Monthly Payment*	*Interest (%)*	*Monthly Payment*
2.5	$6.67	7.5	$ 9.27
3.0	6.90	8.0	9.56
3.5	7.15	8.5	9.85
4.0	7.39	8.0	10.14
4.5	7.65	9.5	10.44
5.0	7.91	10.0	10.75
5.5	8.17	10.5	11.05
6.0	8.43	11.0	11.37
6.5	8.71	11.5	11.68
7.0	8.99	12.0	12.00

[1] Term = 15 years.

In contrast to the 30-year fixed-rate payment examples calculated above, the respective 15-year monthly payments would be: (1) 145 × $10.44 = $1,514; (2) 225 × $8.71 = $1,960; and (3) 87 × $9.56 = $832.

Internet Addresses

The Internet is now exploding with real estate information that pertains to neighborhood data, financing programs, for-sale properties, and various news features. The total number of sites easily exceeds 10,000. Here are just a few of the major sites that you may find of interest. Many of these sites are also linked to related sites and information.)

Stop Renting Now (www.stoprentingnow.com): This is my home page and offers a wide variety of information, counseling, and how-to advice for homebuyers.

Home Buyer's Fair (www.homefair.com): First-time buyer information, mortgage qualification calculator, available booklets.

Realtor.com (www.realtor.com): Linked to various real estate agents, real estate terminology, properties for sale.

Homes and Communities (www.hud.gov): This is the primary site for homebuyers who want to learn more about HUD/FHA programs and HUD Homes. Also includes some VA and FDIC foreclosures.

VA *Home Loan Home Page (www.va gov/vas/loan):* Help for veterans to determine eligibility and listings of VA homes.

Mortgage Loan Page (www.loanpage.com): This site includes links to lenders located throughout the country.

Home Path.com (www.homepath.com): This is Fannie Mae's site and includes nearly everything a first-time buyer would want to know about Fannie's programs, as well as much useful general information.

U.S. Census Bureau (www.census.gov): This site provides great information on neighborhood demographics, price ranges, and other data collected and disseminated by the U.S. government.

Mortgage Market Information Services, Inc. (www.interest.com/mmis.html): Compares interest rates and lenders, links to newspaper articles, gives guidelines for credit-impaired borrowers, late-breaking mortgage news.

Internet Real Estate Directory (www.ired.com): Plan to spend hours at this site as it weaves you through a wealth of real estate and mortgage information. Links with 10,000 other sites including lenders, Realtors, and government agencies.

Terms You Can Use

Abandonment. A tenant who "walks away" from a valid lease agreement before its expiration date.

Abstract of title. A legal document that shows the recorded history of a property's conveyances, mortgages, liens, easements, and other obligations or liabilities that affect the rights of ownership.

Acceleration clause. A clause that permits lenders to demand full payment of an outstanding mortgage if a borrower does not (1) make scheduled payments, (2) maintain the property in satisfactory condition, (3) pay all property taxes when due, or (4) request written lender approval prior to undertaking major (sometimes minor) renovations or improvements to the mortgaged property.

Acceptance. A valid real estate contract requires a signature or other act that firmly binds the offeree.

Accessibility. The convenience with which movement to and from a site can be achieved; accessibility depends on egress and ingress, modes of transport, and proximity to places of importance.

Acre. A measure of land, 160 square rods. (4,840 square yards; 43,560 square feet).

Adaptive use. Creative improvement of older buildings into new uses.

Addendum. Usually a separate rider or amendment to a written contract. Addendums typically modify an original agreement and should be signed by all parties to the agreement.

Adjustable rate mortgage (ARM). A mortgage whose interest rate is adjusted periodically.

Ad valorem. A tax set as a percentage of value.

Adverse possession. The right of an occupant of land to acquire valid title against the owner of record, where the occupant's possession has been actual, continuous, hostile, visible, and distinct for the statutory period.

Affidavit. A statement of declaration reduced to writing, and sworn or affirmed to before some office who has authority to administer an oath or affirmation.

Agency. A contractual relationship in which one party (the principal) authorizes another party (the agent) to act on his behalf.

Agreement of sale. A written agreement whereby the purchaser agrees to buy certain real estate and the seller agrees to sell upon terms and conditions set forth therein. Also called *contract of sale*.

Air rights. The ownership of the right to use, control, or occupy the air space over a designated property.

Alienation. The transfer of real property rights by one person to another.

Amortization. The periodic reductions of a principal balance over time, i.e., paying off a loan.

Analysis. The breaking of a whole into its separate elements. Analysis leads to better understanding of a property, neighborhood, or method of financing.

Annual percentage rate (APR). The interest rate as calculated under Regulation Z of the federal truth-in-lending legislation. Included in this calculation is not only the nominal interest rate but also various associated costs of financing. APR only applies accurately to a fixed-rate mortgage held for its entire term. Early payoffs (property sale, refinance) increase the true APR. Reported APRs for ARMs do not accurately reflect the costs of that type of mortgage. No one knows (or can predict) the future interest costs of an *adjustable* rate mortgage.

Appraisal. An estimate of value. In real estate, an estimate of value of specific rights in a specific parcel of real estate as of a specific date for a specific purpose. Also called *valuation*.

Appraisal report. A report (usually written) of the estimated value of a property, along with pertinent information, evidence, and analysis that lead to the reported value estimate.

ARM ceiling. The maximum rate of interest allowable on an ARM regardless of how high the applicable index increases.

ARM indexes. ARM interest rates are tied to one of several types of indexes such as COFI, LIBOR, one-year treasury, six-month CD, or the prime rate.

ARM margin. A specified percentage (e.g., 2.5, 2.75) that is added to an ARM index to calculate the ARM's current interest rate.

ARM rate cap. The maximum allowable increase in an ARM's interest rate at each periodic rate adjustment.

As-is sale. A transaction whereby the sellers make no warranties or representations to a buyer concerning a property's condition. However, as-is sales typically do not relieve the seller of complying with any applicable disclosure laws.

Asking price. The seller's opening price. In hot markets, buyers sometimes make offers above the seller's asking prices. In cold markets, or with "overpriced" properties, buyers often open their offers substantially below the asking price.

Assemblage. The act of bringing two or more separate parcels of land under a single ownership.

Assessed value. A value set upon real estate by governmental assessors for the purpose of computing taxes.

Assessment. A one-time charge levied against a property for some specific purpose such as the installment of sewers or the widening of streets.

Assessor. A government official charged with the responsibility for valuing real estate for purposes of property taxation.

Assignee. The person to whom an agreement or contract is assigned.

Assignment. The method by which a right or contract is transferred from one person to another.

Assignor. One who makes an assignment.

Assumption fee. A fee charged by a lender when a buyer assumes the seller's mortgage with lender approval.

Assumption of mortgage. When a buyer takes ownership to real estate encumbered with a mortgage and assumes responsibility for the unpaid balance.

Balloon loan. A debt that does not amortize fully via periodic payments. It leaves a lump sum (a balloon) to be paid at the end of its term. (Also called a *bullet loan*.)

Bargain and Sale Deed. In this deed, there is no representation or guarantee of good title, but the grantor's title is conveyed absolutely.

Basic employment. The employers within an urban area who bring in income such as a tourist attraction or export manufacturer. Without strong basic employment, an area's real estate values tend to stagnate or fall.

Basis. Original cost of property plus the value of improvements less accrued depreciation. A property's basis enters into the computation of taxes on capital gains.

Bill of sale. A written contract given to pass title of personal property.

Binder. A brief contract used to bind parties until a more detailed contract can be drawn up.

Blanket mortgage. A mortgage that applies simultaneously to two or more properties.

Broker. In real estate, one who enters into an agency agreement to lease, buy, or sell real estate.

Building code. Statutes or regulations that prescribe construction materials, building techniques, or performance standards.

Building residual. An appraisal technique that calculates the value of a property's man-made improvements as the difference between total property value and the value of its site.

Bullet loan. A loan or mortgage that does not fully amortize over its term and falls due within a short period (one to five years).

Bull's-eye marketing. A strategy of designing and promoting a property's benefits to a selected type of tenants or buyers.

Bundle of rights. The divisible rights associated with ownership of a parcel of real estate.

Buy-down. A lump-sum payment to a lender that is given in exchange for a lower interest rate on a mortgage loan. (Also called *discount points*.)

Buyer's agent (broker). A real estate salesperson who owes a fiduciary duty to act in the primary interest of buyers (subject to professional ethics and rules of fair dealing).

Bylaws. General regulations that govern the management and operation of a legally established homeowners' association.

Capacity. The financial ability of a borrower to fulfill a mortgage or other credit agreement as promised.

Capital gain. The income that results from the sale of an asset for a price in excess of its book value (basis).

Cash reserves. Extra cash that lenders sometimes require borrowers to have on hand at closing to cover the amount of two months of mortgage payments.

Caveat emptor. Let the buyer beware. Formerly a general rule of law, now largely replaced by the rule "let the seller beware."

CC&Rs. The covenants, conditions, and restrictions that govern property owners through deeds and homeowners' associations.

Certificate of occupancy. A government certificate that must be issued before a newly constructed or rehabilitated building can be legally occupied for use.

Circuit breaker. A device in the electrical system to interrupt the circuit when an overload occurs; an automatic switch that can be reset is used instead of a fuse to protect each circuit.

Closing. A meeting in which a final accounting for sales proceeds, mortgage monies, closing costs, and property rights conveyed is made.

Closing statement. The form on which closing proceeds and disbursements are stated.

Cloud on title. A legal claim against a property that prevents an owner from conveying clear title.

Collateral. A property that serves as security for a mortgage (or other type of) loan.

Common element. The physical areas within a condominium or cooperative building jointly owned by all (or some) individual unit owners.

Community property. Property that by state law is owned jointly by husband and wife regardless of which spouse actually earned or purchased it.

Comparables. Properties that provide similar benefits and costs to tenants or buyers. Analyzing comparables, or comps, is a primary technique in both appraisals and competitive market analyses.

Compensating factor. A borrower's good points that can be used to help persuade a lender to approve a mortgage loan.

Competition. All properties (or substitute goods) that provide benefits similar to those offered by a subject property at approximately equal or lower prices.

Competitive edge. A product difference that distinguishes a property from comparables or substitutes.

Competitive market analysis. Shopping substitute properties to learn their relative prices, features, and benefits.

Concessions. Typically, seller concessions that "sweeten" the purchase agreement for buyers (e.g., interest rate, buy downs, personal property, payment of closing costs, repair allowances).

Condemnation. A government act that removes a property from the control and use of its owner and tenants. Properties may be condemned for purposes of public health and safety, or as a precedent to government taking for public use.

Condominium. A type of property ownership in which individuals hold individual ownership of designated units of a building and joint ownership of various common elements.

Conforming mortgage. A mortgage that meets the underwriting standards of Freddie Mac and/or Fannie Mae (i.e., the secondary mortgage market).

Consideration. The values exchanged in a contractual agreement.

Contingencies. Terms in a real estate contract that condition performance upon certain named conditions: e.g., an offer to purchase subject to obtaining a termite inspection or a mortgage loan commitment.

Contract. A court-enforceable agreement between two or more parties.

Contract for deed. *See* **Land contract.**

Contract of sale. *See* **Agreement of sale.**

Conventional mortgage. A mortgage that is neither insured nor guaranteed by an agency of the U.S. government (e.g., FHA, VA, FmHA).

Convertable ARM. An adjustable-rate mortgage that can be switched into a fixed-rate mortgage at specified times (e.g., after three, five, or seven years).

Convey. The act of deeding or transferring title to another.

Conveyance. A written agreement that passes specified rights in real estate from one person to another, including land contracts, leases, mortgages, etc.

Cooperative. A type of property ownership (co-op) that vests title in a corporation, with individual shareholders (property owners) receiving leasehold rights to various specific units within the building.

Corner influence. The effect of street intersections upon adjacent property—the cause of a different value for real estate adjacent to a corner as compared with property away from the corner. Corner influences may add or detract from value.

Cost approach. An appraisal technique that assumes a property's value equals its construction costs, less building depreciation, plus land value.

Covenant. A promise to perform or not to perform a specified act or acts.

Creative financing. Any type of home financing that involves creativity.

Credit scoring. A quantitative method that uses statistical analysis to rate a potential borrower's creditworthiness. Credit scoring may not be used as the single criterion upon which a mortgage loan is denied.

Debt service. The periodic amount of mortgage payments required under a mortgage agreement.

Deed. A written conveyance of title to real estate.

Deed restriction(s). Restrictions that in some way limit a property owner's right of use, possession, or transfer.

Default. The failure of a party to fulfill one or more covenants of a contract.

Deferred maintenance. Necessary repairs, replacements, and improvements that have not been made. Deferred maintenance leads to a rundown property.

Demographics. The study of potential buyers, tenants, or neighborhood residents in terms of age, income, household size, marital status, race, sex, occupation, and other observable characteristics.

Density. The ratio of people or building space to a given area of land, such as 100,000 persons per square mile, or six units per acre.

Depreciation. A decline in a property's ability to produce benefits for a given use. Depreciation may be physical, functional, or locational (external).

Direct Endorsement (DE). A lender who can directly process and approve FHA loans without first submitting the loan documents to the FHA.

Discount points. Money paid at closing to buy down (discount) the interest rate on a mortgage loan.

Discrimination. In law, refusal to rent, sell, or loan money to a person because of race, creed, religion, nationality origin, sex, marital status, or other legislatively specified characteristics.

Distressed property. A property that suffers serious physical and functional depreciation.

Documentary stamp. A revenue stamp issued for the payment of a tax on documents, deeds, checks, or wills.

Down payment. The initial cash or other consideration payable at the time a property is purchased.

Down zoning. A zoning ordinance that decreases the extent to which a site may be developed. Down zoning is an attempt to decrease density.

Dual agency. A situation in which a real estate agent represents both buyers and sellers within the same transaction. Agents must disclose dual agencies to both parties.

Due on sale. A mortgage provision (historically, paragraph 17) that accelerates the payment of the mortgage debt if the mortgaged property is sold or placed under a long-term lease.

Duplex. A single structure designed for two-family occupancy.

Earnest money. Monies pledged to secure the performance of a real estate purchase or rental contract.

Easement. An interest in land that permits a party to use (but not permanently occupy or possess) the property of another for a designated purpose.

Economic base. The major economic support of a community; economic activities that enable it to grow and prosper. *Also see* **Basic employment.**

Economic base analysis. A technique for analyzing the major economic supports of a community; analysis of basic employers, population, income, and other variables that affect real estate value, land utilization, and the economic prosperity of a community (present or forecasted).

Economic life. The period over which a property may be profitably utilized. The period during which a building is productive.

Effective age. The age of a property based on physical condition and economic life, as opposed to simple chronological age.

Eminent domain. The authority of government to take private property for public use. To exercise eminent domain, government is required to pay just compensation.

Encroachment. Usually one owner's building, fence, or driveway that illegitimately transgresses upon the rights of an owner of an adjacent property.

Environment. A dimension of location that may be further classified as (1) aesthetic, (2) physical, (3) legal, (4) socioeconomic, (5) political-economic, (6) fiscal, and (7) climate.

Environmental laws. In addition to zoning and building codes, many properties are now subject to environmental restrictions (e.g., lead paint, asbestos, heating oil tanks, radon).

Equity. The difference between a property owner's indebtedness on a property and the value of his property rights.

Escrow. Funds or legal instruments placed in trust pending performance of certain specified contract provisions or other contingencies.

Escrow (impound) account. A lender-administered escrow account that accumulates monthly payments from borrowers for purposes of paying the borrower's homeowners insurance and property taxes.

Fannie Mae. The Federal National Mortgage Association, the largest buyer of mortgages in the secondary mortgage market.

Fee simple. The most comprehensive private estate or quality of title recognized in law. All other private rights in realty flow from the fee simple estate.

FHA mortgage. A mortgage whose repayment is insured by the Federal Housing Administration.

FICO. A specific type of credit scoring developed by the Fair-Isaacs Company.

Finder's referral fee. A fee or commission paid to a realty agent for referring a homebuyer (mortgage loan customer) to a lender. Such fees may be illegal if the realty agent provides no mortgage loan services.

First-time buyer. Someone who has never owned a home, or, in some mortgage programs, a person who has not owned for at least three years. Also may include some recently divorced, separated, or widowed individuals.

Fiscal policy. Government tax and spending policies that affect inflation, interest rates, and the aggregate amount of economic activity.

Fixed-rate mortgage. A mortgage whose interest rate remains constant during the entire period of amortization.

Fixer-upper. A property in rundown condition that offers opportunity for value-creating improvements.

Fixture. Personal property that by use (or means of attachment) has become a part of realty.

Floor-area ratio (FAR). The ratio of the total floor area of a building to the area of the site on which it is (to be) built. FAR regulations are often included in zoning ordinances.

Foreclosure. A lender-initiated legal procedure against a mortgage borrower who has defaulted on a mortgage obligation. A successful foreclosure action results in the sale of the foreclosed property. If the sales proceeds are inadequate to cover legal costs and mortgage indebtedness, a court may enter a deficiency judgment against the mortgagor.

Fraud. The intentional and successful employment of any cunning, deception, collusion, or artifice used to circumvent, cheat, or deceive another person, whereby that person acts upon it, to his or her detriment, loss, or disadvantage. For example, property sellers who knowingly cover up the fact that water seeps into their basement during the rainy season.

Freddie Mac. The Federal Home Loan Mortgage Corporation, a secondary mortgage market participant who primarily purchases conventional mortgages from mortgage bankers, savings institutions, mutual savings banks, and commercial banks.

Functional depreciation. A loss of property value due to outdated design, floor plan, or other features.

Funding fee. An up-front expense levied by VA for issuing a VA loan guarantee.

Garbage fees. Various indirect loan processing expenses that are often inflated in cost and excessive in number (e.g., fax fees, couriers, photocopying, document handling, sales commission overages, wire transfers).

Gentrification. The movement of higher-income households into neighborhoods currently occupied by households further down the socio-economic scale. This process is usually associated with neighborhood revitalization.

Grace period. A 15-day (or otherwise specified) period during which a lender will forgive late payments without imposing a late fee. For purposes of *credit history,* though, payments received by lenders during the grace period are still considered late payments.

Graduated payment mortgage (GPM). A mortgage that periodically schedules increases in the amount of the monthly payments, according to a predetermined schedule.

Greenlining. As opposed to redlining, greenlining refers to a lender's commitment of mortgage funds to help revitalize a neighborhood or urban area.

Growth management. Government land-use policies that attempt to weigh the economic and environmental costs of real estate development against the need for economic growth and respect for private property rights.

Handyman special. *See* **Fixer-upper.**

Homeowners' association. The association of unit owners in a condominium, townhouse, or subdivision development.

Homestead. The land and dwelling used as a home. In many states, homestead laws protect all or a portion of a homeowner's equity against claims of creditors.

Household formations. The rate at which new households are forming in a community. Migration, maturation, marriage, divorce, and death are leading determinants of household formation statistics.

HUD/VA homes. Foreclosed properties that are now owned by HUD or VA. These properties may be offered for sale with bargain terms, bargain prices, or both (or neither, as well).

Improvements. The man-made physical additions to a site, including not only buildings, but also sewers, sidewalks, driveways, fencing, etc.

Infrastructure. Site improvements that are prerequisites to building construction. They include sewers, utility connections, streets, and municipal services such as fire, police, and sanitation.

Installment sale. The sale of a property that calls for payments over time rather than a lump sum at purchase. Installment sales can offer income tax advantages.

Jumbo mortgage. A mortgage loan that exceeds the Fannie Mae/Freddie Mac conforming limit of around $215,000.

Just compensation. The amount of compensation granted to a property owner who has suffered a taking. The actual amount granted is determined by negotiation between owner and government, or that failing to yield agreement, by court award.

Land. Typically broadly defined to include the earth's surface, attachments, subterranean rights, and air rights.

Land contract. A contract given to a purchaser of real estate who pays a portion of the purchase price when the contract is signed but agrees to pay additional sums at intervals and in amounts specified in the contract until the total purchase price is paid and the seller gives a deed. Sometimes called *contract for deed.*

Land-use controls. Government laws and regulations that limit a property owner's rights of use, occupancy, discharge, construction, improvements, etc.

Lease-option. A realty contract often used by homebuyers who lack sufficient cash for a down payment; also used as a seller incentive to attract potential buyers.

Legal description. A property description that is recognized by the courts for purposes of conveying property rights.

Leverage. The use of borrowed funds to magnify the positive (or negative) returns of a given amount of equity investment.

Lien. A hold or claim that one person has upon property of another as security for a debt, judgment, mortgage, or taxes.

Life estate. An interest in real property that continues until the death of a specified person or persons.

Lis pendens. Suit pending; usually recorded so as to give constructive notice of pending litigation.

Listing contract. The agency agreement that authorizes a real estate broker to find a tenant or buyer for an owner-principal.

Listing price. The price at which a real estate firm lists a seller's property for sale. See also asking price.

Loan-to-value ratio. An outstanding mortgage balance expressed as a percentage of a mortgaged property's market value.

Location. A major property feature influencing utility. The concept of location should be analyzed in terms of its basic elements of accessibility, environment, investment potential, and possibilities for revitalization.

Lock-in. A period of time (e.g., 30 to 60 days) whereby a lender commits to making a mortgage loan at a specified interest rate—even if market interest rates increase.

Manufactured house. A house prefabricated, and sometimes partly assembled, before delivery to a site. Sometimes called a *prefab.*

Market. The interaction of buyers and sellers (lessees and lessors) to establish prices, terms of sale, and benefits traded. Sometimes the word *market* may also be used to designate either demand or supply independently of each other— "Those high-priced condominiums missed the market," or "The market is glutted."

Marketable title. A title to real estate sufficiently clear of liens and encumbrances so that it is acceptable to a title insurer and a majority of potential buyers.

Market area. The geographic boundaries that mark the limits of supply and demand for a subject property. In some instances the market areas for supply and demand will differ from each other.

Market value. The price of a property as established through arms-length negotiations of adequately informed buyers and sellers.

Mechanic's lien. A lien created by statute that exists in favor of persons who have performed work or furnished materials in the construction, renovation, or repair of a building.

Millage rate. One mill equals 1/10 of a cent or 1/1,000 of a dollar. Property tax rates are typically stated in terms of millage per dollar of assessed value; hence the millage rate.

Misrepresentation. A misleading or deceptive statement wrongfully made to induce a party to make or accept an offer.

Mixed-use development. A real estate development that combines several different uses, such as single-family residential, multi-family residential, retail, office, and light industrial.

Monetary policy. Government control of the supply of money designed to regulate inflation, interest rates, and aggregate economic activity.

Mortgage. An interest in realty created to secure a debt.

Mortgage bond programs. Typically, first-time buyer mortgages funded through state housing finance agencies at below-market interest rates.

Mortgage credit certificates (MCCs). A government-sponsored first-time buyer program that gives borrowers a mortgage interest tax credit of 20 percent. This tax credit is in addition to the normal tax deduction for mortgage interest.

Mortgagee. A mortgage lender, the party to whom a mortgage is given.

Mortgage note. A promissory note signed by a borrower that establishes personal liability for the indebtedness above or in lieu of the mortgaged property (collateral). A *nonrecourse* mortgage omits personal liability.

Mortgagor. The borrower, the party that grants the mortgage in exchange for a loan or other consideration.

Neighborhood revitalization. The process of rehabilitating city areas by demolishing, remodeling, cleaning up, or repairing existing buildings, parks, sidewalks, streets, and subways. Revitalization leads to an increase in property values. *See also* **Gentrification.**

Nonconforming use. A land use that conflicts with current zoning or other land-use ordinances. Nonconforming uses are typically permitted under grandfather exemptions.

Nonrecourse financing. A mortgage that pledges a property as the sole security of the debt. The borrower assumes no personal liability for repayment.

Nuisance. A property owner or use that creates harmful effects to neighbors. A nuisance may be illegal under the common law without reference to specific statute or ordinance.

Option. A contract that gives one party the right to buy or lease a described property on specified terms within a stated period of time.

Origination fee. A one-time fee charged by a lender when providing a mortgage loan.

OWC. An abbreviation for owner-will-carry financing. *See* **Seller financing.**

Personal property. All property that is not realty; also, under federal income tax law, property (realty and nonrealty) held for consumption, as opposed to property held for use in trade or business or for investment.

PITI. An acronym that stands for principal, interest, (property) taxes, and insurance (PMI and homeowners).

Plottage value. A more-than-proportional increase in total site value that can result from assembling two or more parcels into one larger parcel.

Points. A cost in addition to interest that a lender charges for making a loan. Each point represents one percent of the original amount loaned.

Police power. The power of state and local governments to legislate and regulate behavior and land use for the purpose of promoting public health, safety, morals, and welfare.

Portfolio lender. Mortgage lenders who retain loans in their own account rather than sell them into the secondary market (portfolio lenders can exercise more underwriting flexibility than conforming lenders).

Preapproval. A type of mortgage prequalifying where the lender commits to making a homebuyer a loan on specified terms within a stated period of time.

Prefab. *See* **Manufactured house.**

Prepayment penalty. A penalty some lenders levy against borrowers who pay off their loan principal ahead of schedule.

Prequalification. A mortgage lender's affordability analysis for a borrower without a commitment to approve that borrower for a mortgage loan.

Principal. A capital sum; also, a person who employs an agent.

Private mortgage insurance (PMI). Insurance offered by private mortgage insurance companies that protects lenders against losses that result from borrower default.

Property. The bundle of legal rights associated with personalty and realty.

Pro rata. Apportioning revenues or expenses according to time or some other criterion.

Psychographics. The study of needs, habits, attitudes, lifestyles, motivations, and other psychological dispositions. Psychographics complements demographics in the study of housing demand and neighborhood residents.

Puffing. Exaggerating the positive features of a product or property. Puffing may be poor or unethical salesmanship, but, if it does not cross the line to misrepresentation, deception, or fraud, it is not illegal.

Purchase agreement. A contract of sale; a contract that sets forth the terms and provisions of a real estate purchase.

Purchase money mortgage. Seller financing to help a buyer purchase a property. Usually purchase money mortgages are junior (second or third) mortgages.

Qualifying. The process of determining whether a potential purchaser, mortgage borrower, or tenant has the necessary financial capacity, character, and credit-worthiness to fulfill a financial commitment.

Qualifying ratios. A ratio (percentage) of a borrower's income that is used to estimate mortgage affordability. The housing cost (front) ratio applies to PITI; the total debt (back) ratio applies to PITI plus monthly payments on installment debt.

Quit-claim deed. A conveyance of property rights without warranty; i.e., "I convey to you all of my rights in the described property whatever those rights may be." Quit-claim deeds are typically used to clear up potential clouds against a property's title.

Real estate. Land, improvements, subsurface space, air space. Technically, *real estate* refers to physical space dimensions and improvements; *real property* refers to rights. However, in common usage the terms often are used interchangeably.

Realtor®. A person who is a member of the National Association of Realtors®.

Realty. Real estate, real property.

Recording. Registering in the appropriate public records a claim or right in realty.

Redlining. Eliminating all properties in certain designated neighborhoods (usually those that are run down) from consideration as security for mortgage loans. Redlining is illegal. *See also* **Greenlining.**

Replacement costs. The current construction costs necessary to replace a site's existing improvements using materials and methods of similar quality.

Reproduction costs. The current construction costs necessary to replicate exactly existing site improvements.

RESPA. The Real Estate Settlement and Procedures Act. A federal law that regulates mortgage lender disclosures and the preparation of closing statements in the purchase and sale of one- to four-family residences.

Reverse annuity mortgage. Generally, a refinancing plan that pays homeowners who borrowed funds in monthly payments over an extended period. Most often used by retirees to help cover living expenses.

Satisfaction. An acknowledged payment of a mortgage or other indebtedness. Mortgage satisfactions should be recorded in the public records.

Secondary mortgage market. A market in which existing mortgages are bought and sold.

Second mortgage. A junior lien that stands second in line to a first mortgage.

Seller financing (OWC). Mortgage financing provided by a property owner to a buyer to facilitate a sale of the owner's property. *See also* **Purchase money mortgage.**

Seller's agent (broker). A real estate salesperson who owes a fiduciary duty to act in the primary interests of property owners (sellers), subject to professional ethics and rules of fair dealing.

Setback. The distance from curb, sideyard, or backyard boundaries within which no building may be erected.

Settlement. A term synonymous with closing.

Shared equity purchase. A purchase agreement whereby an owner-occupant and an investor hold joint ownership of a residence.

Short-fuse mortgage. A bullet loan; a mortgage whose principal balance becomes due within a short period of years.

Specific performance. A lawsuit or contract clause that requires a party to comply with the terms of an agreement.

Statute of frauds. A basic requirement of law that certain contracts should be in writing as a prerequisite to court enforcement.

Subject property. A property that is the focus of an appraisal or other market study.

Survey. The physical measurement and setting forth the boundaries of a site; also a market research technique used to discover market data.

Sweat equity. A down payment provided in the form of personal labor and materials instead of cash. Also, creating property value through personal work of rehab or renovation.

Takings. A question of how strictly government can regulate private property without having to meet the requirement of just compensation.

Teaser rate. A temporarily low starting interest rate on an ARM.

Title. The actual quality of ownership rights.

Title examination. An examination to determine the quality of legal rights and claims against realty.

Title insurance. An insurance policy that protects lenders and/or homeowners against losses due to later-discovered title liens, encumbrances, or defects.

Townhouse. Refers primarily to single-family homes with common walls and zero lot lines. Townhouses usually are part of a homeowners' association that owns common elements (pool, grounds, parking, clubhouse) within a development.

Trust deed. A contingent conveyance of a property's deed to a lender as security for a loan. During the repayment period, the deed is held in trust. Satisfactory completion of the debt voids the conveyance. Default activates it. In some states, trust deeds are used in lieu of mortgages.

Truth-in-lending. A federal law that requires lenders to disclose borrowing costs and annual percentage rates (APRs). Stated APRs do not apply accurately to most borrowers.

Underwriting. The process of evaluating a mortgage loan application with respect to the borrower's creditworthiness, character, collateral, and financial capacity.

Useful life. *See* **Economic life.**

Valuation. *See* **Appraisal.**

VA mortgage. A mortgage whose payments are guaranteed by the U.S. Department of Veterans Affairs.

Variance. A permit granted by government to allow a property owner to deviate from an otherwise applicable land-use regulation.

Warranty deed. Conveyance of title that contains certain assurances and guarantees by the grantor that the deed conveys a good and unencumbered title. Conveyances vary from state to state but generally assume (1) a good title to land; (2) no encumbrances except those listed in the deed; and (3) that a grantee will not be evicted or disturbed by any person with superior rights.

Win-win. A negotiating style in which buyers and sellers work together to structure an agreement that pleases both parties. With win-win negotiating neither party feels disadvantaged by the agreement.

Zoning. Ordinances and regulations that may govern site size, building use, occupancy, height, setbacks, floor area, architectural design, pollutant discharges, and density.

Zoning map. A map depicting the various sections of a community, and the division of these sections into zones of permitted land uses under the zoning ordinance.

Recommended Reading

Bell, Frazier, *How To Get the Best Home Loan* (New York: John Wiley & Sons, 1992). This is one of the best mortgage guides on the market. It is written in a lively style and includes many helpful tips on qualifying.

Bruss, Robert, "Real Estate Mailbag," syndicated columns carried in many newspapers across the country, including *Chicago Tribune* (Sundays), *San Francisco Examiner* (Sundays), and the *Washington Post* (Saturdays). This column is written in a reader question-and-answer format. It addresses many buyer issues and concerns. If your regular paper doesn't carry this column (though you could ask it to), read the column at your local library in one of the papers cited. Bruss has also written a number of valuable reports on lease-options and other special real estate topics. For a current listing write to: Robert Bruss, 251 Park Road, Burlingame, CA 94010.

Eldred, Gary W., *Yes! You Can Own the Home You Want* (New York: John Wiley & Sons, 1995). This book goes further in helping you put together your home-buying possibilities and priorities. It also lists and explains the many initiatives of the National Home Ownership Strategy.

Eldred, Gary W., and Andrew McLean, *Investing In Real Estate* (New York: John Wiley & Sons, 1996). This book is intended for homebuyers and investors in small residential income properties. It goes further into the topics of shopping for bargains, buying HUD/VA foreclosures, and ways to make value-enhancing improvements. It also explains the appraisal process in greater depth. If you really want to make money on your home and other real estate investments, this book will give you the knowledge you need.

Garton-Good, Julie, *All About Mortgages* (Chicago: Dearborn Financial Publishing, 1994). This is another of my favorite books on mortgages. Although not written with the style of Bell's *The Best Home Loan,* Garton-Good does a great job of laying out the specific details and underwriting guidelines of a large variety of loan programs.

Washington Post. For anyone interested in staying current in real estate, the Saturday *Washington Post* real estate section is a great resource. In addition to Robert Bruss, the *Post* carries real estate columnists Kenneth Harney and Benny Kass, both well worth reading. It also reports the various legislative and regulatory changes facing home buyers and sellers. And for human interest, the Saturday *Post* nearly always writes up the experiences of various homebuyers, sellers, or homeowners that illustrate current real estate topics.

Index